LIQUIDS AND SOLIDS

Michael Sprackling took his PhD at Bristol University and was Assistant Master at King Edward VI School, Stourbridge, before taking up an Assistant Lectureship at Queen Elizabeth College, University of London. He is currently Senior Lecturer in Physics at King's College, University of London, and is the author of *The Mechanical Properties of Matter* (1970) and *The Plastic Deformation of Simple Ionic Crystals* (1976).

STUDENT PHYSICS SERIES

Series Editor:
Professor R.J. Blin-Stoyle, FRS
Professor of Theoretical Physics, University of Sussex

Advisory Editors:
Professor E.R. Dobbs, *University of London*
Dr J. Goddard, *City of London Polytechnic*

The aim of the *Student Physics Series* is to cover the material required for a first degree course in physics in a series of concise, clear and readable texts. Each volume will cover one of the usual sections of the physics degree course and will concentrate on covering the essential features of the subject. The texts will thus provide a core course in physics that all students should be expected to acquire, and to which more advanced work can be related according to ability. By concentrating on the essentials, the texts should also allow a valuable perspective and accessibility not normally attainable through the more usual textbooks.

'At a time when many undergraduate textbooks illustrate inflation in poundage, both in weight and cost, an interesting countertrend is established by the introduction from Routledge of a series of small carefully written paperbacks devoted to key areas of physics. The enterprising authors are E.R. Dobbs (*Electricity and Magnetism*), B.P. Cowan (*Classical Mechanics*), R.E. Turner (*Relativity Physics*) and Paul Davies (*Quantum Mechanics*). The student is offered an account of a key area of physics summarised within an attractive small paperback, and the lecturer is given the opportunity to develop a lecture treatment around this core.' — Daphne Jackson and David Hurd, *New Scientist*

Already published

Quantum Mechanics, *P.C.W. Davies*
Electricity and Magnetism, *E.R. Dobbs*
Classical Mechanics, *B.P. Cowan*
Relativity Physics, *R.E. Turner*
Electromagnetic Waves, *E.R. Dobbs*

LIQUIDS AND SOLIDS

M.T. Sprackling

Senior Lecturer in Physics,
King's College,
University of London

ROUTLEDGE & KEGAN PAUL
London, Boston, Melbourne and Henley

First published in 1985
by Routledge & Kegan Paul plc

14 Leicester Square, London WC2H 7PH, England

9 Park Street, Boston, Mass. 02108, USA

464 St Kilda Road, Melbourne,
Victoria 3004, Australia and

Broadway House, Newtown Road,
Henley on Thames, Oxon RG9 1EN, England

Set in IBM Press Roman
by Hope Services, Abingdon, Oxon
and printed in Great Britain
by Cox & Wyman Ltd
Reading, Berkshire

Library of Congress Cataloging in Publication Data

Sprackling, M. T. (Michael Thomas)

Liquids and solids.
(Student physics series)
Includes index.
1. Liquids.   2. Solids.   I. Title.   II. Series.
QC145.2.S67   1985   530.4   84-27740

ISBN 0-7102-0484-1

Contents

Preface

Most of the matter in the world is in a condition described as solid or liquid. In both of these conditions adjacent constituent particles – ions, atoms or molecules – are so close together that they may be described as being in contact.

The aim of this book is to give an elementary account of the properties of solids and liquids and, in particular, of their response to applied forces. Their behaviour is examined on the large scale, that is, in terms of quantities that are measured in the laboratory, and also from the atomic standpoint. An attempt is made to show how the bulk properties are related to what the constituent particles are doing, that is, to the properties of a large assembly of strongly interacting particles. (The properties of gases, kinetic theory, and a more detailed treatment of atoms, molecules and interatomic forces, are discussed in a separate volume in this series.)

The treatment is essentially rough and ready and tries to bring out the essential features by a simple-minded approach. Further, the treatment is largely restricted to the properties of solids and liquids consisting of small molecules, though there is a brief introduction to the behaviour of high polymers and liquid crystals.

The text contains a number of worked examples and also exercises for the reader. Many of the quantities discussed have directional properties, but vector notation is used only where it is considered helpful or where vector algebra is used.

Chapter 1
Condensed phases

1.1 Introduction

The three phases of matter — solid, liquid and gas — are the result of competition between the internal energy and the intermolecular forces of a large assembly of molecules. It is this competition which determines whether a given substance, under given conditions, is a solid, liquid or gas.

This book gives an account of the bulk properties of solids and liquids (and, particularly, their response to external forces) and an attempt is made to show how many of these properties can be explained in terms of the intermolecular forces and the internal energy. In this chapter a simple account is given of the most important properties of solids and liquids in terms of intermolecular forces. No detailed account of the origin of these forces is given, but the basic features are described and characterised.

The idea that matter is composed of very small, discrete basic particles is the essence of the kinetic theory of matter. This idea is a very old one but was only put on a quantitative basis early in the nineteenth century, when such a view was seen to give a ready explanation of the laws of chemical combination. These laws suggest that each unit mass of a given chemical element is proportional to the mass of some basic particle of that element, and that chemical reactions involve the joining together of these basic particles in definite and reproducible small numbers.

The basic postulates of Dalton's theory (1803) are that:

1. the chemical elements consist of discrete particles called atoms, which cannot be subdivided by any known chemical process and which preserve their identity in chemical changes;

2. all atoms of the same element are identical in all respects; different elements are distinguished by having atoms of different mass;
3. chemical compounds are formed by the joining of atoms of different elements in simple numerical proportions.

The distinction between the smallest particle that can take part in a chemical reaction (the atom) and that which can exist in the free state (the molecule) was made by Avogadro in 1811. Studies of the electrolysis of matter, largely performed by Faraday in the years immediately before 1833, showed that atoms may exist in a charged condition, when they are called ions.

Since the early nineteenth century it has become clear that however the particular properties of atoms may be modified in the light of new discoveries and ideas the concept that matter is composed of discrete entities is an essential feature of (classical) physical theory.

1.2 The three phases of matter

One way of classifying substances in bulk is according to their condition of aggregation, or phase. Three phases are usually recognised: solid, liquid and gas. Traditional descriptions of these three phases are as follows. A solid is an aggregation of matter that occupies a definite volume at a given temperature and pressure and, in the absence of external forces, has a definite shape. A liquid has a definite volume at a given temperature and pressure, but its shape is determined by that of the containing vessel, except in the case of very small drops. In contrast, a gas fills completely all the space made available to it and necessarily takes the shape of the boundaries of the space. The term phase is also used to describe different modifications of the arrangement of the constituent particles of a given solid.

All materials are gaseous at sufficiently high temperatures and all condense into liquids as the temperature is lowered. In addition, all except helium form solids under their own vapour pressure as the temperature is lowered still further. Condensation indicates that there must be attractive forces between the basic particles to make them cohere, though this force must become repulsive at very short interparticle distances, otherwise all matter would coalesce.

For some substances the change from one phase to another as, say, the temperature is changed at constant pressure, is not very distinct, but for a simple pure substance, i.e. one consisting of a single chemical species, a clear distinction can usually be made between the solid, liquid and gaseous phases. Consider a given mass of such a substance contained in a cylinder by means of a frictionless piston. Any equilibrium condition, or state, of this substance is specified by a certain set of values of the pressure p, volume V and temperature T. The totality of equilibrium states for a given mass of a particular chemical species is represented by a continuous surface in p-V-T space. Since the surface is usually of a complicated shape, it is often more useful to project sections of the p-V-T surface on to one of the principal planes. The two most useful projections are shown in Fig. 1.1. In the p-V projection (Fig. 1.1(a)) the full lines shown join states having a common temperature, giving a pattern of isotherms, while the dotted lines indicate where phase boundaries occur. This plot shows clearly the states of mixed phase equilibrium. The lines shown in the p-T projection (Fig. 1.1(b)) are the phase boundaries, since in the p-T plane the regions of mixed phases project into lines.

From these two projections it can be seen that for all temperatures above T_c, known as the critical temperature, the substance remains in the gaseous phase, whatever the value of the applied pressure.

At temperatures T_c and below it is always possible to produce a liquid or a solid phase of the substance by the application of pressure. The production of liquid or solid from the gaseous phase is called condensation, and liquids and solids are referred to as condensed phases. When the temperature of the substance is the triple-point temperature T_t, condensation from the gaseous phase produces both liquid and solid so that, along the horizontal portion of the T_t isotherm in the p-V plot, solid, liquid and gas coexist in equilibrium. For temperatures in the range $T_t < T \leqslant T_c$ condensation from the vapour phase is to the liquid phase and the application of sufficient pressure in this temperature range results in

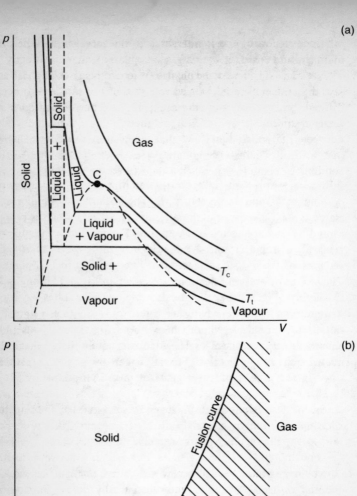

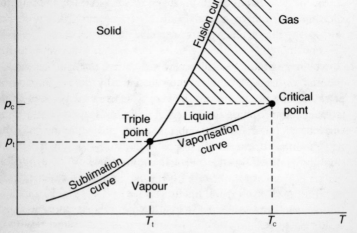

Fig. 1.1

4   Condensed phases

the conversion of the liquid phase to the solid phase. When the temperature is below T_t the gaseous phase condenses directly to the solid phase. (It is convenient to refer to the gaseous phase as a gas when $T > T_c$ and as a vapour when $T \leqslant T_c$; a vapour can always be condensed by the application of pressure at constant temperature.)

Quantitative studies show that solids usually expand slightly on melting whereas liquids always expand considerably on becoming gaseous. In general, the density of the solid phase at the melting point is hardly greater than that of the liquid phase at the same temperature; both phases are almost incompressible and both show cohesion. This implies that the atoms, ions or molecules comprising the substance are hardly more closely packed in the solid than in the liquid: in both solids and liquids the basic constituent particles are effectively in contact. This is the physical basis for the classification of solids and liquids as condensed phases.

A major difference between solids and liquids is that solids show rigidity whereas liquids do not; in solids the basic particles maintain their positions relative to each other while in liquids they are free to move relative to each other. Further, some samples of simple solids show very regular external surfaces and split or cleave in a regular geometrical way. These properties suggest that the particles making up the solid are arranged in a regular three-dimensional pattern, a result confirmed by X-ray diffraction, even in cases where regular external surfaces are not obtained.

The mobility of the particles in a liquid prevents a regular three-dimensional arrangement from being set up, and yet the density and compressibility requirements indicate that the environment of any particle cannot be very different whether it be in the solid or liquid phase. These considerations suggest that a liquid may be pictured as an assembly of small clusters of particles that are randomly oriented with respect to each other. Crudely, a liquid may be pictured as a very broken-up solid, and X-ray diffraction patterns from simple liquids do show the same essential features as those obtained from finely powdered solids, but are more blurred, a consequence of the smallness of the solid-like clusters and their transient nature.

In gases, in contrast, the constituent particles move about quite freely, only constrained by the wall of the container, the pressure arising from the bombardment of the wall by the gas particles.

A simple calculation shows that, for a model gas made up of point particles, each of mass m and exerting zero attractive forces on the other particles (known as an ideal gas), the pressure p exerted by the gas is given by:

$$p = \frac{1}{3} mn\overline{c^2} \qquad [1.1]$$

where n is the number of particles per unit volume and $\overline{c^2}$ is the mean value of the squares of the speeds of the particles.

If N_A is the Avogadro constant and V_m is the volume occupied by 1 mole of molecules, equation [1.1] may be written:

$$pV_m = \frac{1}{3} mN_A\overline{c^2}. \qquad [1.2]$$

It may be shown that the equation of state of an ideal gas is:

$$pV_m = RT \qquad [1.3]$$

where R is the gas constant and T is the thermodynamic temperature. Equations [1.2] and [1.3] are consistent if:

$$RT = \frac{1}{3} mN_A\overline{c^2}$$

which may be written as

$$RT = \frac{2}{3} \cdot \frac{1}{2} m\overline{c^2}$$

or, putting $R/N_A = k$, the Boltzmann constant:

$$kT = \frac{2}{3} \cdot \frac{1}{2} m\overline{c^2}. \qquad [1.4]$$

Therefore, for ideal gases, the temperature is proportional to the mean kinetic energy per particle or, alternatively, the mean kinetic energy per particle of an ideal gas at a temperature T is $\frac{3}{2}kT$.

It is not difficult to extend this model to give a discussion of the properties of gases with particles of finite size. Estimates of the diameter of gas particles (assumed spherical) can then be obtained from, for example, the flow properties of the gas. In this way values for the particle diameter of about 10^{-10} m are obtained.

Liquids are formed by supplying energy to solids to produce melting, and the further sufficient supply of energy will convert the liquid to the gaseous phase. For ideal gases all the energy of the particles is kinetic energy, but in real substances the interactions between the particles means that the energy of an assembly of particles is partly kinetic and partly potential. It is reasonable to infer that the total energy of a given collection of matter macroscopically at rest (the internal energy of the sample) increases as the temperature increases, though not necessarily proportionally as in the case of the ideal gas.

Introducing the concept of internal energy modifies the models of solids and liquids in the following way. The particles in a solid are arranged in a regular pattern, but the particles vibrate about mean positions. In a liquid the vibrations are sufficient to break up the extended regular pattern of particles, but the attractive forces are still able to hold the particles together, though not able to prevent them from wandering slowly from point to point. When the motion of the particles is so violent that they can break away completely from the attractive forces of neighbouring particles the gaseous phase is formed.

The different phases arise from the competition between the interparticle forces, which try to produce a regular arrangement of the particles, and the internal energy, which tries to destroy such an arrangement. Applied pressures affect the role played by the interparticle forces so that the phase in which a particular substance exists depends on both the temperature and pressure.

1.3 Intermolecular forces

The actual nature of the force between the constituent particles of matter depends on the electronic structures of the interacting particles, i.e. on whether they are atoms, ions or molecules. For example, the ionic interaction arises when electrons are transferred from atoms of one type to those of a second type, so that the material is composed of positive and negative ions, giving a force that is central and unsaturated (i.e., one positive ion can attract several negative ions around it and the force exerted by the positive ion on each negative ion is not affected by the presence of the other ions). In the covalent interaction valence electrons are shared between two atoms to an appreciable extent, giving an interaction that is saturated and has marked directional properties. The van der Waals interaction is a weak electrostatic interaction which occurs even in atoms and molecules showing no permanent dipole moment. It arises from the fluctuating dipole moment associated with the instantaneous positions of the electrons in the atom. In many materials one type of interaction predominates so that, for example, a certain solid may be referred to as an ionic solid. In other cases the nature of the interaction may be less clear-cut.

Despite the differences in the nature of the interactions between the constituent particles, most simple materials show similar properties of aggregation as the temperature is changed, and similar responses to balanced applied forces. Therefore, qualitatively, the form of the interaction between the constituent particles in condensed matter must be the same in all cases. In view of this, the precise nature of the particles is unimportant for the purposes of this book and the constituent particles will generally be referred to as molecules, even though they are frequently ions or atoms. Distinctions will be made in particular cases where necessary.

Figure 1.1(a) shows that to produce even a small reduction in volume of the solid and liquid phases needs a very large increase in the applied pressure. This implies that, for small molecular separations, the intermolecular forces are repulsive and that they increase rapidly as the separation is reduced.

Solids (and under certain conditions liquids) can also resist extension up to some limiting value at which rupture occurs. Therefore, for larger molecular separations the intermolecular forces are attractive. The attractive force must increase with molecular separation for small changes in separation, since the force needed to extend a solid increases with the extension, at least for a small range of increase. However, at still larger molecular separations the attractive force must fall off rapidly, since gases obey Boyle's law reasonably well under conditions in which the density is not very different from that of the liquid, yet Boyle's law can be deduced using the kinetic theory of gases only if the attractive intermolecular force is zero.

These simple observations concerning intermolecular forces can be represented in the following way. Consider the interaction between two molecules. If one of the molecules is taken as the origin of coordinates, repulsive intermolecular forces will be in the direction of increasing separation and will be counted positive; attractive intermolecular forces will be counted negative. Then, for simple substances generally, the variation of intermolecular force F with intermolecular distance r for a molecule and a single neighbour will take the form shown in Fig. 1.2(a). The force is repulsive for small intermolecular distances, becoming stronger as this distance decreases, and is attractive at larger distances, reaching a maximum and then falling practically to zero when the separation is a few molecular diameters. At some value r_0 of the intermolecular distance the value of F is zero. This is the equilibrium separation of the two molecules, provided that neither has any kinetic energy. For identical molecules r_0 is equal to the molecular diameter. The equilibrium is stable since, if the value of r is reduced, the molecules repel each other while if it is increased they attract. Therefore, if the molecules have a small amount of kinetic energy they will vibrate, with r_0 as the mean separation. The amplitude of this vibration will increase with temperature.

It is generally more rewarding to discuss interactions in terms of energies rather than forces. The potential energy of a pair of molecules is defined as the work done by forces external to the two molecules in changing their relative positions from some standard configuration to the given one. This standard configuration then constitutes a zero which must be stated when potential energy values are quoted. With two molecules an obvious standard configuration is when they are an infinite distance apart, so that their interaction is negligible. Then, if F_e is the external force needed to maintain the intermolecular distance at a value x, the work dw done by this force when one molecule moves so that the separation increases by dx along the line of centres is (assuming central forces):

$$dw = F_e dx$$

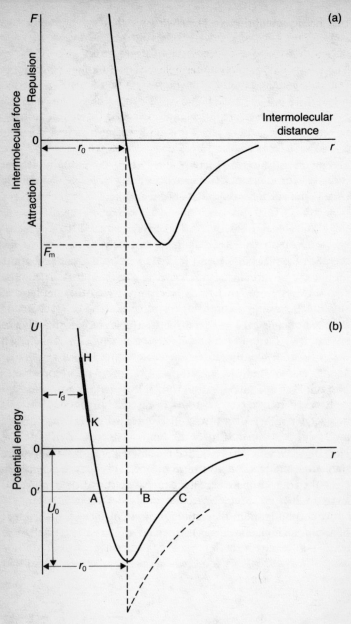

Fig. 1.2

or, since in equilibrium $F_e = -F$:

$$dw = -F dx .$$ [1.5]

Therefore, to reach an intermolecular separation r from the standard configuration, the work that must be done by the external force is:

$$w = \int_{\infty}^{r} F_e dx = - \int_{\infty}^{r} F dx$$

and this is equal to the potential energy U of the pair of molecules when they are a distance r apart. Strictly, the energy resides in the field of force between the molecules. Therefore:

$$U = - \int_{\infty}^{r} F dx; \quad dU \left[= -F dx \right]$$ [1.6]

and the force law shown in Fig. 1.2(a) can be equally well represented by the potential energy variation shown in Fig. 1.2(b). The equilibrium separation r_0 here corresponds to the minimum in the U–r curve.

To determine the exact shape of the U–r curve the precise nature of the intermolecular interaction is required, but often an empirical representation is sufficient. When the intermolecular forces are spherically symmetric, probably the simplest representation is the equation proposed by Mie in 1907:

$$U(r) = -\frac{A}{r^m} + \frac{B}{r^n} .$$ [1.7]

Here A, B, m and n are positive constants and n must be greater than m so that the positive term dominates when r is very small, but falls to zero more rapidly than the negative term when r is larger.

At the equilibrium separation of the molecules (in the absence of appreciable kinetic energy)

$$\frac{dU}{dr} = 0 \quad \text{and} \quad r = r_0$$

so that

$$\frac{mA}{r_0^{m+1}} - \frac{nB}{r_0^{n+1}} = 0$$

or $\quad B = \frac{m}{n} A r_0^{n-m}.$ [1.8]

Therefore, equation [1.7] may be written

$$U(r) = -\frac{A}{r^m} + \frac{mAr_0^{n-m}}{nr^n}.$$ [1.9]

The binding energy of a pair of molecules is U_0, the value of U when $r = r_0$, that is

$$U_0 = -\frac{A}{r_0^m} + \frac{B}{r_0^n} = -\frac{A}{r_0^m}\left(1 - \frac{m}{n}\right).$$ [1.10]

Many molecules behave rather like rigid spheres and, consequently, the term in equation [1.7] representing the repulsion is not very sensitive to the value of n, provided that it is large, and a value in the range 9–12 is often used. In contrast, the attractive term is very sensitive to the nature of the interaction. For the ionic interaction A is very large and for monovalent ions m has the value unity (corresponding to the usual Coulomb potential), while for the van der Waals interaction A is very small and m has the value 6. In the covalent interaction A is very large but, since the interaction cannot be described in classical terms, a simple power law is not adequate to describe the variation of U over a wide range of r.

In an assembly of molecules any given molecule experiences forces due to those molecules that are very close to it and also to those that are further away. However, since the intermolecular forces are very short-range, the interactions between any molecule and those that are very close to it will be dominant. Then, provided that negligible changes in the form of the force law result from the presence of the other molecules, it is reasonable to expect that the F–r curve for a pair of molecules in a large assembly will take the form shown in Fig. 1.2(a), though the detailed shape of the curve and, in particular, the value of r_0, will be slightly different. Further, the total energy of the assembly will then be the sum of the energies of every molecular pair, given by the pair potential.

To dissociate an isolated pair of molecules, i.e. to separate them at infinity with zero kinetic energy, requires the binding energy U_0. In an assembly of molecules constituting a solid phase, the molecules will pack so that each has a certain definite number of other molecules that are at a mean distance r_0. These molecules are termed nearest neighbours and their number is the coordination number q. If there is one mole of molecules in the assembly and only nearest neighbour interactions are important, the molar binding energy U_m will be given by the number of interacting pairs of molecules in one mole multiplied by the binding energy per pair of molecules, i.e.:

$$U_m = \frac{1}{2} N_A U_0 q .$$ [1.11]

The factor of a half is included because it takes two molecules to give one interaction.

Liquids can be similarly treated, but the number of near neighbours, though intuitively obvious, is best expressed through the radial distribution function (see section 1.5).

For the liquid phase U_m is very approximately the molar enthalpy of vaporisation, while for solids it is approximately the molar enthalpy of sublimation. Corrections must be applied for the energy of the molecules in the condensed phase and for the work done in expanding the vapour against the atmosphere, so that the best simple approximation to U_0 is obtained from the value of U_m extrapolated to absolute zero. For example, the extrapolated value of U_m for liquid argon is about 6400 J mol^{-1}, and taking q as 10 gives a value for U_0 of about 21×10^{-22} J.

As an illustration of the use of the intermolecular potential consider the following example.

Example 1.1

The interaction energy between nearest neighbours in a long-chain molecule composed of identical atoms equally spaced is given by

$$U(r) = -\frac{A}{r^6} + \frac{B}{r^{12}}$$

where A and B are positive constants and r is the distance between neighbouring atoms. Calculate the equilibrium separation of atoms in the chain at low temperatures and the energy needed to break bonds in the chain, assuming that only nearest neighbour interactions are important.

At low temperatures kinetic energy effects may be neglected. The equilibrium separation r_0 is obtained from the condition that:

$$\frac{dU}{dr} = 0 \quad \text{when} \quad r = r_0.$$

Now

$$\frac{dU}{dr} = \frac{6A}{r^7} - \frac{12B}{r^{13}}$$

so that

$$\frac{6A}{r_0^7} = \frac{12B}{r_0^{13}}$$

which gives:

$$r_0^6 = \frac{2B}{A}.$$

Therefore, the equilibrium separation is:

$$r_0 = \left(\frac{2B}{A}\right)^{\frac{1}{6}} = 1.12 \left(\frac{B}{A}\right)^{\frac{1}{6}}.$$

The bond energy U_0 is the value of U when $r = r_0$. Substituting for r_0 in the expression for U gives:

$$U_0 = -\frac{A}{r_0^6} + \frac{B}{r_0^{12}} = -\frac{A^2}{2B} + \frac{A^2 B}{4B^2}$$

$$= \frac{A^2}{2B}\left(\frac{1}{2} - 1\right) = -\frac{A^2}{4B}.$$

Since, experimentally, B is usually more difficult to measure than r_0, the expression for U_0 might better be written:

$$U_0 = -\frac{A}{2r_0^6}.$$

1.4 Solids

If the intermolecular force F is spherically symmetric, in any large assembly of molecules at fairly low temperatures the molecules will take up positions relative to their neighbours such that all the time-averaged intermolecular distances are constant and approximately equal to r_0. Arranging molecules in this way produces a regular three-dimensional array as shown in Figs. 1.3(a) and (b). Such an array, existing over distances large compared with r_0, gives a crystalline material, the characteristic of which is the long-range ordering in the molecular arrangement. Note that Figs. 1.3 and 1.4 show the mean positions of the molecule centres only, and not the way in which space is filled.

Provided that interactions with molecules other than nearest neighbours can be neglected, the potential energy of a molecule in the bulk of a solid is approximately q times that resulting from the interaction with one near neighbour at a separation close to r_0, where q is the number of nearest neighbours. A molecule in the surface, however, has approximately half the number of nearest neighbours of one in the bulk. Therefore, provided that no substantial rearrangement takes place in the surface, the potential energy of a surface molecule is very approximately half that of a molecule in the bulk.

Figs. 1.3(a) and (b) are constructed on the assumptions that all the molecules are identical and are, in fact, spherical, that only nearest-neighbour interactions are important and that the force F is central and conservative. Then, $U(r)$ is a function of the separation of the molecules only. In practice, however, the exact nature of the intermolecular force depends on the electron arrangement in the molecules and, in many cases, even though the intermolecular forces are central, or very closely so, $U(r)$ does depend on orientation. Such cases will not be considered here. Further, where different molecules are combined into a crystal, the molecular arrangement must be such as to accommodate the different radii and give bulk neutrality if the molecules are, in fact, ions. These considerations influence the mean equilibrium positions taken up by the molecules. Every crystal exhibits two different features, namely, the recurring motif, known as the basis, and the way the mean (or time-averaged) position of the basis is repeated

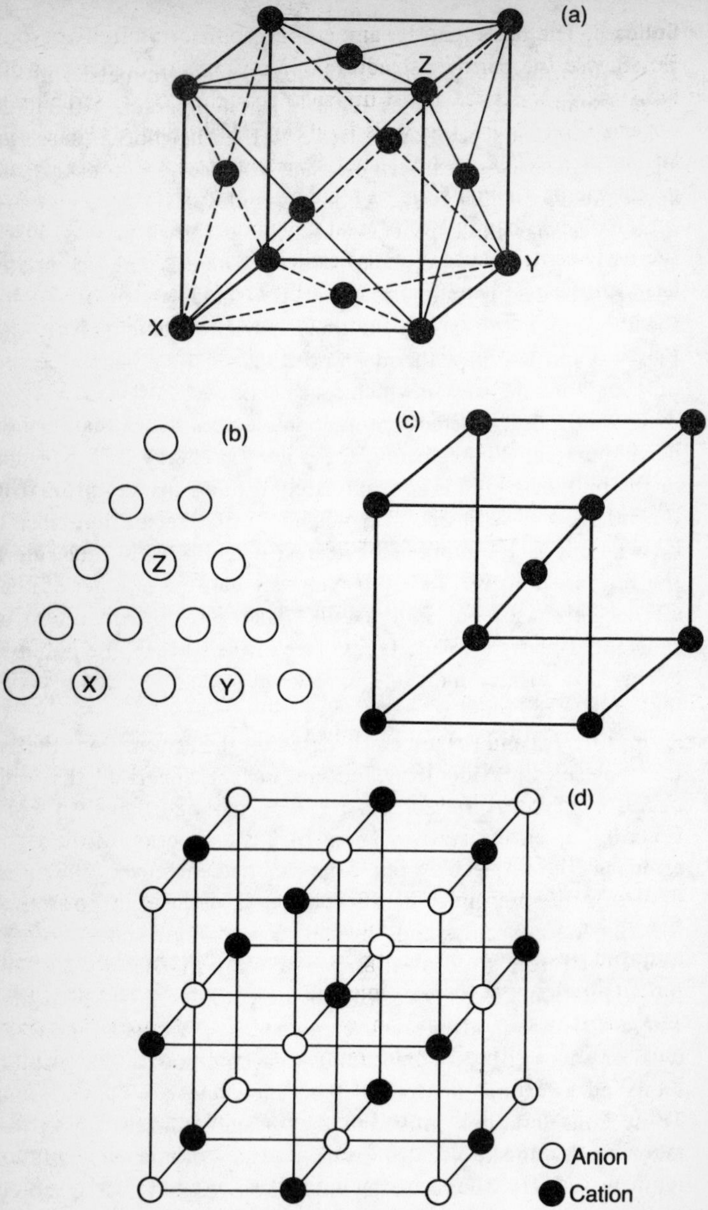

Fig. 1.3

in space. The basis may be any atomic, ionic or molecular group. To analyse the periodic structure of a crystal a reference coordinate system or lattice is set up, such that the crystal structure is obtained by placing the basis in an identical orientation on each lattice point. The crystal structure shown in Figs 1.3(a) and (b) is known as the face-centred cubic (f.c.c.) structure, in which each molecule has twelve nearest neighbours. Figure 1.3(c) shows the body-centred cubic (b.c.c.) structure, in which each molecule has eight nearest neighbours, while Fig. 1.3(d) shows the rock salt structure, composed of sodium and chloride ions, in which each ion is surrounded by six of the opposite electrical charge.

The axes of the reference coordinate system or lattice are known as crystallographic axes, and are usually chosen to be directions of small intermolecular distance. In general, a crystalline solid can be divided into regions in each of which the crystallographic axes have different orientations from those in adjacent regions. Each such region where a regular three-dimensional arrangement can be identified is called a grain, and the contact zone between two differently oriented grains is a grain boundary. A grain boundary is a zone, a few molecular diameters across, in which the regular molecular arrangement is distorted and the molecules occupy equilibrium positions that are a compromise between the normal positions in the grains in contact. Figure 1.4 shows a section through a grain boundary in a monatomic crystal. When a specimen consists of a single grain it is called a single crystal.

In general, the internal energy of a fixed mass of any substance increases with temperature. In the solid phase this energy causes the molecules to oscillate about fixed positions (the mean or time-averaged positions), the energy of any one molecule being totally potential energy at the extreme ends of the vibrational movement. The variations in separation of a pair of molecules that occur during this vibration may be represented in Fig. 1.2(b) using the line $0'ABC$. It is assumed that one molecule of the pair is fixed at $0'$, while the relative position of the other changes between A and C, the line $0'ABC$ being drawn at a height above the minimum in the U–r curve corresponding to the energy of vibration. The mean separation of the molecules is $0'B$, where B is midway between A and C. If the U–r curve is symmetrical about the minimum, the mean molecular separation will remain at r_0, even though the vibrational energy of the pair of molecules (and, therefore, the temperature of a large assembly of molecules) increases. However, if the curve is asymmetrical about r_0, as shown in Fig. 1.2(b), increasing the vibrational energy causes the mean separation to increase and the assembly of molecules then shows thermal expansion.

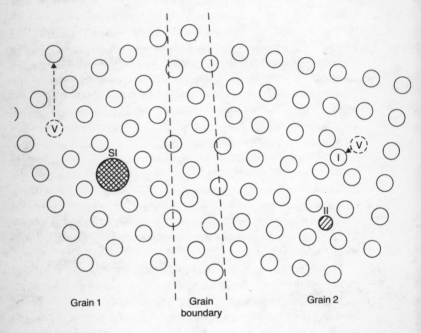

Fig. 1.4 V = vacancy, I = interstitial, II = interstitial impurity, SI = substitutional impurity.

The molecules in the solid phase interact strongly with each other and, consequently, at any instant they will not all have the same energy; there will be a distribution of energies among them, and the energy of any particular molecule will vary rapidly with time. This leads to two related effects. At any temperature the most energetic molecules close to the surface of the solid will have enough energy to escape through the surface of the solid, despite the attractive forces of the others. This is the process of sublimination and is responsible for the (generally very low) vapour pressure of solids. These fluctuations in molecular kinetic energy also result in some molecules being removed from their normal positions in the crystal structure. When the displaced molecule may be considered as being placed on the surface of the solid, a vacant lattice site or vacancy (sometimes called a Schottky defect) is produced, shown schematically for a simple atomic crystal in Fig. 1.4. Alternatively, the displaced molecule may be pushed into a site between normal crystal positions, again leaving a vacancy. The displaced molecule is termed an interstitial and the interstitial–vacancy pair is known as a Frenkel defect.

Schottky and Frenkel defects are continuously created by fluctuations in the molecular energy (thermal fluctuations) and destroyed by recombination. An equilibrium concentration of defects is established, the value of the concentration being a rapidly increasing function of temperature.

In most crystals the energies of formation of Schottky and Frenkel defects are very different so that one type of defect predominates, the concentration of the other being negligible.

In addition to Schottky and Frenkel defects, impurities (foreign molecules) may be present, either occupying normal crystal sites (substitutional impurities) or interstitial sites (interstitial impurities) as shown in Fig. 1.4.

Most solids are crystalline, but not all are so; some are amorphous and others partially crystalline. In amorphous solids there is no long-range order, though nearest-neighbour bonds are normal. The structure of an amorphous solid is similar to what would be expected in an instantaneous photograph of the liquid, but there is, of course, negligible molecular movement. One way of producing simple materials in amorphous form is to lower the temperature of the melt so rapidly that the molecules do not have time to take up the true equilibrium positions predicted by the intermolecular potential. For this reason they are sometimes referred to as supercooled liquids.

Partially crystalline solids are those that have some regions where long-range order is found and others where it is absent. Many polymers in bulk show this property. Polymer molecules consist of long chains of atoms, often with small side groups at intervals. The chains may be held together by strong covalent bonds or by the much weaker van der Waals bonds. Partially crystalline regions occur when polymer chains lie side by side over a definite area. Since polymers behave rather differently from 'ordinary' substances of low relative molecular mass they will be dealt with separately in Chapter 8.

1.5 Liquids

As the temperature of a solid rises, so does the mean amplitude of the oscillations of the molecules and, even when the mean energy is less than U_0, this leads to the break-up of the long-range order and the material becomes a liquid. At the melting point a liquid has almost the same density as the solid at that temperature, showing that the molecules in the liquid are still more or less closely packed, but have a very much greater mobility than those in the solid.

Some indication of the distribution of molecules in a liquid in equilibrium may be obtained from X-ray diffraction studies. Monatomic liquids give an intensity pattern having the same essential features as that from finely powdered crystalline material, but much more diffuse.

One way of interpreting the X-ray results is to consider the average number density of molecules in the liquid $\rho(r)$, relative to some chosen origin. If one particular molecule is taken as the origin of coordinates, $\rho(r)$ is the mean number of molecules per unit volume at a radius r and may be obtained, in principle, by averaging over a large number of instantaneous photographs of molecular positions. Then the average number of molecules found within a shell of radius r and thickness dr is $4\pi r^2 dr\rho(r)$. The total number of molecules in this shell at any instant may also be written as $g(r)dr$, so that:

$$g(r) = 4\pi r^2 \rho(r).$$ [1.12]

$\rho(r)$ is the radial distribution function. (It should be noted that other, slightly different definitions are in use.)

Now $g(r)$ may be obtained by X-ray diffraction and a slightly idealised representation of $g(r)$ for a monatomic liquid is given by the full line in Fig. 1.5(a). This curve may be considered to represent a series of overlapping peaks, each peak arising from one 'layer' of molecules surrounding the molecule at the origin. The

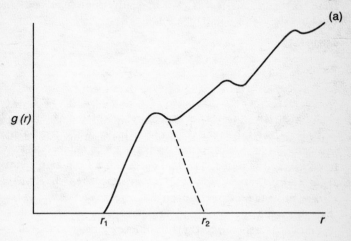

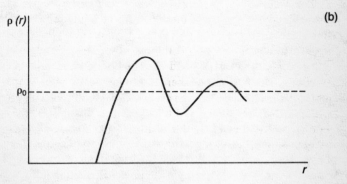

Fig. 1.5

area under the first peak can be estimated by reflecting the leading edge of the curve in the vertical through the peak, giving the curve shown dotted. Then the number of nearest neighbours of the molecule at the origin can be determined from the area under the first peak as follows. The number of molecules in the shell lying between radii r_1 and r_2 is:

$$\int_{r_1}^{r_2} 4\pi r^2 \rho(r) \, dr$$

which is simply:

$$\int_{r_1}^{r_2} g(r) \, dr$$

i.e. the area under the first peak.

Alternatively, the results can be represented by plotting $\rho(r)$ against r, which shows the peaks more clearly. The curve obtained is shown in Fig. 1.5(b), where ρ_0 is the mean number density of molecules in the liquid. The $\rho(r)$ curve starts from zero and rises sharply at a finite value of r as a consequence of the molecular repulsions. It then passes through a maximum and oscillates about the value ρ_0, tending to the value ρ_0 at large values of r. The first maximum corresponds to the shell of nearest neighbours and gives the approximate molecular diameter.

An analysis of this type shows that, for simple liquids, the order gradually disappears as the temperature rises; the number of nearest neighbours decreases slightly on going from the solid to the liquid phase. One interpretation of the results described in this section is to treat a liquid as a broken-up solid. This is the essence of the cell model of a liquid, in which each molecule is assumed to be constrained by its neighbours to move in a small volume of space called a cell, but is not so firmly held as to eliminate small irregular movements. The model will be discussed in greater detail in section 4.7.

The potential energy curve of Fig. 1.2(b) gives no direct information about the change from the solid to the liquid phase. Lindemann suggested that the melting temperature could be obtained from this curve by assuming that melting occurs when the amplitude of the molecular vibration exceeds a critical fraction of the intermolecular distance. At that stage numerous collisions occur between neighbours and the long-range structure of the solid is destroyed. Simple models of this sort are not really adequate to describe the melting process and more recent approaches will be mentioned in section 4.8.

When the temperature of the liquid is raised sufficiently so that the mean value of the internal energy per molecule pair is U_0 the molecules can escape completely from their nearest neighbours. This produces the gaseous phase, in which the separations of the molecules are sufficiently great for the intermolecular forces to be ineffective except during collisions. Let a target molecule, assumed fixed at the original coordinates, make a head-on elastic collision with a moving similar molecule, the projectile. The projectile will approach the target until all its kinetic energy has been converted into potential energy; the projectile is then instantaneously at rest before moving away from the target. The separation r_d of the two molecules when the projectile is instantaneously at rest will correspond to a point on the part KH of the U–r curve (see Fig. 1.2(b)), the precise value of r depending on the speed of the projectile molecule. This value r_d is a measure of the molecular diameter in the gaseous phase and will decrease slowly as the speed of the projectile increases; the molecules behave as slightly soft spheres. In the hard sphere approximation the U–r curve becomes that shown dashed in Fig. 1.2(b), with the repulsive force rising abruptly to infinity at $r = r_0$, the equilibrium separation of a pair of molecules.

Chapter 2

The elastic properties of matter

2.1 Forces and equilibrium in a finite body

Much of this book is concerned with the response of solids and liquids in bulk to applied forces and is, therefore, concerned with the application of Newton's laws of motion to such bodies. Newton's laws of motion as usually stated (see, for example, *Classical Mechanics* by B.P. Cowan in this series) describe the effect of forces on particles, i.e. on entities so small that their size plays no role in the description of their behaviour. Matter in bulk can be treated as an assembly of such particles and, as a first step in the study of the response of bulk matter to applied forces, some of the implications of Newton's laws for a finite body will be examined.

As a specific example, consider a right circular cylinder of area of cross-section α and length L, initially at rest, that is acted upon by a force F_a applied in the direction of its axis, as indicated in Fig. 2.1. If ρ is the density of the material of the cylinder (so that its mass is $\rho\alpha L$) and u is its velocity (which here is in the same direction as F_a), the equation of motion of the body as a whole is

$$F_a = \rho\alpha L \, \frac{\mathrm{d}u}{\mathrm{d}t} \tag{2.1}$$

where t is the time.

Newton's laws can be applied to any part of the body. In particular, consider the behaviour of that part, shown shaded in Fig. 2.1, of length l. Since the acceleration of this part of the body is the same as that of the body as a whole, the force F_i acting on the shaded part of the body because of the presence of the remainder of the body is

$$F_i = \rho a l \frac{du}{dt}. \qquad [2.2]$$

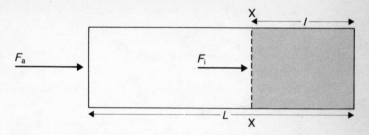

Fig. 2.1

According to Newton's third law of motion, that part of the body corresponding to the shaded region in Fig. 2.1 exerts a force $-F_i$ on the remainder of the body. Therefore, the equation of motion of that part of the body is

$$F_a - F_i = \rho a (L - l) \frac{du}{dt}. \qquad [2.3]$$

Notice that when $l = L$, $F_a = F_i$ and when $l = 0$, $F_i = 0$.

This analysis shows that the force acting on a finite body must be considered as being transmitted through that body, and that to specify the value of that force the part of the body under consideration must be specified. The force F_i is the response of the body to the applied force F_a and arises from the interactions of the molecules making up the material. These forces, which resist the applied, or external, forces are called internal forces.

The situation illustrated in Fig. 2.1 is one in which equal and opposite forces act across the section plane XX of the body and, since this was chosen arbitrarily, across each parallel section plane. This condition may be described by saying that a load is acting across the section plane under consideration. It should be noted that there is no resultant force acting across the section plane itself since the forces are equal and opposite. The term load indicates a mutual action across the section; the measure of the load is the amount of force on one side of the section. This load is compressive when the two equal and opposite forces on either side of the section are each toward the section, and is tensile when their directions are each away from the section.

Loads that are produced by external forces acting directly on the surface of the body are transmitted throughout the body by the interactions of the constituent molecules; any element of the body exerts a force on neighbouring parts. The forces exerted on the surface of any element of the body by the material surrounding it are known as contact or surface forces, and are proportional to the surface area of the element. That the interaction of one part of a body with an adjacent part can be regarded as a contact or surface force across the common boundary is, of course, a consequence of the short-range nature of the intermolecular forces.

In addition, there may be forces that act throughout the body on all its elements. The magnitudes of these forces are proportional to the volume of the element and are called body forces. An example of a body force is that due to gravity. Generally, the effects of body forces are negligible compared with those of surface forces, but see, however, example 2.2.

A finite body is still under load when it is in statical equilibrium while subject to external forces. The conditions for equilibrium are that the vector sum of all the external forces acting on the body is zero and the sum of all the external moments acting on it is zero. These conditions must hold for any portion of the body so that the internal force system must also be in equilibrium. Any arrangement of applied forces that is in equilibrium to give zero translational and rotational accelerations will be called a set of balanced forces.

2.2 Elasticity

When a crystalline solid is acted on by a system of balanced forces the molecules of the solid are displaced from their equilibrium positions. As soon as the applied forces produce changes in the molecular separations from the equilibrium value, intermolecular forces are brought into play that resist the external forces. This is the origin of the internal forces by which the applied forces are effectively transmitted through the body. The restoring forces build up almost instantaneously when the molecular separation is changed, to values that balance the applied forces, giving an equilibrium state. These intermolecular forces are maintained as long as the external forces are applied and, when the external forces are removed, they return the molecules almost instantaneously to their original positions.

This property of solids and, in some circumstances, of liquids and gases, to suffer deformation under applied forces and then to recover completely their original shape when the forces are removed is called elasticity. The behaviour of real materials can be extrapolated to prescribe an ideal elastic material, which is one that:

1. responds instantaneously to a change in the applied forces;
2. has a deformation that does not vary with time when the applied forces remain constant; and
3. has an instantaneous and complete recovery of its original form when the applied forces are removed.

In the immediate neighbourhood of the equilibrium separation, the graph of intermolecular force against intermolecular distance may be treated as a straight line (Fig. 1.2(a)). Small changes in molecular separation in any region of the solid are then proportional to the load produced in that region by the external forces, and this is true for both compressive and tensile loads. Figure 1.2(a) shows that further increases in load result in a behaviour that is still elastic but no longer linear. If no other processes occur first, the maximum tensile load that any region of the solid can withstand is F_m. Any attempt to exceed this value results in a catastrophic separation of the molecules since the equilibrium is no longer stable.

2.3 Stress

The effect of a load of given magnitude in producing distortion in a body depends on the area over which it acts. When comparing the effects produced in different materials the appropriate measure is the load per unit area, which is known as the stress, and which has, therefore, units of N m^{-2} or Pa. It is important to remember that stress is a measure of what is a mutual interaction. The term stress is also used more generally so that a body in which one part exerts a force on a neighbouring part is said to be in a state of stress.

At a point O in a body that is in a state of stress take a definite direction OP and a small plane area $\delta\alpha$ normal to OP and containing O, as in Fig. 2.2. OP is the normal to $\delta\alpha$ and the side of $\delta\alpha$ from which OP projects is taken as the positive side. Treating the material as continuous, at each point of the surface $\delta\alpha$ the material on one side exerts a definite force on the material on the other. Conditions in the solid as a whole would be unchanged if a cut were made across $\delta\alpha$ and these forces inserted. The resultant of all forces exerted by the material on the positive side of $\delta\alpha$ on that on the other side will be a force, δF, say, that is the measure of the load acting across $\delta\alpha$. Then, the stress at the point O across the plane whose normal is in the direction OP is defined as:

$$\underset{\delta\alpha \to 0}{\mathrm{Lt}} \ \frac{\delta F}{\delta\alpha} \, .$$

There is a difficulty at the molecular level in that the discrete nature of the matter makes taking the limit as $\delta\alpha \to 0$ meaningless. However, if attention is focused on an infinitesimal area of a condensed phase, this contains such a large number of molecules that the material is effectively continuous and the definition can be used.

The stress in a body is described as homogeneous if, for a surface element within the body of fixed shape and orientation, the value is independent of the position of the element in the body.

The force δF may make any angle θ with the normal to $\delta\alpha$, as in Fig. 2.2. The direct or normal stress component has a direction normal to the surface element across which it acts and is denoted by σ. When the direction of the normal stress is outwards from the surface element under consideration the stress is termed tensile. Applied forces that give rise to a tensile stress are counted positive, as is the stress, considered as the transmission of the load per unit area through the body, though the resisting intermolecular forces brought into play are negative.

When the direction of the normal stress is towards the surface element it is termed compressive and is considered negative, as are the applied forces giving rise to the stress.

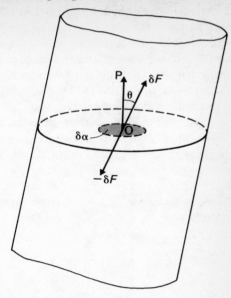

Fig. 2.2

If OP in Fig. 2.2 is the outward normal to the surface $\delta\alpha$, the normal stress σ acting over $\delta\alpha$ is:

$$\sigma = \underset{\delta\alpha \to 0}{\mathrm{Lt}} \frac{\delta F \cos\theta}{\delta\alpha}. \qquad [2.4a]$$

The direction of a normal stress relative to Cartesian axes is denoted by a suffix notation: σ_x is the normal stress component in the x direction, etc.

The component of the load per unit area acting in the plane of $\delta\alpha$ is termed a tangential or shear stress and is denoted by τ. Then:

$$\tau = \underset{\delta\alpha \to 0}{\mathrm{Lt}} \frac{\delta F \sin\theta}{\delta\alpha}. \qquad [2.4b]$$

To denote the directions of shear stresses a two-suffix notation is needed. In the usual convention the first suffix denotes the direction of the normal to the plane in which the stress acts and the second gives the direction of the shear stress component. For example, τ_{xy} is a shear stress acting in the y direction on a plane with its positive normal in the x direction. When the directions of both normal and stress have the same sign the stress component is counted positive; when they have different signs it is counted negative.

The conditions for the equilibrium of a body subject to shear stresses are most simply examined by considering the case of a unit cube within a stressed body. Let the edges of the cube be parallel, respectively, to the axes $0x, 0y, 0z$. The material outside the cube exerts a force on the material inside the cube across each face of the cube. Consider a section of the cube perpendicular to the $0z$ axis, as shown in Fig. 2.3. When a stress τ_{yx} acts on the

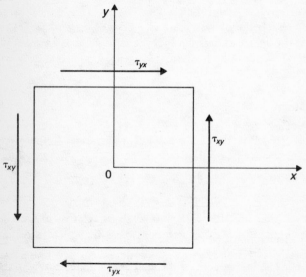

Fig. 2.3

face with its outward normal in the positive y direction, a stress τ_{yx} must also act on the face with its outward normal in the negative y direction, as shown in Fig. 2.3, to maintain translational equilibrium. In addition, to prevent rotation of the cube, complementary shear stresses τ_{xy} must be present as shown. Let the stresses be homogeneous, body forces be absent and the cube be in equilibrium. Then, taking moments about an axis parallel to the z axis and passing through the centre of the cube gives:

$$\tau_{yx} = \tau_{xy} \qquad [2.5a]$$

so that the presence of a shear stress on one plane necessitates a complementary shear stress of the same sign and magnitude on a perpendicular plane. Similarly:

$$\tau_{yz} = \tau_{zy} \text{ and } \tau_{xz} = \tau_{zx}. \qquad [2.5b]$$

(The results contained in equations [2.5] are, in fact, still true when the stress is inhomogeneous, body forces are present and the body is not in statical equilibrium, though such cases are not considered here.)

A special state of stress that occurs occasionally with solids is the hydrostatic stress, in which a body is subject to external forces that produce a stress that has the same value in all directions. Negative values of hydrostatic stress correspond to uniform pressures.

2.4 Strain

For a given material the deformation of different bodies subjected to a particular load is a function of size. Therefore, comparisons of deformation are best made by expressing the deformation as a non-dimensional quantity called strain and defined as:

$$\text{strain} = \frac{\text{change in dimension}}{\text{original dimension}}.$$

The application of a set of balanced forces to a body in general produces translation, rotation and change in shape of individual elements of the body. Translations and rotations (as a rigid body) do not involve strain, which is a measure of the relative change of shape.

The simplest situations to deal with are those in which the strain of an element of a body of constant size and orientation is independent of its position in the body. This implies that the state of strain is the same at all points in the body and the strain is said to be homogeneous. The tests for homogeneous strain are that lines on the body that were originally straight should remain straight after deformation and lines that were originally parallel should remain parallel, though their direction may be changed.

In general a cube of material that has undergone a homogeneous strain is distorted into a parallelepiped, which suggests that strains should be specified in terms of the changes in length of the cube edges and the changes in the angles between the edges of the cube. This suggestion turns out to be well-founded, though in practice three basic strains are found to be convenient for describing the condition of a body in a state of homogeneous strain. These strains are:

1. linear or extensional strain;
2. bulk strain;
3. shear strain.

Linear or extensional strain

When a prismatic bar of undeformed length L_0, with free (i.e. unloaded) prismatic surfaces, is deformed by balanced forces applied along its axis its length changes to a value L. The linear strain ϵ is then defined as

$$\epsilon = \frac{L - L_0}{L_0}. \qquad [2.6]$$

ϵ is positive when the load produced in the material is tensile and negative when it is compressive. Sometimes it is more convenient to use a logarithmic (or natural) linear strain ϵ^*, defined as:

$$\epsilon^* = \ln(L/L_0) . \qquad [2.7]$$

It follows that:

$$\epsilon^* = \ln(1 + \epsilon)$$

so that, when the extension $L - L_0$ is small, $\epsilon \approx \epsilon^*$.

Balanced axial forces applied to a prismatic bar not only produce a linear strain but also give rise to a change in cross-sectional area. Tensile loading gives a decrease in area while compressive loading gives an increase. A lateral or transverse strain ϵ_1 can be defined as:

$$\epsilon_l = \frac{\text{change in lateral dimension}}{\text{original lateral dimension}}.$$

For a material with properties that are homogeneous and isotropic ϵ_l is independent of direction in the cross-sectional plane. It is found experimentally that the quantity ν, defined by

$$\nu = -\frac{\epsilon_l}{\epsilon}, \qquad [2.8]$$

is a material constant. This is known as the Poisson's ratio of the material.

Bulk strain

When the balanced applied forces produce a hydrostatic stress in an isotropic solid, so that the volume changes from an initial value V_0 to a value V, the bulk strain θ is defined as

$$\theta = \frac{V - V_0}{V_0}. \qquad [2.9]$$

Shear strain

Let a cube of a homogeneous, isotropic material have two lines at right angles inscribed on one face. When the cube is subjected to balanced forces that produce shear stresses with directions parallel to the edges of this face the angle between the two lines changes. The tangent of the change in the angle between the two lines is taken as the measure of the strain, in this case a shear strain. When the shear strain is very small the change in the angle itself (expressed in radians) is taken as the measure of the shear strain. The shear strain is considered as positive when the angle between the inscribed lines decreases on straining and negative when it increases. For very small strains, a shear strain does not involve a change in the volume of the specimen (see section 2.9), so that there is no lateral effect.

2.5 Infinitesimal strain

When the strains are small (infinitesimal strains in the limiting case of the strain approaching zero) more precise definitions of the strain can be given. A suffix notation can also conveniently be introduced. Consider a section of a body in the xy plane, as in Fig. 2.4. Set up perpendicular lines in space to be the x and y

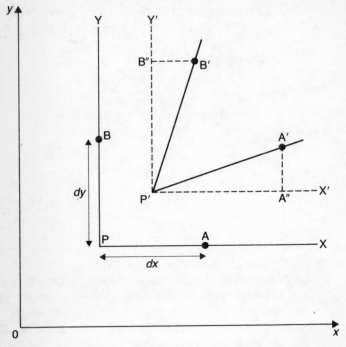

Fig. 2.4

coordinate axes and mark lines PX and PY on the specimen parallel to $0x$ and $0y$ respectively. Let A be a point on PX, a distance dx from P and B be a point on PY, a distance dy from P. When the body is deformed elastically by a small amount let P be displaced to P′, A to A′ and B to B′. The lines P′X′ and P′Y′ are parallel to $0x$, $0y$ respectively, A′A″ is perpendicular to P′X′ and B′B″ is perpendicular to P′Y′.

The extensional or linear strain in the x direction is:

$$(P'A'' - PA)/PA$$

and may be denoted by ϵ_x. Similarly, the linear strain in the y direction is ϵ_y, given by:

$$(P'B'' - PB)/PB.$$

There will be a similar expression for ϵ_z in three-dimensional strain.

If U, V, W are respectively, the displacements of P in the x, y and z directions, referred to the original axes, the respective displacement of A in the x direction is:

$$U + (\partial U/\partial x)dx$$

so that

$$\epsilon_x = \partial U/\partial x$$

and similarly:

$$\epsilon_y = \partial V/\partial y$$

and: $\epsilon_z = \partial W/\partial z$.

The displacement of the point A in the y direction is V + $(\partial V/\partial x)dx$ while that of the point B in the x direction is U + $(\partial U/\partial y)dy$. These displacements cause the inscribed line P'A' to make an angle equal to $\tan^{-1}(\partial V/\partial x)$ with the initial direction. Similarly, P'B' is inclined to its original direction by the angle $\tan^{-1}(\partial U/\partial y)$. Therefore, the angle between the inscribed lines, initially the right-angle APB, is reduced by the angle $\tan^{-1}(\partial V/\partial x + \partial U/\partial y)$. This is the shear strain between the planes xz and yz and may be denoted by γ_{xy}. For very small angles $\tan \gamma \approx \gamma$ and the infinitesimal shear strain is:

$$\gamma_{xy} = \frac{\partial V}{\partial x} + \frac{\partial U}{\partial y}.$$

Similarly, the infinitesimal shear strains between the zx and yx planes is:

$$\gamma_{yz} = \frac{\partial W}{\partial y} + \frac{\partial V}{\partial x}$$

and that between the zy and xy planes is:

$$\gamma_{zx} = \frac{\partial U}{\partial z} + \frac{\partial W}{\partial x} .$$

The six infinitesimal strains are collected together for convenience as equations [2.10]:

$$\epsilon_x = \frac{\partial U}{\partial x} \; ; \; \epsilon_y = \frac{\partial V}{\partial y} \; ; \; \epsilon_z = \frac{\partial W}{\partial z}$$

$$[2.10]$$

$$\gamma_{xy} = \frac{\partial V}{\partial x} + \frac{\partial U}{\partial y}; \; \gamma_{yz} = \frac{\partial W}{\partial y} + \frac{\partial V}{\partial z}; \; \gamma_{zx} = \frac{\partial U}{\partial z} + \frac{\partial W}{\partial x} .$$

Note that it does not matter whether, for example, γ_{xy} or γ_{yx} is used, since the shear strains at all four corners of an initially rectangular element are equal.

Any component of shear strain, e.g. $\partial V/\partial x$ in γ_{xy}, is counted as positive if a particle of the solid moves, during deformation, in the direction of an axis that has the same sign as the axis on which the particle lies.

2.6 The relationship between stress and strain

When the strain produced in a simple solid is small it is found experimentally that

strain $\propto$ stress

or, including a constant of proportionality,

stress = constant $\times$ strain.

This is Hooke's law, first stated in connection with the extension of a loaded spring. The constant in the equation as it is written is called a modulus of elasticity. For an isotropic material the modulus depends on temperature only, but for an anisotropic material it also depends on the direction in the sample in which the measurement is made. The graph of stress against strain for such small strains is a straight line passing through the origin; it has the same slope in tension and in compression and is followed in both loading and unloading. A modulus of elasticity has the dimensions of stress and has, therefore, units of N m^{-2} or Pa.

2.7 Moduli of elasticity

The three strains commonly used to describe the deformation of bodies give rise, respectively, to three moduli of elasticity. In each case the modulus is, in general, temperature-dependent and has a single value at a given temperature only if the material can be treated as elastically isotropic.

A bar of uniform cross-section α and unstretched length L_0 becomes of length L when acted on by balanced forces, F_a applied uniformly over the end sections. The extension is $L - L_0$ and the linear strain ϵ, which here is homogeneous, is $(L - L_0)/L_0$. Since the stress σ, which here is also homogeneous, is given by F_a/α, when Hooke's law is obeyed

$$\sigma = F_a/\alpha = E\epsilon = E(L - L_0)/L_0. \qquad [2.11]$$

E is a material constant, at constant temperature, known as Young's modulus.

When a cube of material is subject to a uniform hydrostatic stress as a result of equal forces F_a being applied in the same sense to each surface, of area α, a change in volume from V_0 to V is produced. The stress is given by F_a/α and the bulk strain is:

$$\theta = (V - V_0)/V_0.$$

When Hooke's law is obeyed

$$\sigma = F_a/\alpha = K\theta = K(V - V_0)/V_0 \qquad [2.12]$$

where K is a material constant, at constant temperature, called the bulk modulus. The most important applications of this modulus involve a solid subjected to an applied hydrostatic pressure. A pressure has a negative sign but produces a decrease in volume so that K is positive.

When a cube of material is sheared by applied couples produced by forces F_a acting tangentially over surfaces of area α the angle of shear γ is taken as the measure of the strain. Then, when Hooke's law is obeyed:

$$\tau = F_a/\alpha = G\gamma \qquad\qquad [2.13]$$

where G is a material constant at constant temperature known as the rigidity modulus or the shear modulus.

Some typical values of elastic moduli are given in Table 2.1. They refer to room temperature measurements and in the case of crystalline materials, to isotropic (fine-grained) specimens.

Table 2.1 *Elastic moduli and Poisson's ratio of some common materials*

Materials	E(GPa)	G(GPa)	K(GPa)	ν
Aluminium	70	26	76	0.35
Cadmium	50	19	42	0.30
Copper	130	48	138	0.34
Gold	78	27	217	0.44
Lead	16	5	46	0.43
Mild steel	212	82	169	0.29
Crown glass	71	29	41	0.22
Granite	46	19	26	0.21

2.8 The theorem of superposition

When the state of stress in a body is other than a simple, normal shear or hydrostatic stress, the resulting strain may be determined by application of the theorem of superposition, which may be stated as follows.

For a deformed body, in the linear elastic range of behaviour, the strain produced by a complex system of stresses (of the same type) is given by the sum of the strains produced by the component stresses acting separately. A simple proof of the theorem, as applied to elastic deformation, is given in *The Mechanical Properties of Matter* by A.H. Cottrell but, essentially, if the theorem were not true, the energy stored in a body deformed by a complex stress system would depend on the order of loading, so that an elastic device could be produced that would release more elastic energy on unloading than was stored during loading.

In section 2.9 the theorem will be applied to complex stress systems in the linear, isotropic solid to obtain relations between the various elastic constants of such a material.

2.9 The linear, isotropic, elastic solid

A model substance that represents closely the deformation behaviour for small strains of a wide range of materials is the linear isotropic, elastic solid. As the name implies, the substance is isotropic, satisfies Hooke's law for all strains and shows perfect elasticity.

Consider a cube of such a material with its edges parallel, respectively to the coordinate axes $0x$, $0y$, $0z$ and let balanced forces be applied that produce stresses σ_x, σ_y and σ_z simultaneously. The total effect of these stresses can be determined by means of the principle of superposition: the effect of each stress acting separately is determined and the total effect of the stresses acting simultaneously is obtained by adding together the separate effects.

When σ_x alone acts, a linear strain is produced in the x direction equal to σ_x/E, where E is Young's modulus for the material. This is accompanied by a strain in the y direction equal to $-\nu\sigma_x/E$ and an equal strain in the z direction, where ν is Poisson's ratio for the material. Similar results are obtained for σ_y and σ_z acting separately. When all three stresses act simultaneously, the theorem of superposition gives, for the total strains in the three coordinate directions:

$$\epsilon_x = \frac{\sigma_x}{E} - \nu\frac{\sigma_y}{E} - \nu\frac{\sigma_z}{E} = \frac{1}{E}(\sigma_x - \nu(\sigma_y + \sigma_z))$$

$$\epsilon_y = \frac{1}{E}(\sigma_y - \nu(\sigma_z + \sigma_x)) \qquad\qquad [2.14]$$

$$\epsilon_z = \frac{1}{E}(\sigma_z - \nu(\sigma_x + \sigma_y)) \ .$$

If the unstrained edge length of the cube of material is L_0, the unstrained volume is L_0^3. When the cube is subjected to the balanced external forces its volume is $(L_x L_y L_z)$, where:

$$L_x = L_0(1 + \epsilon_x); \ L_y = L_0(1 + \epsilon_y); \ L_z = L_0(1 + \epsilon_z).$$

These expressions follow from the definition of linear strains. When the linear strains are small, as is normally the case in practical situations of elastic deformation, the deformed volume is closely equal to $L_0^3(1 + \epsilon_x + \epsilon_y + \epsilon_z)$, an expression obtained by neglecting terms of the type $(\epsilon_x \epsilon_y)$ and higher terms. Therefore, the change in volume per unit volume is $(\epsilon_x + \epsilon_y + \epsilon_z)$, a quantity known as the dilatation and denoted by Δ, i.e.:

$$\Delta = \epsilon_x + \epsilon_y + \epsilon_z . \tag{2.15}$$

Adding equations [2.14] shows that

$$\Delta = \frac{1}{E}(1 - 2\nu)(\sigma_x + \sigma_y + \sigma_z) . \tag{2.16}$$

If all three stresses are equal the cube is subjected to a hydrostatic stress and the dilatation becomes the bulk strain θ.

Put: $\sigma_x = \sigma_y = \sigma_z = \sigma$.

Then, from equation [2.16]

$$K = \frac{\sigma}{\theta} = \frac{E}{3(1 - 2\nu)}$$

where K is the bulk modulus. Therefore, for an isotropic linear elastic material:

$$E = 3K(1 - 2\nu) . \tag{2.17}$$

Since E and K must both be positive, equation [2.17] indicates that the value of ν cannot be greater than $\frac{1}{2}$.

Now let the cube of isotropic, linear elastic material be subjected to external forces giving the stress system:

$$\sigma_x = +\sigma; \ \sigma_y = -\sigma; \ \sigma_z = 0.$$

Then, considering the effect of each stress component acting separately and using the theorem of superposition, gives for the linear strains when both stress components act simultaneously:

$$\epsilon_x = \frac{\sigma}{E} + \nu\frac{\sigma}{E} = \frac{\sigma}{E}(1 + \nu)$$

$$\epsilon_y = -\frac{\sigma}{E}(1 + \nu)$$

$$\epsilon_z = \nu \frac{\sigma}{E} - \nu \frac{\sigma}{E} = 0.$$

The dilatation produced by this stress system is:

$$\Delta = \epsilon_x + \epsilon_y + \epsilon_z$$

$$= \frac{\sigma}{E}(1 + \nu) - \frac{\sigma}{E}(1 + \nu) = 0$$

i.e. when the strains produced by the separate stress components are small, there is no volume change produced by this deformation.

Consider a section through the cube of material, parallel to the xy plane, as shown in Fig. 2.5(a). The midpoints of the sides of the sections are, respectively, A,B,C,D. Then:

$$BF = FC = L_0/2$$

and: $BC = L_0/\sqrt{2}$.

The prism of material with cross-section BFC must be in equilibrium under the applied forces acting on the surfaces represented by BF and FC, together with the load acting across the surface represented by BC and arising from the presence of the remainder of the stressed solid. Figure 2.5(b) shows the forces acting on unit thickness of the prism of material; τ is the tangential stress acting on the prism across the surface BC, while σ_n is the stress component normal to BC.

Resolving forces normal to BC gives:

$$\sigma_n \frac{L_0}{\sqrt{2}} + \frac{\sigma L_0}{2\sqrt{2}} - \frac{\sigma L_0}{2\sqrt{2}} = 0$$

giving:

$$\sigma_n = 0.$$

Resolving forces parallel to BC gives:

$$\tau \frac{L_0}{\sqrt{2}} = \frac{\sigma L_0}{2\sqrt{2}} + \frac{\sigma L_0}{2\sqrt{2}}$$

which gives:

$$\tau = \sigma.$$

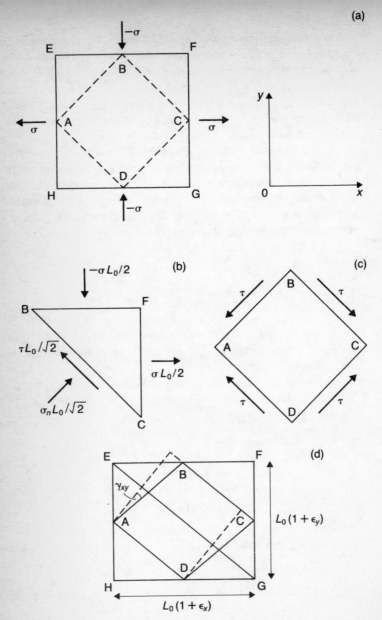

Fig. 2.5

A similar analysis may be applied to the other three prisms of material with cross-sections ABE, CDG and ADH. Then, the stresses acting on the material contained in the section ABCD are shown in Fig. 2.5(c). Only equal shear stresses act on the surface of this section, giving a state of affairs known as a pure shear stress. There is no associated change in volume for small strains, only a change in shape.

In the above discussion the distortion of the cube was neglected in the calculation of the stresses because it is very small. The shape of the distorted cube is, however, as shown in Fig. 2.5(d), and this must be examined in more detail if the relationship between linear and shear strains is to be determined.

Consider the similar triangles EFG and BFC of the section EFGH. The strain EG must equal the strain of BC. Using the theorem of Pythagoras:

$$EG = L_0 [(1 + \epsilon_x)^2 + (1 + \epsilon_y)^2]^{\frac{1}{2}}.$$

If it is assumed that both ϵ_x and ϵ_y are very small:

$$EG = L_0(2 + 2\epsilon_x + 2\epsilon_y)^{\frac{1}{2}}$$

and, since $\epsilon_x = -\epsilon_y$ under these small strain conditions, therefore:

$$EG = \sqrt{2} . L_0 .$$

However, $\sqrt{2} . L_0$ was the original length of EG, so that, despite the applied forces, EG and BC are unchanged in length. In the triangle ABD:

$$B\hat{A}D = \pi/2 - \gamma_{xy}$$

where γ_{xy} is the shear strain. Also:

$$(EH)^2 = (BD)^2 = L_0^2(1 + \epsilon_y)^2$$

$$= (AB)^2 + (AD)^2 - 2(AB)(AD) \cos B\hat{A}D$$

$$= \frac{L_0^2}{2} + \frac{L_0^2}{2} - 2\left(\frac{L_0\sqrt{2}}{2}\right) \sin \gamma_{xy} ..$$

Therefore:

$$(1 + \epsilon_y)^2 = 1 - \sin \gamma_{xy}$$

and, when ϵ_y and γ_{xy} are both small, this becomes:

$$1 + 2\epsilon_y = 1 - \gamma_{xy}$$

or: $\quad \gamma_{xy} = -2\epsilon_y = 2\epsilon_x$

that is, numerically, the shear strain is twice either linear strain.

The shear stress τ and shear strain γ are related through equation [2.13] when Hooke's law is obeyed. Therefore, for an isotropic, linear solid in which the elastic strains are very small:

$$G = \frac{\tau}{\gamma_{xy}} = \frac{\sigma}{2\epsilon_x} = \frac{\sigma E}{2\sigma(1 + \nu)} = \frac{E}{2(1 + \nu)}. \qquad [2.18]$$

Since G and E must be positive, ν must be greater than -1. Therefore, for a linear, isotropic solid at small strains:

$$E = 3K(1 - 2\nu)$$

$$E = 2G(1 + \nu).$$

These results may be written in various ways — for example

$$\frac{1}{E} = \frac{1}{9K} + \frac{1}{3G} \qquad [2.19]$$

$$\nu = \frac{\dfrac{1}{6G} + \dfrac{1}{9K}}{\dfrac{1}{3G} + \dfrac{1}{9K}}. \qquad [2.20]$$

The linear isotropic approximation is widely used in calculations on the elastic behaviour of solids and the equations [2.14] are often expressed in terms of two material parameters known as the Lamé elastic constants.

Equations [2.14] may be written in the form:

$$\epsilon_x = \frac{\sigma_x}{E}(1 + \nu) - \frac{\nu}{E}\Theta \qquad [2.21]$$

$$\epsilon_y = \frac{\sigma_y}{E}(1 + \nu) - \frac{\nu}{E}\Theta \qquad [2.22]$$

$$\epsilon_z = \frac{\sigma_z}{E}(1+\nu) - \frac{\nu}{E}\Theta \qquad [2.23]$$

where $\Theta = \sigma_x + \sigma_y + \sigma_z$. The dilatation Δ is given by:

$$\Delta = \epsilon_x + \epsilon_y + \epsilon_z$$

and therefore:

$$\Delta = \frac{(1+\nu)}{E}(\sigma_x + \sigma_y + \sigma_z) - \frac{3\nu}{E}\Theta$$

$$= \frac{(1+\nu)}{E}\Theta - \frac{3\nu}{E}\Theta = \frac{(1-2\nu)}{E}\Theta . \qquad [2.24]$$

Substituting for Θ in equation [2.21] from equation [2.24] gives:

$$\epsilon_x = \frac{\sigma_x(1+\nu)}{E} - \frac{\nu E\Delta}{E(1-2\nu)}$$

or: $$\sigma_x = \frac{E\epsilon_x}{(1+\nu)} + \frac{\nu E\Delta}{(1-2\nu)(1+\nu)} . \qquad [2.25]$$

Putting:

$$2\mu = \frac{E}{(1+\nu)}$$

and: $$\lambda = \frac{\nu E}{(1-2\nu)(1+\nu)}$$

gives:

$$\sigma_x = 2\mu\epsilon_x + \lambda\Delta$$

where μ and λ are the Lamé elastic constants. In fact, μ is the rigidity modulus of the material. The complete set of equations using the Lamé constants is then:

$$\sigma_x = 2\mu\epsilon_x + \lambda\Delta$$
$$\sigma_y = 2\mu\epsilon_y + \lambda\Delta \qquad [2.26]$$
$$\sigma_z = 2\mu\epsilon_z + \lambda\Delta .$$

Using the techniques involving the principle of superposition it is a straightforward matter to show that the following relations hold between the Lamé constants and the quantities used earlier:

$$K = \frac{2\mu + 3\lambda}{3}$$

$$E = \frac{\mu(3\lambda + 2\mu)}{\lambda + \mu} \tag{2.27}$$

$$\nu = \frac{\lambda}{2(\lambda + \mu)}.$$

For many solid materials λ and μ are almost equal and, if this simplifying assumption is made, equations [2.27] become

$$K = 5\mu/3; \quad E = 5\mu/2; \quad \nu = 1/4 . \tag{2.28}$$

An alternative simplifying assumption is to treat the material as incompressible. This gives:

$$\lambda = K = \infty; \quad \nu = 1/2; \quad \mu = E/3. \tag{2.29}$$

A simple illustration of the use of linear, isotropic elasticity theory is given in example 2.1.

Example 2.1

A right circular solid cylinder made of copper is surrounded by a coaxial brass tube of the same length. Both stand on a rigid base with the common axis vertical. A large slab of mass M is placed symmetrically so that it rests on both cylinder and tube. If the cross-sectional area of the cylinder is α_c and that of the tube wall is α_b, determine the stress in both tube and cylinder. The copper and brass may be assumed isotropic with Young's modulus E_c and E_b respectively.

Essentially, there are three conditions that must be satisfied in a problem dealing with elastic deformation. These are: the equilibrium condition, the geometry of deformation and the stress–strain relation. In this problem both stress and strain are homogeneous and these conditions lead to the following equations.

1. *Equilibrium*

   If F_c and F_b are the forces exerted on the copper and brass respectively by the slab, then:

   $$-Mg = F_c + F_b \qquad [2.30]$$

   where the negative sign indicates that the applied forces produce a compressive load, and g is the acceleration of free fall.

2. *Geometry of deformation*

   Let L_c and L_b be the undeformed lengths of the copper and brass respectively. Since both components suffer the same change in length:

   $$\delta L_c = \delta L_b. \qquad [2.31]$$

3. *Stress–strain relationship*

   Letting σ be the stress in a component and ϵ be the corresponding linear strain:

   $$\sigma_c = E_c \epsilon_c \qquad \text{for the copper;}$$
   $$\sigma_b = E_b \epsilon_b \qquad \text{for the brass.} \qquad [2.32]$$

   Equations [2.30], [2.31] and [2.32] may now be combined to give the solution. Introducing the areas, equation [2.30] may be written:

   $$-Mg = \alpha_c \sigma_c + \alpha_b \sigma_b \qquad [2.33]$$

   and, substituting for σ from equation [2.32] gives:

   $$-Mg = \alpha_c E_c \epsilon_c + \alpha_b E_b \epsilon_b. \qquad [2.34]$$

   Since the initial lengths of tube and cylinder are equal, equation [2.31] gives:

   $$\epsilon_c = \epsilon_b = \epsilon$$

   say, so that, from equation [2.34],

   $$\epsilon = -\frac{Mg}{\alpha_c E_c + \alpha_b E_b}.$$

Therefore:

$$\sigma_c = E_c \epsilon = -\frac{MgE_c}{\alpha_c E_c + \alpha_b E_b}$$

and

$$\sigma_b = E_b \epsilon = \frac{MgE_b}{\alpha_c E_c + \alpha_b E_b}.$$

2.10 Elastic moduli and intermolecular forces

An elementary discussion of the relationship between the macroscopic and microscopic elastic properties of a crystalline solid may be based on a model solid in which the molecules are arranged in a simple cubic array, as shown in Fig. 1.4. Let the x direction be parallel to a row of molecules. If the equilibrium separation of the molecules is r_0, the effective area of cross-section of this row of molecules is r_0^2, and if there are N molecules in the row its unstretched length is $(N - 1)r_0$. Now let balanced forces F_a be applied to each row of molecules of the crystal. When these forces are positive they produce an increase δr in the separation of the molecules in the x direction which results in the setting up of attractive intermolecular forces. These forces have a negative sign using the convention for such forces adopted in section 1.3. Now assume that each row of molecules in the x direction can be treated separately from the others and that, in each row, only nearest neighbour interactions are important. If the intermolecular potential energy (for two molecules) is modelled by the Mie potential:

$$U = -\frac{A}{r^m} + \frac{B}{r^n}$$

the intermolecular force F is given by:

$$F = -\frac{dU}{dr} = \frac{mA}{r^{m+1}} + \frac{nB}{r^{n+1}}.$$

When $r = r_0$, $F = 0$, so that:

$$B = \frac{m}{n} A r_0^{n-m}.$$

Now the response of the solid to balanced applied forces is governed by the slope of the F–r curve in the neighbourhood of the equilibrium separation r_0. For this part of the curve the force F set up when the intermolecular separation increases by δr (from the value r_0) is given by:

$$F = \left(\frac{dF}{dr}\right)_{r=r_0} \delta r \qquad [2.35]$$

where the derivative is evaluated at $r = r_0$. The corresponding applied force is F_a, which is equal to $-F$. On the assumption that the effective area of cross-section of the row of molecules is r_0^2, the stress on the row of molecules is:

$$\sigma = \frac{F_a}{r_0^2} = -\frac{F}{r_0^2}$$

and the strain is:

$$\frac{(N-1)\,\delta r}{(N-1)\,r_0} = \frac{\delta r}{r_0}.$$

Therefore, Hooke's law for this solid in tension is:

$$\sigma = -\frac{F}{r_0^2} = E\frac{\delta r}{r_0}. \qquad [2.36]$$

Now, in the neighbourhood of r_0:

$$\left(\frac{dF}{dr}\right)_{r=r_0} = \frac{m(m+1)A}{r_0^{m+2}} - \frac{n(n+1)B}{r_0^{n+2}} = \frac{mA(m-n)}{r_0^{m+2}}$$

so that:

$$F = \frac{mA(m-n)\,\delta r}{r_0^{m+2}}. \qquad [2.37]$$

Substituting in equation [2.36] gives:

$$E = \frac{A(mn-m^2)}{r_0^{m+3}} \qquad [2.38]$$

for Young's modulus.

With the approximations made in this model the intermolecular force F may be written:

$$F = \phi \delta r \qquad [2.39]$$

where ϕ is a constant characteristic of the molecules concerned, and known as the force constant. Let one molecule in a row parallel to the x direction be displaced by a small amount δr, the others remaining fixed. Since only nearest neighbour interactions in the row are being considered, the restoring force on the displaced molecule due to the fixed molecule on one side is $-\phi \delta r$, and that due to the fixed molecule on the other side is also $-\phi \delta r$, though one force is attractive and the other repulsive. The net restoring force on the displaced molecule is $-2\phi \delta r$ and the equation of motion of the displaced molecule is:

$$\text{Acceleration} = -\frac{2\phi}{M} \delta r$$

where M is the mass of the molecule. This equation represents a simple harmonic motion of frequency:

$$\nu_0 = \frac{1}{2\pi} \sqrt{\frac{2\phi}{M}}$$

which is the natural frequency of the vibration of the molecules in this model of a solid. It is often referred to as the Einstein frequency.

Comparing equations [2.36] and [2.39] shows that ϕ is equal to Er_0 on this model. Typically E is of the order of 10^{11} Pa and r_0 is of the order of 0.5 nm, which gives a value of 50 N m for ϕ and, using the expression for ν_0, gives a value of the order of 10^{12} Hz for the Einstein frequency.

2.11 Strain energy

Work must be done by the external forces acting on a body when the latter deforms and in the case of an elastic solid all this work is stored as potential energy of the distorted solid, or strain energy. The whole of this stored energy may be recovered when the external forces are removed from the elastic solid reversibly.

Consider a rod deformed in tension by balanced forces F_a applied at its ends, such that an extension e is produced. If the rod extends a further amount de while F_a remains sensibly constant, the work that the external forces do on the rod is:

$$dw = F_a \, de . \qquad [2.40]$$

Let the rod be perfectly elastic, which means that F_a is a single-valued function of e. When the changes in the extension take place reversibly, the work done by the external forces as the extension is changed from e_i to e_f is:

$$w = \int_{e_i}^{e_f} F_a \, de . \qquad [2.41]$$

If Hooke's law is obeyed and the rod has an unstretched length L_0 and area of cross-section α, then:

stress, $\sigma = E\epsilon$

load, $F_a = \sigma\alpha$

extension, $e = \epsilon L_0$

where ϵ is the linear strain and E is Young's modulus of the material. The expression for w then becomes:

$$w = \int_{e_i}^{e_f} \frac{\alpha E e}{L_0} \, de$$

$$= \frac{\alpha E(e_f^2 - e_i^2)}{2L_0}$$

$$= \frac{\alpha E L_0(\epsilon_f^2 - \epsilon_i^2)}{2} \qquad [2.42]$$

provided that α may be treated as a constant. Further, provided that changes in the volume of the rod can be neglected, the volume of the rod is αL_0 and then the energy stored per unit volume of the material is:

$$\frac{E}{2}(\epsilon_f^2 - \epsilon_i^2) . \qquad [2.43]$$

When ϵ_i is zero this may be written as:

$$w = \frac{E\epsilon_f^2}{2} = \frac{\sigma_f^2}{2E} = \frac{\sigma_f \epsilon_f}{2} .$$ [2.44]

2.12 The torsion of a right circular cylinder

This is a simple example of a situation where the stress and strain are not homogeneous. The problem is tackled by considering an element in which stress and strain can be considered as homogeneous and then integrating over the complete solid.

Consider a right circular cylinder of isotropic material, having a length L and radius a. Let one end of the cylinder be twisted relative to the other, about the cylindrical axis, through an angle ϕ radians, as in Fig. 2.6(a). The undeformed shape of a small element of this cylinder at a distance r from the axis is shown as ABCDEFGH in Fig. 2.6(b). After deformation the shape of the same element is ABCDJKLM. Figure 2.6(c) shows the positions of the element on the base of the cylinder before and after deformation.

The surface area of each end of the element is $r\mathrm{d}\theta\,\mathrm{d}r$, where $\mathrm{d}\theta$ is the angle subtended at the axis by the element, and the shear strain suffered by the element is $\phi r/L$. The applied shearing forces needed to produce this strain are of magnitude:

stress $\times$ area $=$ strain $\times$ modulus $\times$ area

$$= \frac{\phi r}{L} \cdot G \cdot r\mathrm{d}\theta\mathrm{d}r$$

where G is the rigidity modulus of the material. The moment of either force about the axis is equal to:

force $\times$ distance from axis $= \dfrac{\phi r^2 G \mathrm{d}\theta\,\mathrm{d}r}{L} \cdot r$.

Therefore, the total moment, which is equal to the couple that must be applied at each end of the cylinder to give equilibrium, is:

$$\Gamma = \int_0^{2\pi} \mathrm{d}\theta \int_0^a \frac{\phi r^3 G}{L} \, \mathrm{d}r$$

$$= \frac{\pi G a^4}{2L} \phi .$$ [2.45]

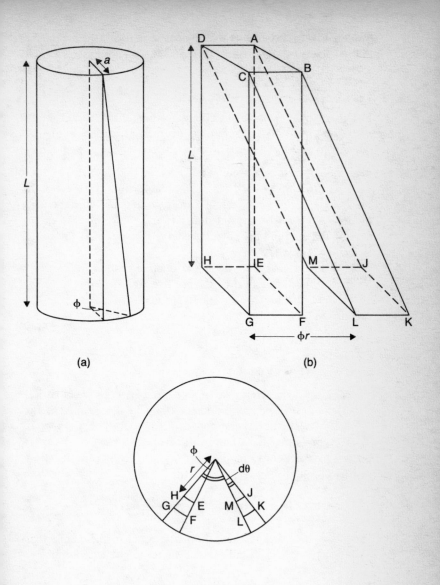

Fig. 2.6

The quantity Γ/ϕ is called the torsional rigidity. If the cylinder is hollow, having an internal radius a_i and an outer radius a_o:

$$\Gamma = \frac{\pi G(a_o^4 - a_i^4)}{2L} \phi. \qquad [2.46]$$

Example 2.2

Another simple example where stress and strain are inhomogeneous is the following. It is also a situation where the load in the deformed body is produced by body forces.

A wire of unstretched length L_0 and area of cross-section α, made of isotropic material of density ρ and having a Young's modulus E, is freely suspended at one end. Find the total extension of the wire and the potential energy stored in it as a result of stretching under its own weight.

Take the origin of coordinates at the fixed end of the wire and let the downward vertical be the positive direction of y. Consider an element of the wire of length dy at a distance y from the origin, and let L be the length of the wire in tension.

The equilibrium condition is that the force F acting on the element dy is equal to the weight of the wire below it, that is:

$$F = (L-y)\rho\alpha g$$

where g is the acceleration of free fall. Here the geometrical condition is simply that the linear strain in the element is the change in its length (its extension) divided by dy. The stress–strain relationship is that the strain in the element is equal to the stress divided by the Young's modulus.

Therefore:

$$\text{strain in the element} = \frac{\text{extension of the element}}{dy}$$

$$= \frac{\text{stress}}{E}$$

$$= \frac{E}{\alpha E} = \frac{(L-y)\rho g}{E}.$$

The total extension e of the wire is then:

$$e = \int_0^L \frac{(L-y)\rho g}{E}\, dy \ .$$

Provided that the total change in length is small this may be written as

$$e = \frac{\rho g L_0^2}{2E} \ .$$

The elastic energy stored in the element dy of the wire is given by:

$\frac{1}{2} \times$ load acting on the element $\times$ extension of the element

$$= \frac{1}{2} \cdot (L-y)\rho\alpha g \cdot \frac{(L-y)\rho g}{E}\, dy$$

$$= \frac{(L-y)^2 \rho^2 g^2 \alpha}{2E}\, dy \ .$$

The total elastic energy stored in the wire is:

$$\int_0^L \frac{\rho^2 g^2 \alpha (L-y)^2}{2E}\, dy$$

which is:

$$\rho^2 g^2 \alpha L_0^3 / 6E$$

provided that changes in L and α are negligible.

2.13 Elastic limit and yield stress

When a rod is deformed in tension under an increasing stress, a stage is reached when the further deformation produced by a slight increase in stress is still elastic, but Hooke's law is no longer obeyed, that is, the stress–strain curve ceases to be a straight line, even though there is a complete recovery of the original size and shape when the deforming forces are removed. The stress at which the departure from linearity of the stress–strain curve occurs is called the proportional limit or (linear) elastic limit.

When the stress is increased above the proportional limit a value is reached at which permanent extension occurs: the original size and shape are not recovered completely on removal of the applied forces. The stress at which a permanent extension is first detected is called the yield stress, and the corresponding point on the stress–strain curve is called the yield point. Usually the proportional limit and yield stress have almost the same value and cannot readily be distinguished. The yield stress is characteristic of the material, but also depends on grain size and temperature.

At the molecular level, the departure from linearity of the stress–strain curve can be attributed to the curvature of the F-r curve (Fig. 1.2(a)) once molecular separations differ by more than a very small amount from the equilibrium spacing r_0. Permanent deformation at a similar stress level cannot be interpreted on the same model — a new process intervenes, and this will be discussed briefly in the next chapter.

2.14 The elasticity of liquids

Because of its molecular mobility a liquid cannot sustain a shear stress and the only modulus of elasticity that can be defined for a liquid is the bulk modulus K.

Values for K for simple liquids at constant temperature are about two orders of magnitude less than those for solids and are rather more dependent on pressure. For water at $15°C$, and pressures in the range 1–25 atmospheres, K is 2.05×10^9 Pa, while for mercury at $20°C$, and pressures in the range 8–37 atmospheres, K is 26.2×10^9 Pa.

Solids are almost incompressible and liquids only slightly less so. This is in accord with the simple description given in Chapter 1, in which the molecules in both solids and liquids are effectively in contact, but the molecules in a liquid have a high mobility because of their somewhat smaller number of near neighbours.

Chapter 3

The deformation and fracture of simple crystals

3.1 Introduction

Under the conditions of elastic deformation a specimen of a simple crystalline solid suffers a definite deformation when a definite load is applied; the deformation does not depend on the duration of application of the load and disappears completely when the applied forces are removed. When the strain is small the stress and strain are linearly related. Elastic behaviour can be readily explained in terms of the intermolecular forces existing within a crystal, as discussed in section 2.10, based on the assumption that the force between neighbouring planes of molecules in a simple crystal varies with the separation of the planes in qualitatively the same way as the force between a pair of molecules, shown schematically in Fig. 1.2(a). This figure also indicates that if F reaches the value $-F_m$ the two molecular planes would fly apart and the crystal would separate into two parts. The applied force F_{am}, equal to $-F_m$, would be the tensile force needed to produce rupture between neighbouring molecular planes. In macroscopic terms, the solid would deform elastically in tension and then suddenly split into two parts, a process known as brittle fracture. A number of materials, e.g. rock salt and bismuth, behave approximately in this manner at room temperature.

Not all materials behave in this way; at room temperature many common metals, e.g. copper and aluminium, are ductile, i.e. they are able to undergo large amounts of permanent extension and, when failure occurs, it does not do so by a simple brittle fracture. Rather, when a specimen of such a material in the form of a wire or rod is extended at room temperature, the behaviour is perfectly elastic at very small strains but when the yield stress is reached (see section 2.13) macroscopic permanent deformation occurs, and the material is said to be plastically deformed.

In fact, most simple materials can show both brittle and ductile behaviour, the governing factors being the temperature at which deformation takes place and the rate at which the deformation is produced. Ductility is difficult to express in a quantitative manner, but one measure is the reduction in cross-sectional area before fracture occurs, produced in a specimen undergoing deformation under tension. When a graph is plotted of percentage decrease in area against temperature, keeping the rate of deformation constant, many materials give a curve of the form shown in Fig. 3.1. This allows a ductile–brittle transition temperature T_{DB} to be defined. For many common metals T_{DB} is about $0.1 \, T_m$, while for non-metallic crystals and intermetallic crystals it is frequently about $0.5 \, T_m$, where T_m is the melting temperature.

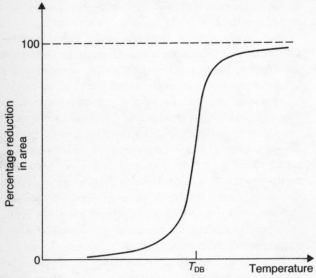

Fig. 3.1

The evidence presented in this section indicates that there are two alternative processes that can occur when the strain in a crystal is raised to a sufficiently high value. These processes are brittle fracture, which is effective at low temperatures, and plastic deformation, which is dominant at high temperatures. These two processes will now be examined in a little more detail.

3.2 Plastic deformation

When a fine-grained, polycrystalline wire of a ductile material is deformed under an axial load the stress–strain curve obtained has the form shown by the full line in Fig. 3.2(a), where the initial area of cross-section is used to calculate the stress from the applied forces. Permanent deformation occurs when the stress exceeds the yield stress σ_y so that, on reducing the stress to zero, a permanent deformation results. For example, if the specimen is unloaded when the point B is reached, the unloading path is not BAO but BC, which has approximately the same slope as OA. Of the total strain ϵ_t corresponding to the point B, the elastic strain ϵ_e is recovered, but the specimen retains the plastic strain, or permanent set, ϵ_p.

Along the region of the curve ABD the stress increases with the total strain, which indicates that the material becomes progressively harder (though not usually at a constant rate) as it is deformed plastically, a phenomenon known as work hardening. If the test specimen is a suitably squat cylinder the behaviour observed in a compression test is very similar to that observed in tension over the range of strain represented by the curve ABD: there is a range of purely elastic deformation and, at a stress closely equal to the yield stress in tension, plastic deformation occurs and the material work hardens.

Plastic deformation takes place at effectively constant volume of the specimen and, therefore, a cylinder under an axial stress undergoes a considerable change in cross-sectional area when the strain exceeds a few per cent. This is a much greater change in area than that observed in elastic deformation and it necessitates a more careful definition of stress. Two definitions are in common use.

1. Conventional stress σ_c is defined as:

$$\sigma_c = \frac{\text{load at any extension}}{\text{original area of cross-section}}.$$

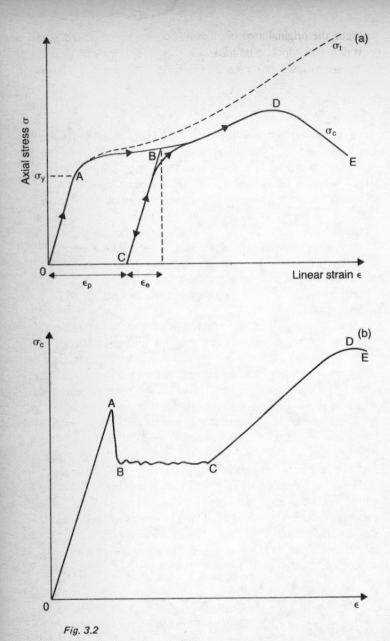

Fig. 3.2

Since the original area of cross-section is a constant, this stress is directly proportional to the load.

2. True stress σ_t is defined as:

$$\sigma_t = \frac{\text{load at any extension}}{\text{area of cross-section under that load}}.$$

σ_c and σ_t are almost equal for the small strains encountered in practical situations involving purely elastic deformation, which is why the distinction was ignored in Chapter 2. However, in a tensile test where extensive plastic deformation occurs, the stress–strain curves obtained using the two stresses show some different features. The graph of σ_c against ϵ (the full line in Fig. 3.2(a)) rises until D is reached and then starts to fall, fracture occurring at the point E on the stress–strain curve. At the point D the load has the maximum value that the specimen can support and the value of the conventional stress at this point is known as the ultimate tensile strength or ultimate stress σ_u.

Over the range of strain represented by OABD in Fig. 3.2(a) the deformation is macroscopically homogeneous but at D a neck forms in the specimen; subsequent plastic extension is restricted to this neck and the load needed to produce further extension falls. The neck gets progressively narrower until fracture occurs under conditions corresponding to the point E. Necking is a characteristic of deformation in tension and is not observed in compression. It arises because the work hardening resulting from the extension is not sufficient to offset the geometrical softening that occurs because of the decrease in the area of cross-section.

When σ_t is plotted instead of σ_c (the dotted curve in Fig. 3.2(a)) there is very little difference at small strains, though σ_t is always larger than σ_c in tension. When the point of instability D is reached, if σ_t is measured in the neck of the specimen, i.e. $\sigma_t = $ load $\div$ area of cross-section of the neck, σ_t continues to increase right up to the instant of fracture.

Some materials, notably annealed mild steel, show a rather different yielding behaviour, indicated schematically in Fig. 3.2(b). Starting at 0, a long elastic range is sharply terminated at A, when the stress reaches a value known as the upper yield stress. There is an abrupt partial unloading and macroscopic plastic deformation begins locally in regions called Lüders bands. As the extension of the specimen proceeds, the Lüders bands spread along its length until at C they cover the whole specimen. During this process the value of σ_c oscillates about a relatively constant value known as the lower yield stress. At C the stress starts to rise.

Stress–strain curves for single crystal specimens show the same basic features as those for polycrystals under similar conditions, but the detailed features depend on the orientation of the crystal structure relative to the tensile stress direction.

The values obtained experimentally for such quantities as σ_y and σ_u are material parameters, though they depend, to some extent, on a number of variables including purity of the material, grain size, temperature of testing and rate of deformation. Some values for pure polycrystalline materials in the form of wires and tested in tension at room temperature are given in Table 3.1.

Table 3.1 *Yield stress (σ_y) and ultimate stress (σ_u) values for polycrystalline specimens at room temperature*

Material	σ_y (MPa)	σ_u (MPa)
Aluminium	26	.60
Copper	40	160
Lead	12	15
Nickel	60	300
Mild Steel ($\approx$1% carbon)	400 (upper yield stress) 300 (lower yield stress)	460

Example 3.1

When the results of a tensile test are plotted on a graph of true stress against linear strain, show that the point at which necking starts is the point of contact of the tangent to the curve that passes through the point on the strain axis where the strain equals -1. This is the construction of Considère.

When balanced axial forces F_a act on a specimen the true stress σ_t is given by:

$$\sigma_t = F_a/\alpha$$

where α is the area of cross-section. Necking occurs when the load reaches a maximum, that is, when:

$$dF_a = d(\alpha\sigma_t) = 0 .$$

Therefore, when necking occurs:

$$\frac{d\sigma_t}{\sigma_t} = -\frac{d\alpha}{\alpha} .$$

In plastic deformation the volume V of the specimen remains constant so that, if L is the length of the specimen:

$$V = \alpha L = \text{Constant}$$

or: $\quad dV = d(\alpha L) = 0 .$

Therefore:

$$\frac{d\alpha}{\alpha} = -\frac{dL}{L}$$

so that:

$$\frac{d\sigma_t}{\sigma_t} = \frac{dL}{L} .$$

The linear strain ϵ is:

$$\frac{L - L_0}{L_0} = \frac{L}{L_0} - 1$$

where L_0 is the unstretched length. Therefore:

$$\frac{dL}{L} = \frac{dL}{L_0} \cdot \frac{L_0}{L} = \frac{d\epsilon}{1 + \epsilon}$$

giving:

$$\frac{d\sigma_t}{\sigma_t} = \frac{d\epsilon}{1 + \epsilon}$$

or: $\quad \dfrac{d\sigma_t}{d\epsilon} = \dfrac{\sigma_t}{1 + \epsilon}$ [3.1]

which is the required result. Notice that this construction assumes that purely elastic deformation is negligible.

3.3 Plastic deformation by slip

One fundamental experimental observation on simple crystals is that, except at very high pressures, the application of a uniform hydrostatic pressure to a crystal does not lead to plastic deformation. Application of the methods of section 2.9 shows that, when an isotropic solid is subjected to a uniform hydrostatic pressure, the shear stress on any plane in the solid is zero. From this it may be surmised that plastic deformation of a crystalline solid occurs as the result of shearing processes.

Microscopic and X-ray studies on deformed crystals bear this out. When a crystalline specimen with polished surfaces is deformed plastically and then examined under a low-power light microscope, the surfaces are, in general, found to be crossed by a large number of fine dark lines, known as slip lines. They result from a process in which adjacent blocks of molecules slip past each other. Because of the periodic nature of the molecular structure of crystals, it is expected that the blocks will slip over each other by one or more complete intermolecular distances. This would leave the crystal structure essentially unchanged by the slipping process, a result confirmed by X-ray diffraction.

When the relative displacement of two adjacent blocks is large enough, a small slip step is produced on the polished surface of the crystal, and this appears in the light microscope as a fine dark line. A surface on which slip has taken place is known as a slip surface; in many situations this surface is planar, when it is referred to as a slip plane.

Experiment shows that the relative displacement of two adjacent blocks of molecules in the slip process is always in a particular crystallographic direction, usually that along which the molecules are most closely packed. This direction is known as the slip direction and is characteristic of the material. The slip plane is less characteristic. In a given material different slip planes (different, that is, in a crystallographic sense) may operate at different temperatures, though the operative planes are invariably planes of high molecular density. When slip lines are examined in the electron microscope they often show a fine structure, consisting of a number of slip lines closely grouped. The total relative displacement in one of these groups is typically a few thousand intermolecular spacings, while the groups are a few micrometres apart.

Plastic deformation is produced by the shear stresses set up in the material and another basic law of plastic deformation, applicable most simply to single crystals, is that the plastic strain depends only on the shear stress in the slip plane, resolved parallel to the slip direction. Further, appreciable plastic deformation by slip starts when this resolved shear stress reaches a fairly well-defined value called the critical resolved shear stress (c.r.s.s.). This is Schmidt's law and it embodies the result that the yield stress is a characteristic of a given material, other conditions being the same.

A single crystal under tension will slip as shown in Fig. 3.3 and in this case it is a straightforward matter to calculate the resolved

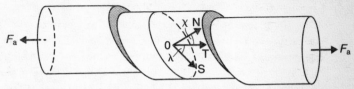

Fig. 3.3 OT = tensile axis, ON = normal to slip plane, OS = slip direction.

shear stress. The cylindrical specimen shown has a cross-sectional area α and tensile forces F_a are applied at each end. If the normal to the active slip plane makes an angle χ, and the slip direction an angle λ, with the tensile axis, the component of F_a parallel to the operative slip direction is $F_a \cos \lambda$ and acts over an area $\alpha/\cos \chi$. Therefore, the value of the resolved shear stress τ_R is given by:

$$\tau_R = \frac{F_a \cos \lambda}{\alpha/\cos \chi} = \frac{F_a}{\alpha} \cos \lambda \cos \chi = \sigma \cos \lambda \cos \chi \quad [3.2]$$

where σ is the tensile stress. Macroscopic plastic deformation by slip is observed when τ_R reaches a critical value τ_y (= c.r.s.s.) for a given material at a given temperature. Values of the c.r.s.s., τ_y, at room temperature for some single crystals are given in Table 3.2, together with the rigidity modulus. It will be noted that τ_y is always several orders of magnitude less than G.

The laws stated also govern the slip behaviour in polycrystalline specimens, but there the active slip planes and directions in

The deformation and fracture of simple crystals 65

different grains will make different angles with the tensile axis, and, in addition, the presence of grain boundaries may inhibit slip and modify the stress distribution in any particular grain.

Table 3.2 *Critical resolved shear stress and rigidity modulus at room temperature for materials in the form of single crystals*

Material	τ_y(MPa)	G(GPa)
Aluminium	0.86	25
Copper	1.0	46
Iron	3.0	77
Zinc	0.50	40
Gold	0.80	27

3.4 The theoretical critical resolved shear stress

The theoretical or ideal shear strength of any perfect crystal may be estimated using a method due originally to J. Frenkel (1926). He considered a crystal at absolute zero, neglected the zero-point energy, and assumed that, when slip occurs, all the molecules in one block of the crystal slide simultaneously over those in an adjacent block.

Consider a single crystal of a simple material in which the spacing between planes of molecules is a, and that between molecules in a row in a plane is b. It is assumed that the planes chosen are the slip planes and that the chosen rows of molecules in these planes are parallel to the slip direction. Let the slip direction coincide with the x coordinate direction and let τ be the shear stress necessary to displace one block of molecules a distance x with respect to an adjacent block. Taking the origin to coincide with a molecule, the value of τ will be zero when $x = 0, b, 2b \ldots$, since the molecules are then at their normal equilibrium positions in the crystal. Also, when $x = b/2, 3b/2 \ldots$, the displaced molecules are in metastable positions and τ is again zero. Therefore, τ must be a periodic function of x with period b. Frenkel assumed that τ could be represented by:

$$\tau = C \sin \left(\frac{2\pi x}{b} \right) \qquad [3.3]$$

where C is a constant whose value is obtained from the condition that Hooke's law is obeyed when the displacement x is very small.

When x is very small:

$$\tau \approx C\frac{2\pi x}{b} \qquad [3.4]$$

the shear strain γ is given by:

$$\gamma = \frac{x}{a} \qquad [3.5]$$

so that, if G is the rigidity modulus:

$$C\frac{2\pi x}{b} = G\frac{x}{a}$$

or: $\quad C = Gb/2\pi a$.

Therefore:

$$\tau = \frac{Gb}{2\pi a} \sin\left(\frac{2\pi x}{b}\right) . \qquad [3.6]$$

The c.r.s.s. is the maximum value of τ, since this is the condition for the displacement to become unstable and change from recoverable to permanent. Since the maximum value of the sine function is unity:

$$\tau_y = \frac{Gb}{2\pi a} . \qquad [3.7]$$

Equation [3.7] predicts that slip will take place in the direction for which b is a minimum and a is a maximum, that is, it predicts slip on close-packed planes in close-packed directions. For many crystals $a \approx b$ and the theoretical c.r.s.s. on this model is, therefore, about $G/10$. Table 3.2 shows that this is about 10^4 or 10^5 times greater than the observed values for annealed crystals. Refinements of the above calculation using more realistic laws of force between molecules only reduce the predicted value of τ_y to about $G/30$, which is still much larger than that observed. It should be noted, however, that this model only deals with molecular behaviour well inside the crystal. The calculation gives no information about the shear strength of the surface layers and, in particular, whether the surface regions of a crystal are intrinsically weaker or stronger than the interior.

3.5 Dislocations

Surface and X-ray observations indicate that plastic deformation occurs by slip in many crystalline solids, but the Frenkel calculation suggests that slip is not achieved by the simultaneous movement of all the molecules in the slip plane. The only real alternative is that slip takes place by the consecutive movement of molecules in one plane over those in the adjacent plane.

If slip occurs over a complete slip plane in a single crystal, the only consequence is that there is a shear displacement of one block of molecules, relative to the adjacent block, by a whole number of molecular spacings. However, when slip takes place over part of the slip plane only, a line may notionally be drawn in the slip plane separating those parts where slip has occurred from those where it has not. This line is termed a line of crystal dislocation or, simply, a dislocation line. Except in the immediate neighbourhood of the dislocation line the molecules of the crystal are in perfect register across the slip plane.

When a dislocation line passes through a region of crystal, blocks of molecules on either side of the slip plane undergo a certain relative displacement which can be represented by a vector **b**, known as the Burgers vector. The Burgers vector is associated with the whole of the dislocation line and must be constant along it. When the Burgers vector is everywhere perpendicular to the dislocation line, the dislocation is called an edge dislocation; when **b** is everywhere parallel to the dislocation line it is a screw dislocation. In general, dislocations are neither pure edge nor pure screw and are termed mixed dislocations. This idea that slip is the result of the movement of dislocations through a crystal was put forward independently by Taylor, Orowan and Polanyi in 1934.

By its definition, the movement of a dislocation produces slip. It must now be shown that a dislocation in a crystal possesses the property of moving under a very small applied stress. To do this it is necessary to examine the force exerted on a dislocation line by an applied stress and also the mobility of a dislocation.

Consider first the force exerted on a dislocation line by a stress set up in the crystal. Under the action of a shear stress a dislocation in a crystal will try to move in a direction that allows the crystal to give way to the force. If the dislocation line is treated as a physical entity, this result may be described by saying that the dislocation line experiences a force in the presence of the shear stress. Let a straight edge dislocation line of length L_1 be located in the surface of a crystal. When the dislocation line moves completely across the crystal, of width L_2, it produces a relative displacement of the two parts of the crystal on opposite sides of the slip plane of magnitude b. Let F be the force per unit length of the dislocation line and acting perpendicular to the line. The work done by this force in producing the displacement is FL_1L_2 and this must equal the work done by the shear stress τ. This stress exerts a force $\tau L_1 L_2$ and moves its points of application a distance b in the direction of the Burgers vector. Therefore:

$$\tau L_1 L_2 b = FL_1L_2$$

or: $\quad F = \tau b.$ [3.8]

This force acts in the slip plane, is perpendicular to the dislocation line and is directed towards the unslipped part of the crystal.

The stress necessary to move a single dislocation through an otherwise perfect crystal is known as the Peierls–Nabarro stress. Its exact calculation is difficult and needs a detailed knowledge of the molecular arrangement in the crystal and the intermolecular force law. A simplified discussion will, therefore, be given in terms of dislocations in a simple cubic crystal. First, the molecular arrangement around a dislocation in a simple cubic crystal will be considered qualitatively.

An edge dislocation in such a structure is shown schematically in Fig. 3.4, where the plane of molecules shown contains the slip direction and is normal to the slip plane, the trace of which is **AB**. Figure 3.4(a) shows the molecular arrangement in the perfect, undeformed crystal. Since the crystal structure provides a periodic field of force, molecules will slip from one equilibrium position to the next under a shear stress, so that the Burgers vector will be

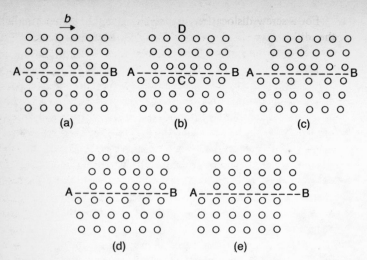

Fig. 3.4

in the direction AB and its magnitude will be the intermolecular spacing in that direction, i.e. b. Let slip take place over that part of the slip plane represented by AC, but not over CB, as in Fig. 3.4(b). Then C represents the position of the dislocation line in the plane of molecules shown. If all parallel planes suffer the same distortion the dislocation line is perpendicular to the plane of molecules shown. The Burgers vector is then perpendicular to the line so that such a dislocation has pure edge character. Figure 3.4(b) shows that the introduction of an edge dislocation into a crystal is equivalent to making a cut in the perfect crystal, ending on the slip plane, and inserting an extra half-plane of molecules, represented by DC. The dislocation line lies along the edge of the inserted material. Close to a dislocation line the molecules are displaced from their normal positions so that a dislocation is a region of molecular misfit and a source of elastic strain.

As an edge dislocation passes through a simple cubic structure the molecular configuration takes up, successively, the arrangements shown in Figs 3.4(b), (c) and (d). When the dislocation passes completely through the crystal (Fig. 3.4 (e)) the result is a relative displacement of two blocks of crystal by an amount b, producing two surface steps, each of height b, and leaving the crystal structure undistorted.

For a screw dislocation, crystal shearing takes place parallel to the dislocation line so that, in a simple cubic structure, the molecular arrangement is as shown schematically in Fig. 3.5. Slip has occurred over the plane ABCD, the Burgers vector being **b**, and CD the screw dislocation line. Starting at molecular site E, say, and following a path, from molecule to molecule, which passes once completely around the screw dislocation, such as EFGHKE, it can be seen that the crystal planes are really part of a helix even though, well away from the dislocation line, the displacement of molecules from their normal positions is so small that the layers of molecules in such regions are effectively planar.

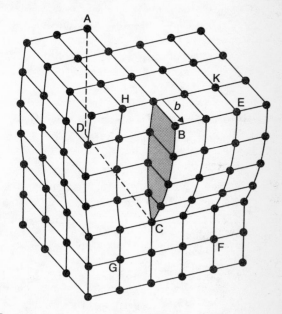

Fig. 3.5

Returning now to the question of dislocation mobility, the following argument shows, in a general way, why the slip motion of an isolated dislocation can occur under a low force per unit length. Figures 3.4 and 3.5 suggest that molecules that are sufficiently behind or far ahead of the dislocation will be in their normal equilibrium positions, while those close to the dislocation line are sheared out of their normal positions.

Those molecules that have almost completed the slip process repel the dislocation away from them, so that they may occupy the next equilibrium positions. In contrast, those molecules that have just started the slip process repel the dislocation in the opposite direction so that they may return to their original normal positions. Further, when the molecular arrangement around a dislocation is symmetric, as it is in Figs. 3.4 (b), (c) and (d), these two forces are equal and opposite so that, to a first approximation, the crystal offers no resistance to the slip of a dislocation from such a position. When the molecular arrangement is no longer symmetric these forces do not balance and a small force is needed to move the dislocation through the crystal. Even though b is typically less than 1 nm, from equation [3.8] it might reasonably be expected that an isolated dislocation will move through a (ductile) crystal under a low stress, and dislocations could then satisfy the requirements of a mechanism for slip.

3.6 The critical resolved shear stress and work hardening

Detailed calculations indicate that, for simple crystals, the Peierls–Nabarro stress is, in fact, smaller than the observed c.r.s.s. However, since the yield stress refers to a plastic deformation of, say, 0.1%, and the Burgers vectors of dislocations in most simple crystals are less than 1 nm, a shear strain of 0.1% corresponds to the passage of a very large number of dislocations, about 10^6, completely through a crystal of dimensions of a few mm, and the movement of even larger numbers if the dislocations do not pass completely through the crystal. Therefore, the c.r.s.s. is the stress needed to set large numbers of dislocations in motion. τ_y is, essentially, a property of the interactions of large numbers of dislocations rather than a property of an individual dislocation, which is why τ_y is a material characteristic, though the smallness of the c.r.s.s. must be a reflection of the smallness of the Peierls–Nabarro stress.

Through the associated strain field, a dislocation is able to interact with other dislocations and also with point defects such as vacancies and impurities. The c.r.s.s. can be affected by the presence of these defects so that the c.r.s.s. is, to some extent, a property of the purity of a specimen and the way it has been prepared.

Once plastic deformation has started in a specimen an increase in stress is needed to produce further deformation. In microscopic terms this means that as deformation proceeds, the movement of dislocations on their slip planes becomes progressively more difficult. This hardening of the material may arise from elastic interactions between dislocations, through their strain fields, it may arise from dislocation reactions that produce segments that cannot slip and it may also arise from interactions with other defects such as vacancies, impurities and grain boundaries.

Grain boundaries, in particular, are regions of considerable crystal distortion and, like edge dislocations, are preferred regions for the segregation of impurities that distort the normal crystal structure. Also, grain boundaries are often able to hold up slip dislocations because of the change in orientation of the slip plane that occurs in crossing the boundary. For reasons of this nature, polycrystalline specimens of a given material usually work harden more rapidly than single crystal ones.

3.7 Brittle fracture

At sufficiently low temperatures crystalline solids respond to high stresses through brittle fracture rather than large-scale plastic deformation. Single crystals showing brittle fracture often part on a crystallographic plane of high molecular density. When the fracture occurs after little or no plastic deformation the fracture obeys, in general, Sohncke's law, namely, that cleavage occurs when the normal component of stress acting across the cleavage plane reaches a critical value. Therefore, brittle fracture is, in effect, a pulling apart of two blocks of crystal. The normal tensile stress needed to produce brittle fracture is called the brittle strength of the material.

Many single crystals, especially of metals, though fracturing in essentially a brittle manner when the temperature is low enough, do undergo some plastic deformation before fracture occurs. For these materials Sohncke's law does not usually hold.

When polycrystalline specimens undergo brittle fracture the

fracture surface is macroscopically the plane of maximum tensile stress, though individual grains break on crystallographic planes, giving a fracture surface made up of facets.

3.8 The theoretical brittle strength

When a single crystal is under tension, ideal brittle fracture occurs when the tensile stress reaches the value necessary to pull one block of molecules completely away from the adjacent block.

Consider a specimen of area of cross-section α under a tensile stress σ and assume that the extension is stable until the brittle strength σ_B is reached. When fracture occurs the elastic energy in the neighbourhood of the fracture surface must provide the surface energy of the two fracture surfaces produced (surface energy is discussed in Chapter 7). In terms of chemical bonding, the elastic energy must be sufficient to break the bonds between the molecules across the fracture surface.

Let r_0 be the intermolecular distance in the direction of tension and assume that fracture occurs at small strains so that, when σ equals σ_B, r is closely equal to r_0, the equilibrium intermolecular distance.

When a stress σ produces a linear strain ϵ in a Hookean solid of volume V, the strain energy in the solid is $\sigma \epsilon V/2$, which is equal to $\sigma^2 V/2E$, where E is Young's modulus of the material. If γ is the specific surface free energy of the material (see Chapter 7), the total surface energy of the surfaces created by the fracture process is $2\alpha\gamma$.

A large fraction of this energy $2\alpha\gamma$ must be present at the moment of fracture between the molecules immediately adjacent to the fracture surface. Thus:

$$V \approx r_0 \alpha$$

and: $\sigma_B^2 \, r_0 \alpha/2E \approx 2\alpha\gamma$

so that:

$$\sigma_B \approx 2 \left(\frac{\gamma E}{r_0}\right)^{\frac{1}{2}}. \hspace{2cm} [3.9]$$

Since the behaviour is not Hookean when σ is other than very small, a better approximation to σ_B is:

$$\sigma_B \approx \left(\frac{\gamma E}{r_0}\right)^{\frac{1}{2}}. \qquad [3.10]$$

For many materials σ_B is, in fact, approximately $E/10$, a value which reflects the high strength of intermolecular forces.

This approximate calculation gives values for σ_B about one thousand times greater than those observed. For example, sodium chloride fractures on its cube plane under a stress of 2.2 MPa, whereas the value of σ_B is 5 GPa.

To explain this discrepancy, A.A. Griffith assumed that the low observed value of the brittle strength was a consequence of the presence of minute cracks or other flaws in the material. Very high stress concentrations could occur in the neighbourhood of such cracks, while the mean, or bulk, stress remained low. Fracture then occurred through the movement of one of these cracks under a mean (observed) stress much smaller than the brittle strength.

If a crack is treated as an elliptical hole and a plate containing such a hole of major axis $2L$ is subjected to a mean stress σ, normal to the major axis, the highest local tensile stress σ_t occurs at the ends of the major axis. In an isotropic linear elastic material σ_t is given by:

$$\sigma_t = 2\sigma \sqrt{\frac{L}{\rho}} \qquad [3.11]$$

where ρ is the radius of curvature of the hole at the ends of its major axis. Fracture would then be expected to occur when σ_t reaches the value σ_B. This would give the macroscopic fracture stress, i.e. the observed brittle strength σ_{obs}, as:

$$2\sigma_{obs} \sqrt{\frac{L}{\rho}} = \sigma_B = \sqrt{\frac{\gamma E}{r_0}}$$

or: $$\sigma_{obs} = \sqrt{\frac{\gamma E \rho}{4 L r_0}}. \qquad [3.12]$$

The problem is to know what value to put for ρ for a crack in a crystalline solid, since the separation of the molecules across the crack takes all values from r_0 to a value so large that the molecules on opposite sides of the crack do not interact.

Griffith got round this problem by assuming that the crack spreads through the crystal if the rate of release of elastic strain energy stored in the material is at least equal to the rate of increase of surface energy resulting from the production of new areas of crack surface.

Consider a surface crack of length L in a solid stressed by applied forces that produce a bulk stress σ, as shown in Fig. 3.6. If it is assumed that all the deformation is purely elastic and that

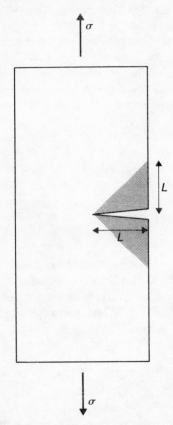

Fig. 3.6

the formation of a crack of length L releases the strain energy in the regions shown shaded, the energy released per unit thickness of the specimen is:

$$\frac{1}{2}\sigma\epsilon L^2 = \frac{\sigma L^2}{E} \qquad [3.13]$$

provided that the bulk stress remains σ. When the tip of the crack moves by a distance dL, under conditions such that the applied forces do no work, the accompanying release of elastic energy is $2\sigma^2 L dL/E$ per unit width of crack. At the same time the new crack surfaces gain energy $2\gamma dL$ per unit width. Therefore, the crack will extend if:

$$\frac{2\sigma^2 L dL}{E} \geqslant 2\gamma dL$$

which defines a critical crack length L_c given by:

$$L_c = \frac{\gamma E}{\sigma_{obs}^2}. \qquad [3.14]$$

The observed brittle strength is, therefore:

$$\sigma_{obs} = \sqrt{\frac{\gamma E}{L_c}}. \qquad [3.15]$$

When σ is equal to that needed to make the longest crack grow the fracture occurs.

In many metals showing brittle behaviour L_c would have to be several millimetres. No visible pre-existing cracks or flaws of this size are observed in these materials, yet the brittle strength is still low. However, it has been assumed that the deformation during the spreading of the crack is purely elastic, whereas in many metals some plastic deformation occurs before the material fractures. This has two important effects. The small cracks that spread rapidly to give brittle fracture may be formed by the coalescence of edge-type slip dislocations and also the effective specific surface free energy will be changed if the deformation is not purely elastic. In ductile materials sharp cracks are blunted by plastic deformation, which is localised at the crack tip, and this renders the crack ineffective for facture.

Theoretical brittle-fracture conditions may also be approached through the intermolecular force law. Example 3.2 illustrates how the theoretical fracture strain may be estimated. It is then a simple matter to determine the fracture stress.

Example 3.2

The potential energy of two krypton atoms may be written in the form:

$$U = -\frac{A}{r^6} + \frac{B}{r^{10}}$$

where A and B are constants and r is the separation of the two atoms. If solid krypton is assumed to be a simple cubic solid in which only nearest neighbour interactions are important, estimate the strain at which brittle fracture will occur in a krypton crystal.

Assume that the temperature is low enough for the kinetic energy of the atoms to be ignored. The equilibrium separation of the atoms is r_0, obtained from the condition that $r = r_0$ when $dU/dr = 0$. Fracture of the crystal will occur when the interatomic force F reaches its maximum value, and, since $F = -dU/dr$, this will be when $d^2U/dr^2 = 0$.

Now:

$$\frac{dU}{dr} = \frac{6A}{r^7} - \frac{10B}{r^{11}}$$

so that:

$$r_0{}^4 = \frac{10B}{6A} \quad \text{or, } B = 0.6Ar_0{}^4.$$

$$\frac{d^2U}{dr^2} = -\frac{42A}{r^8} + \frac{110B}{r^{12}}$$

$$= -\frac{42A}{r^8} + \frac{110 \times 0.6Ar_0{}^4}{r^{12}}.$$

When fracture occurs let $r = r_f$. Then:

$$42A/r_f{}^8 = 110 \times 0.6Ar_0{}^4/r_f{}^{12}$$

or: $r_f = 1.12r_0$.

The linear strain at which facture occurs is:

$$\frac{r_f - r_0}{r_0} = 1.12 - 1 \approx 12\%.$$

3.9 Ductile fracture

Crystals of ductile materials usually fracture in one of two ways. Either:

1. a neck develops so that the crystal tapers down to a chisel edge, known as rupture if the reduction in cross-sectional area is 100%; or
2. slip is concentrated in a narrow zone making an angle of about 45° with the tensile axis, which leads to what is called slipping off or shearing.

Rupture is characteristic of single crystals of high purity, while shearing is more commonly observed in single crystals of alloys and also in pure polycrystalline materials.

In materials of nominal purity small holes and cracks are formed when necking starts. These holes and cracks are produced during deformation at inclusions and, possibly, by dislocation inter-actions. In cylindrical specimens the formation of the neck is accompanied by the setting up of a triaxial stress system in the neck: the forces between adjacent transverse sections of the neck have trajectories that follow the profile of the neck and will, therefore, have components normal to the specimen axis. This triaxial stress system may be considered as a hydrostatic stress plus a longitudinal stress. The former does not produce plastic deformation and so the material is effectively hardened. Any holes that are formed in the neck are able to grow transversely more rapidly than they can axially and so are able to coalesce, leading to an internal fracture surface at the centre of the mini-mum cross-section. The formation of this internal surface is followed by shearing on a surface of maximum shear stress. This surface is conical and the result is the so-called cup and cone fracture, typical of the fracture of many metallic materials at room temperature.

3.10 The plastic deformation of brittle solids

Many normally brittle solids can undergo considerable plastic deformation when, in addition to an axial stress, they are subjected to a hydrostatic pressure. If the brittle strength of the material is σ_B and the specimen has a hydrostatic pressure p applied to it, the tensile stress needed to produce brittle fracture is $\sigma_B + p$. This tensile stress gives rise to a shear stress resolved in the slip direction in the slip plane and if this resolved shear stress reaches a value corresponding to the axial yield stress σ_y before it reaches $\sigma_B + p$ the material will deform plastically without brittle fracture taking place.

This change in behaviour under a confining pressure accounts for the macroscopic plastic deformation of many materials normally considered brittle. Many rocks, for example, deform plastically under a sufficiently high confining pressure.

Chapter 4
The liquid phase

4.1 Introduction

A liquid was defined in section 1.2 as an aggregation of matter that has a definite volume at a given temperature and pressure, but no definite shape, the chief difference between the liquid and solid phases being the very much greater fluidity of the liquid. Under the effect of gravity, the liquid phase flows so that, ultimately, it takes up the shape of the containing vessel up to a certain definite level that is the surface of the liquid.

For pure substances a better definition of a liquid may be given in terms of the pressure–temperature diagram or phase diagram (Fig. 1.1(b)). A liquid may then be defined as that condition of a pure substance represented by points that lie between the fusion curve and the vapourisation curve in the temperature range T_t to T_c. The changes from solid phase to liquid phase going across the fusion curve and from gaseous phase to liquid phase across the vaporisation curve both involve the appearance of a meniscus separating the two phases. This is not true for changes from gas to liquid when the pressure is greater than p_c, and so some authorities reserve the term liquid for the condition given, but with p less than p_c, and talk about dense gases in the region shown hatched in Fig. 1.1(b).

Figure 1.1(b) shows the boundaries of the stable states of the three phases. (Note that complex molecules may decompose before melting or boiling occurs, so that parts of the diagram are then unavailable.) Clean liquids can, however, with care, be super-cooled and superheated, giving metastable states that are not shown in the diagram. Some liquids, for example glycerol, supercool so quickly that, on lowering the temperature, there is a continuous transition to the glass phase and the material has the elastic properties of an isotropic solid. Table 4.1 gives the values of T_t and T_c for some common pure substances, showing the relatively narrow range of temperature in which the liquid phase exists.

Table 4.1 *Value of the triple-point temperature T_t and critical temperature T_c for some common pure substances*

Substance	$T_t(K)$	$T_c(K)$
Ammonia	196	406
Carbon dioxide	217	304
Ethylene	104	283
Hydrogen	14	33
Methane	91	191
Nitrogen	63	126
Oxygen	54	154
Water	273.16	647

This chapter continues by looking at some of the macroscopic properties of simple liquids, particularly the tensile strength and flow properties. A brief discussion is then given of some molecular models of simple liquids and, finally, the unusual behaviour of liquid helium is described.

4.2 The tensile strength of liquids

Under certain conditions liquids are able to sustain large tensions. One way in which this can be demonstrated is due to Berthelot. A cylindrical tube is almost filled with liquid, the remainder of the space being air and liquid vapour, and is then sealed. When the temperature of the tube is raised the liquid expands faster than the tube and forces the air into solution so that, at a certain temperature T_f, the liquid fills the tube completely. The tube is then allowed to cool. During this cooling the liquid adheres to the walls of the tube and continues to fill this tube completely until a temperature T_b ($< T_f$) is reached, when the liquid ruptures as a result of the tension set up in it as its temperature is lowered. At the instant at which the rupture occurs the release of tension is accompanied by a 'click' and a sudden increase in the radius of the tube. The nature of the walls of the tube has an important effect on the results obtained in the above experiment, and it is likely that what is being measured is the adhesion of the liquid to the solid rather than the true liquid tensile strength.

An alternative method is to rotate a Z-shaped capillary tube, open at both ends, and containing the liquid, about an axis through the centre and perpendicular to the plane of the Z. As the speed of rotation is gradually increased, the liquid ruptures at the axis of rotation when the tensile stresses set up are no longer able to provide the centripetal force needed to maintain the continuity of the liquid. Experiments of this type show that the tension to cause rupture in water is strongly temperature-dependent, with a maximum tensile strength of about 28 MPa, occurring at 10 °C.

4.3 Liquid flow

A liquid possesses a definite volume at a given temperature and pressure, but no definite shape; it takes up the shape of the containing vessel. This process may be accomplished very rapidly, as in the case of water under normal conditions, or it may take a considerably longer time, as with thick treacle. When a liquid undergoes a continuous deformation under the action of gravity or of an externally applied force, the process is called flow. As a flow process takes time to complete, the liquid must be offering some resistance to flow, which may be called, quite generally, a liquid friction.

Isotherms on the pressure–volume graph for the liquid phase of a pure simple substance are practically straight lines, almost parallel to the pressure axis. This indicates that liquids are almost incompressible so that the changes in shape that occur during flow do so without change in volume; from the discussion of section 2.9, this suggests that liquid flow takes place through a shear deformation. Therefore, a liquid deforms or flows continuously under the action of a shear stress or, in other words, a liquid is incapable of sustaining a shear stress. When a solid is deformed by an applied shear stress system a definite shear strain is produced and, if the solid is Hookean, this shear strain is proportional to the shear stress. On the other hand, when a shear stress is applied to a liquid, the latter deforms continuously and the behaviour is described in terms of the shear stress and the shear strain rate or rate of shear.

When the applied shear stress system is removed from an elastically deformed solid, the solid regains its original shape completely and the work of deformation is also recovered. No such recovery occurs in a liquid; the work done in producing a given rate of shear is completely dissipated against the liquid friction forces. The resistance to flow offered by a liquid when it is subjected to a shear stress is called a viscous force and the liquid is said to possess viscosity.

From a macroscopic viewpoint, a liquid may be treated as an isotropic, continuous medium and, to describe the flow behaviour, attention may be concentrated on a 'liquid particle', that is, an infinitesimal mass of liquid moving with the remainder of the liquid.

The motion of an element of liquid, or liquid particle, may be specified in terms of the velocity of the liquid, which may be defined as follows.

In the region of the liquid under consideration construct a plane surface of area α, and let the direction of the normal to the surface be denoted by a unit vector $\hat{e}$. If, in a time δt, a volume of liquid V crosses the surface from the negative side to the positive side, as given by the direction of $\hat{e}$, the velocity $\mathbf{u}$ of the liquid is defined by:

$$\mathbf{u} \cdot \hat{e} = \underset{\substack{\alpha \to 0 \\ \delta t \to 0}}{\text{Lt}} \left(\frac{V}{\alpha \, \delta t} \right). \qquad [4.1]$$

This velocity is not the velocity of the molecules of the liquid, but is the 'drift' velocity of the liquid particle. It is closely equal to that of a very small solid object carried along by the liquid.

Macroscopically, liquid flow can occur in two basic ways: the liquid may flow so that there is complete mixing or it may flow in layers without mixing. The flow in which there is complete mixing is called turbulent flow and, for a given liquid, is characteristic of high flow rates in broad channels. Flow, in layers, without mixing on the macroscopic scale, is called laminar or streamline flow. Under steady conditions this type of flow is quite stable and, for a given liquid, is characteristic of low flow rates in narrow channels.

The term streamline is also used to describe a line in the liquid, drawn at any instant, such that the tangent at any point is the direction of the velocity vector at that point. A liquid particle must travel along a streamline so that, if s is some parameter along the curve, specified with respect to chosen Cartesian axes:

$$\frac{d\mathbf{r}}{ds} \text{ is parallel to } \mathbf{u}$$

$$\frac{d\mathbf{r}}{ds} = \lambda\mathbf{u}$$

where $\mathbf{r}$ is the position vector of the particle and λ is a constant.

Since λ can be made equal to unity by incorporating it into the parameter s, the equation of the streamline is obtained by solving:

$$\frac{d\mathbf{r}}{ds} = \mathbf{u}(r, t) .$$ [4.2]

If the velocity components in the x, y, z directions are, respectively, u_x, u_y, u_z, the equations of the streamlines are given by:

$$\frac{dx}{u_x} = \frac{dy}{u_y} = \frac{dz}{u_z} .$$ [4.3]

When conditions are steady, the velocity of flow at any point is constant and the streamlines do not vary with time. Under steady conditions streamlines can be observed by scattering very small, light particles into the liquid and following their paths.

In a liquid in which the flow is laminar, adjacent layers of liquid travel with different speeds. The liquid layer immediately in contact with the solid containing surface is, in fact, adsorbed to that surface and is, therefore, from a macroscopic viewpoint, at rest relative to the surface. Microscopically, this adsorbed layer is in dynamic equilibrium, since molecules are continually being removed as a result of collisions with other molecules, while different molecules take their places.

When a liquid at rest starts to flow, the bulk of the liquid begins to move, but the layer adsorbed to the containing wall does not. It tries to prevent the adjacent layer of liquid from moving and, in this process, extracts from it momentum which is transferred to the solid wall. Similarly, each moving liquid layer loses momentum to the adjacent layer nearer the wall and gains momentum from the adjacent layer further from the wall. There is, therefore, a transfer of momentum from layer to layer and finally the momentum is lost to the wall, the rigidity of the wall resisting the tendency of the adsorbed layer to be dragged along. Therefore, the flow velocity of the liquid decreases as the wall is approached and tends to zero at the wall itself.

An adsorbed layer exists even when the liquid flow is turbulent. In this case the adsorbed layer maintains a narrow boundary layer in which the liquid flow is laminar, even though the bulk flow is turbulent. These regions of laminar flow and completely turbulent flow are separated by a narrow buffer layer, in which the flow is neither truly· laminar nor truly turbulent. In the laminar region the liquid velocity increases monotonically with distance from the wall but, in the turbulent region, velocity as defined by equation [4.1] is no longer appropriate. Rather, a mean flow velocity $\bar{u}$ is used, defined by:

$$\hat{e} \cdot \bar{u} = \frac{Q}{\alpha} \qquad \cdot [4.4]$$

where Q is the volume of liquid flowing per second across an area of cross-section α, and $\hat{e}$ is a unit vector in the direction of the normal to α.

4.4 Coefficient of viscosity

Set up fixed coordinate axes in a liquid that is flowing in a laminar manner. Despite the dissipation of energy against the viscous forces, assume that the temperature of the liquid remains constant. Assume further that conditions are steady and let a and b, respectively, be two streamlines close together in a small region of the liquid. Now let two light particles A and B be placed, one on each streamline, at a time t, in such positions that the line joining them is at right angles to the streamlines (which must be closely parallel in this small region of flowing liquid).

The speed of liquid flow will be slightly different along the two streamlines so that, after a further time δt, the line joining A and B will make an angle $\delta\gamma$ with its direction at time t. The liquid between the streamlines has suffered a shear of $\delta\gamma$ and $\delta\gamma/\delta t$ measures the rate of shear or shear strain rate.

Now assume further that the liquid is flowing in the x direction in layers normal to the y axis. The streamlines are then straight and parallel to the x axis and the flow velocity of the liquid is constant along each streamline, the only variation in flow velocity being in the y direction. Assume that streamlines a and b lie in the same xy plane. If the speed of liquid flow along streamline a is u, that along streamline b is:

$$u + \frac{du}{dy}\delta y$$

where δy is the distance between the two streamlines. In the small interval of time δt particle A moves a distance $u\delta t$ while B moves a distance

$$\left[u + \frac{du}{dy}\delta y \right] \delta t.$$

Then, provided that δt and, therefore, $\delta\gamma$ are small:

$$\delta\gamma = \left(\frac{du}{dy}\right)\frac{\delta y\,\delta t}{\delta y} = \frac{du}{dy}\delta t$$

so that, in the limit:

$$\frac{d\gamma}{dt} = \frac{du}{dy}.$$ [4.5]

Therefore, when a liquid is flowing in planar layers and conditions are steady, the rate of shear is equal to the velocity gradient normal to the direction of flow.

For many liquids undergoing steady flow in the manner described, the shear stress τ acting in the direction of flow needed to maintain a given shear rate is proportional to that shear rate. Then:

$$\tau = \eta\frac{d\gamma}{dt} = \eta\frac{du}{dy}$$ [4.6]

where η is a constant for a given liquid at a given temperature and pressure. A liquid for which equation [4.6] holds is termed Newtonian and η is known as the coefficient of dynamic or shear viscosity or, more generally, simply as the viscosity. η has dimension $ML^{-1}T^{-1}$ and its unit is $N\,m^{-2}\,s$ or $Pa\,s$.

Examples of Newtonian liquids are water, ether, glycerine, benzene, mercury and most pure simple liquids. Values of the coefficient of viscosity, measured at 291K are given in Table 4.2.

Table 4.2 *Values of the coefficient of viscosity η of some simple liquids at 291 K*

Liquid	$\eta(\mu Pa\,s)$
Benzene	660
Bromine	993
Carbon tetrachloride	981
Chloroform	569
Glycerol	1.6×10^6
Mercury	1540
Methanol	584
Olive oil	88.3×10^3
Turpentine	1470
Water	1040

More generally, a Newtonian viscous liquid may be defined as one in which the components of stress at a given point in the liquid, at a given time, are linear functions of the first spatial derivatives of the velocity components at the same point and at the same instant. The general equations for Newtonian liquid flow may then be obtained from the elastic equations of an isotropic solid by replacing the strain components with the rate of strain components, remembering that, in a liquid, there is a hydrostatic stress $-p$, where p is the pressure, superposed on the viscous stresses. Equations [2.10] and [2.26] then become:

$$\sigma_x = \lambda'\dot{\Delta} + 2\eta\dot{\epsilon}_x - p$$
$$\sigma_y = \lambda'\dot{\Delta} + 2\eta\dot{\epsilon}_y - p \qquad\qquad [4.7]$$
$$\sigma_z = \lambda'\dot{\Delta} + 2\eta\dot{\epsilon}_z - p$$
$$\tau_{yz} = \eta\dot{\gamma}_{yz}; \quad \tau_{zx} = \eta\dot{\gamma}_{zx}; \quad \tau_{xy} = \eta\dot{\gamma}_{xy}$$

where λ' and η are the constants of proportionality appropriate to the situation of liquid flow and:

$$\dot{\Delta} = \frac{\partial \epsilon_x}{\partial t} + \frac{\partial \epsilon_y}{\partial t} + \frac{\partial \epsilon_z}{\partial t}$$

$$= \frac{\partial u_x}{\partial x} + \frac{\partial u_y}{\partial y} + \frac{\partial u_z}{\partial z} .$$

From equation [4.6], η in equations [4.7] can be identified as the coefficient of dynamic viscosity.

The shear strain rate $\dot{\gamma}$ can be written in terms of the velocity components, using equations [2.12], so that:

$$\tau_{yz} = \eta \left(\frac{\partial u_z}{\partial y} + \frac{\partial u_y}{\partial z} \right)$$

$$\tau_{zx} = \eta \left(\frac{\partial u_x}{\partial z} + \frac{\partial u_z}{\partial x} \right) \qquad [4.8]$$

$$\tau_{xy} = \eta \left(\frac{\partial u_y}{\partial x} + \frac{\partial u_x}{\partial y} \right) .$$

If the liquid is incompressible both Δ and $\dot{\Delta}$ are zero and then the equations of viscosity [4.7] become:

$$\sigma_x = 2\eta \dot{\epsilon}_x - p \; ; \; \tau_{yz} = \eta \dot{\gamma}_{yz}$$
$$\sigma_y = 2\eta \dot{\epsilon}_y - p \; ; \; \tau_{zx} = \eta \dot{\gamma}_{zx} \qquad [4.9]$$
$$\sigma_z = 2\eta \dot{\epsilon}_z - p \; ; \; \tau_{xy} = \eta \dot{\gamma}_{xy} .$$

4.5 Critical velocity

When a liquid flows in a channel the flow is laminar for very small velocities; it remains laminar as the flow velocity is increased but, at a certain, fairly definite, mean flow velocity in the channel, turbulence sets in. The mean flow velocity at which this happens is called the critical velocity u_c. When turbulence occurs the definition of coefficient of viscosity is no longer applicable; η is not defined under turbulent conditions.

Under laminar flow conditions most of the work done by the shearing forces when conditions are steady is dissipated in overcoming the viscous drag between liquid layers moving with different velocities. However, when the flow is turbulent, most of the energy supplied is first used in producing eddies in the liquid. The ease with which eddies are formed is likely to involve a dependence on the density of the liquid, since bulk kinetic energy is given to local regions of the liquid. Therefore, u_c may be expected to depend on the viscosity of the liquid, its density ρ, and on the lateral size d of the channel through which the liquid is flowing, since the effect of the boundary layer is greater the narrower the channel. Dimensional analysis shows that:

$$u_c = \frac{(Re)\eta}{\rho d} = (Re)\frac{\nu}{d} \qquad [4.10]$$

where Re is a dimensionless number known as the Reynolds number and $\nu(=\eta/\rho)$ is known as the kinematic viscosity of the liquid, having dimensions L^2T^{-1} and units $m^2\,s^{-1}$.

If d refers to the diameter of a cylindrical channel, turbulent flow occurs for $Re > 2000$ and laminar flow for $Re < 1000$. When Re lies between 1000 and 2000 the flow is usually laminar provided that there is no undue disturbance at the entrance of the channel.

4.6 Fluidity and solidity

The simple definitions given of solids and liquids are not always appropriate when the latter are subjected to applied forces. Pitch, for example, behaves like a solid, in that it shows a definite and measureable rigidity, when subjected to applied forces for short times, but flows like a liquid when it is subjected to applied forces for very long times.

Generally, a material may be regarded as capable of sustaining and exerting an instantaneous shearing stress, but immediately starts to flow as a viscous liquid. The elastic behaviour diminishes with time (termed fugitive elasticity by Maxwell), the rate of decrease depending on the elastic and viscous properties of the material. The designation of a specimen as solid or liquid will then depend on the rate of decrease of the elasticity relative to the time of observation.

If hysteresis effects are ignored, the shear strain rate $\dot{\gamma}$ of a material that shows flow behaviour may be written:

$$\dot{\gamma} = f(\tau) \qquad\qquad [4.11]$$

where τ is the shear stress acting on the specimen and f is a function characteristic of the material, but including the result that $\dot{\gamma} = 0$ when $\tau = 0$. Assuming that $f(\tau)$ may be written as a power series, the limiting equation for small values of τ may be written:

$$\dot{\gamma} = \phi\tau \qquad\qquad [4.12]$$

where ϕ is a constant. Equation [4.12] is, of course, the Newton law of viscosity for laminar flow and ϕ is identified with the reciprocal of the viscosity η and is known as the fluidity of the material.

Using the Maxwellian idea of fugitive elasticity, let a shear stress τ produce both a shear strain γ_e and a Newtonian shear strain rate $\dot{\gamma}_N$ in a given material. When a shear stress τ_0 is applied abruptly to the material the shear strain instantly becomes $\gamma_e = \tau_0/G$, where G is the rigidity modulus. However, since the material is capable of Newtonian viscous flow, the stress immediately starts to relax, with the elastic strain being replaced by a viscous strain that is given by $\tau = \eta\dot{\gamma}_N$. If it is assumed that the mechanical device producing the initial deformation does not move thereafter, $\dot{\gamma}_e + \dot{\gamma}_N = 0$, i.e. the total applied strain rate is zero. Now $\dot{\gamma}_e = \dot{\tau}/G$ and $\dot{\gamma}_N = \tau/\eta$, so that:

$$\frac{\tau}{\eta} + \frac{\dot{\tau}}{G} = 0 \;\; \text{or,} \;\; \frac{\dot{\tau}}{\tau} = -\frac{G}{\eta}. \qquad [4.13]$$

Integrating equation [4.13] gives:

$$\tau = \tau_0 \exp(-t/t_R) \qquad\qquad [4.14]$$

where $t_R = \eta/G$ and is a time of relaxation that is a measure of the relative importance of the viscous and elastic contributions to the strain rate. If t_0 is the time of observation and $D = t_R/t_0$, liquid behaviour is associated with very small values of D and solid behaviour with very large values of D. Impact loading can make a conventional liquid behave like a solid; a very long observational time can make a conventional solid appear to have liquid properties. When conditions are such that D lies within a few decades of unity the behaviour does not approach either ideal solid or liquid behaviour and is described as viscoelastic, a behaviour that is described in a little more detail in section 8.9. An ideal viscous liquid is, then, a body that constantly changes its form under the smallest applied shear stress, whereas a solid body only suffers a continuous alteration of form when the stress exceeds a certain value.

4.7 Models of simple liquids

From the viewpoint of equilibrium thermodynamics, the macroscopic properties of any closed hydrostatic system are completely specified by the equation of state and the molar internal energy $U_m(p, T)$. For simple liquids it is found that U_m is close to that of the solid phase when T is close to the triple point temperature but close to that for the gas phase when T is close to the critical temperature. Liquids also have the cohesion that is characteristic of solids but, like gases, do not show rigidity. Observations of this sort suggest that liquids are intermediate in their behaviour between solids and gases. Further evidence leading to the same conclusion comes from values for the average coordination number, which can be obtained from X-ray scattering experiments by means of the radial distribution function (see section 1.5). Near the fusion curve the number of nearest neighbours in a simple liquid approaches, but does not equal, that in the crystalline phase. For most of the liquid range the coordination number is about one half of that in the crystalline solid, though near the critical point the value becomes similar to that in the adjacent gas. Further, the nearest neighbour distance is somewhat smaller than in the crystalline phase, a consequence of atmospheric pressure and fluidity, but the bulk density is reduced, so that there must be a larger density of vacancies or holes in the liquid than in the crystal. Consequently, molecular models of liquids often start by treating a simple liquid either as a very dense gas or as a broken-up solid.

Liquids as dense gases

In the gas-like model of a liquid an attempt is made to extrapolate the structure of a gas to temperatures below the critical temperature T_c. The simplest model of a gas assumes that the molecules can be treated as point masses that interact with each other and with the walls of the container only during collisions and then in a crude 'contact' sense. This implies that the attractive forces between the molecules are negligible and that the repulsive forces are of vanishingly short range. This model readily gives the equation of state for the ideal gas:

$$pV_m = RT . \qquad [4.15]$$

Attempts to improve on this model try to allow for the non-zero, but short-range, attractive forces, and also for the finite range of the repulsive force, which, essentially, gives a molecule its size. One well-known attempt to improve on the simple model is that of van der Waals, who wrote the equation of state for a real gas in the form:

$$\left(p + \frac{a}{V_m^2}\right)(V_m - b) = RT \qquad [4.16]$$

where a and b are constants for a particular gas; a is a correction to the attractive interaction and b to the repulsive interaction. Equation [4.16] is an improvement of equation [4.15] since it does predict the existence of a critical point, but it does not predict a triple point. When the isotherms corresponding to equation [4.16] are plotted (Fig. 4.1) it is found that though there is a region where the isotherms look like those for an almost incompressible substance and another where the behaviour is gas-like, in the region where liquid and vapour should coexist in equilibrium, the isotherms have a positive slope, implying an instability. Further, at sufficiently low temperatures, the isotherms reach regions where the pressure becomes negative.

Despite these difficulties this type of model has been used in certain situations. In particular, the negative pressure regions have been interpreted as denoting the liquid phase under tension, and the maximum value of this tension, for a particular temperature, is interpreted as the tensile strength of the liquid phase at that

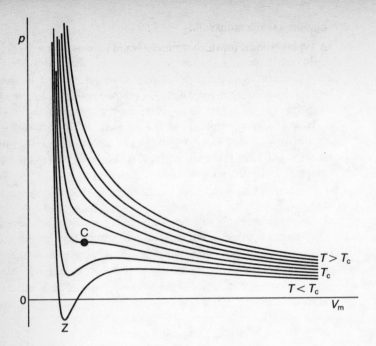

Fig. 4.1

temperature. The pressure at the point Z in Fig. 4.1 is given by:

$$p_Z = \frac{a(V_m - 2b)}{V_m{}^3} \qquad [4.17]$$

and, since V_m tends to the value b as the temperature tends to zero, the limiting value of p_Z (at absolute zero) is $-a/b^2$. The values of a and b can both be expressed in terms of the critical pressure p_c, giving the result for the predicted maximum tensile strength of $27p_c$. For argon p_c is 4.9×10^6 Pa, which gives a predicted maximum tensile strength of 1.3×10^8 Pa. The observed values are only about 10^6 Pa, which is not very good agreement, but this is not unexpected since the liquid should be most like a gas in the neighbourhood of the critical point, whereas the discussion of the maximum tensile strength is located far below C in p–V–T space.

Liquids as broken-up solids

A typical model in which a simple liquid is treated as a broken-up solid is the cell model.

The results described in section 4.7 indicate that the general reduction in bulk density that occurs when a solid changes to a liquid arises from the decrease in coordination number, rather than from a uniform increase in the distance between neighbouring molecules. In the cell model a liquid is treated as a collection of molecules that spend most of their time in small clusters that fit together in a rather loose manner. Each cluster can be treated as a cell, the walls of which are formed by molecules and inside which one molecule is trapped. Any particular molecule can be pictured as a wall molecule of one cell or as a molecule trapped in another cell. This does not affect the analysis and, in any case, the cells are constantly breaking up and reforming.

In the simplest treatment it is assumed that the molecules forming the outside of the cluster (see Fig. 4.2) or cell remain practically fixed, while the molecule trapped in the cell moves around inside and occasionally obtains sufficient kinetic energy,

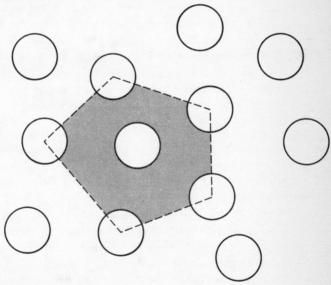

Fig. 4.2

as a result of thermal fluctuations, to escape from its cell, that is, it is able to overcome the potential barrier that represents the force fields of the molecules forming the walls of the cell. When a molecule escapes from a cell it joins another cluster of molecules, either as a wall molecule or as the occupant of a cell. If the height of the barrier is U and the vibration frequency of the molecule in the cell is ν_0, the number of successful attempts at surmounting the barrier per unit time, ν, is approximately:

$$\nu = \nu_0 \exp\left(-U/kT\right)$$

where k is the Boltzmann constant.

The cell model is most useful in discussing transport properties such as diffusion and viscosity and will be developed rather more fully in Chapter 6. In associated liquids it is likely that certain angular orientations between nearest neighbours will be preferred which will complicate matters.

4.8 Melting

Melting is the name given to the transition from the solid to the liquid phase. In pure substances it is characterised by a sharp melting temperature T_m that varies with the pressure. At the melting point the liquid suddenly becomes the phase with the lowest free energy. Melting is a first-order phase change — there is an associated change in specific entropy and also a specific enthalpy of fusion — but the most marked change on melting is the dramatic increase in fluidity displayed by the liquid relative to the solid.

At present the molecular behaviour in melting is not well understood. Most molecular models rely on some form of instability of the solid phase to provide the driving force for melting. A typical example of such a model is that due to Born, who assumed that the rigidity modulus of the solid, which decreases with increasing temperature, becomes zero at the melting point, a suggestion refuted by careful measurement.

An alternative suggestion, due originally to Lindemann, is that melting occurs when the amplitude of the molecular vibrations reaches a critical value that causes the long-range structure of the crystal to break-up. In the Hertzfeld–Mayer model (see exercise 3), the critical separation is taken to be that at which the potential energy versus intermolecular distance curve passes through a point of inflexion. Models of this type have some qualitative value and, experimentally, there is a rough correlation between melting point and rigidity modulus of crystals.

The most recent model of the melting process, and one that has some support from computer simulations, is based on the idea that the melting transition results from a catastrophic proliferation of dislocations in the material. A liquid at its melting point is then pictured as a crystal that is saturated with dislocation lines. The model does not lend itself to a simple quantitative treatment, but it should be noted that the energy of a dislocation line introduced into a crystal depends on the density of dislocation lines existing in the crystal and the greater the density of dislocation lines, the lower the energy needed to create still more. To avoid the production of long-range stresses the dislocations generated in the crystal must be dipoles, that is, close pairs of opposite sign.

4.9 Liquid helium

The structure assumed by a condensed phase is a compromise resulting from the opposing tendencies of the intermolecular forces, trying to produce an ordered structure, and of the internal energy, which opposes the establishment of this order. As the temperature of a substance is reduced the internal energy is lowered and, as the absolute zero of temperature is approached, the study of the properties of matter gives information about ordering forces too weak to be effective at higher temperatures such as room temperature.

Classically it is impossible for a substance to remain in the liquid phase as the temperature approaches absolute zero since the internal energy tends to zero. Quantum mechanically a condensed phase at absolute zero has a zero-point energy (see *Quantum Mechanics* by P.C.W. Davies in this series), but, generally, this is too small to have an important effect on the behaviour. The one known exception to the classical rule is that of helium, which remains liquid down to the lowest temperatures unless subjected to an external pressure in excess of 25 atmospheres (25 × 101 325 Pa). This behaviour is a consequence of the abnormally high zero-point energy of helium; essentially, liquid helium at low temperatures is a macroscopic manifestation of quantum effects.

There are two common stable isotopes of helium, ^{3}He and ^{4}He, with relative abundancies of 10^{-4} and $\approx100\%$, respectively. Neither isotope has a triple point in the phase diagram, and when mixed, they provide the only case in which isotopic mixtures form two liquid phases in equilibrium, the isotopic solutions separating below 0.87 K.

The phase diagram for ^{4}He is shown in Fig. 4.3. There are two liquid phases, HeI and HeII, separated in the phase diagram by a line known as the lambda line (λ line) and shown dashed in Fig. 4.3. The change that occurs at the λ line is marked by a very characteristic anomaly in the specific heat capacity c of the liquid: the specific heat capacity rises to a very high value at the lambda

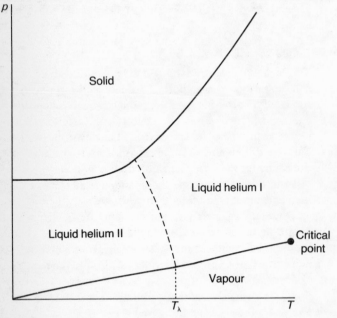

Fig. 4.3

temperature (2.17 K under the saturation vapour pressure) as it is approached from either side, and then falls off rapidly, giving a c–T curve that has the rough form of the Greek letter lambda.

HeI behaves as an ordinary liquid but HeII shows a number of remarkable properties. In particular, it is superfluid, in the sense that it can flow through very fine channels with apparently zero viscosity.

^{3}He shows no lambda transition and is not superfluid, except at very low temperatures, and the condition is reached gradually, rather than abruptly as in the case of ^{4}He. The remainder of this section will deal only with ^{4}He.

When HeII flows through very narrow channels it does so with a velocity of flow that is independent of the pressure head. This result of apparent zero viscosity is valid only if the flow velocity is below some critical value which increases with decreasing channel size and decreasing temperature. However, when the viscosity of HeII is determined from the damping of an oscillating disc, the viscosity falls markedly at T_λ, but not to zero, and then decreases more slowly as T is reduced, becoming zero at absolute zero. Again, this result is true only if the amplitude of the oscillation is below some critical value. For larger amplitudes the damping increases rapidly, as if some form of turbulence sets in.

An unusual feature of HeII is that variations in temperature propagate through the liquid as a true wave motion whose velocity is independent of frequency. These temperature waves are analogous to 'ordinary' sound waves. They can be excited with a heater and detected with a thermometer. This type of heat propagation is known as second sound.

When two vessels A and B containing HeII are joined by a very fine capillary the liquid level in both vessels is the same when the temperatures and pressures are the same. If an excess pressure is applied to the surface of the liquid in vessel A, say, liquid flows through the capillary into the vessel B, as expected, but the temperature of A rises while that of B falls. This is the thermomechanical effect. When the excess pressure is removed the system returns to its original state. The converse effect (the mechanocalorie effect) also occurs. If the levels in A and B are initially the same and the temperature of one vessel is raised, the liquid level rises in that vessel and falls in the other.

When a small beaker containing HeII is suspended in a closed vessel above a bath of HeII at the same temperature, drops of liquid HeII form at the bottom of the beaker and fall into the bath of liquid. This process continues until the beaker is empty. Rollin first showed that this is a consequence of a film of HeII, of about 100 atoms thick, covering the surface of the beaker. It is characteristic of this flow that it takes place at a velocity that depends only on the temperature, and vanishes at T_λ, irrespective of the nature of the walls.

4.10 The two-fluid model of HeII

HeI is a fairly normal liquid, remarkable only for its low temperature and density. The transition to HeII that occurs at the lambda temperature is not an ordinary, first order, phase change since there is no abrupt change in specific volume and specific entropy. Nor is it a formation of molecules or loosely bound complexes (no Raman effect). Further, X-ray studies show no kind of pseudo-crystallisation.

There is now a good quantum model for HeII, but a useful, working description is given by the two-fluid model of Tisza and Landau. This model assumes that, at absolute zero, all atoms have only their zero-point energy of translation. As the temperature is raised some atoms acquire further translational energy through collisions, the fraction of the atoms acquiring some additional energy being zero at absolute zero and unity at T_λ. These are the so-called normal atoms. Since all the other atoms still have only their zero-point energy, at any temperature between absolute zero and T_λ there are some atoms that are energetically at absolute zero. These are the so-called superfluid atoms. The two sets of atoms are assumed to intermingle freely without interaction. Since the superfluid atoms have energy corresponding to absolute zero, if absolute zero is used as the reference temperature, they have an entropy equal to zero.

If the translational energies of the helium atoms are represented on an energy-level diagram, to account for the phenomena shown by HeII there must be a gap in the energy-level spectrum between the lowest level and the next, above which the spectrum of levels is continuous. Atoms in the lowest level cannot then make transitions to a state with a momentum that is higher by an arbitrarily small amount. Therefore, they cannot dissipate momentum and their flow is free from viscosity, that is, they exhibit superfluidity. An atom which makes a transition into any of the levels above the lowest level becomes part of the normal fluid which can dissipate momentum and shows the normal properties of a viscous liquid.

If the normal fluid has a density ρ_n and the superfluid a density ρ_s, the ordinary density of HeII is given by the sum of ρ_n and ρ_s. Both ρ_n and ρ_s are functions of temperature, but the density of HeII ρ varies only slightly with temperature, and this variation can often be ignored. Since the superfluid has zero entropy, the normal fluid has a specific entropy equal to that of HeII.

When HeII flows through very narrow tubes the motion of the normal fluid is restricted by its viscosity, but the superfluid moves readily with zero viscosity and flow without friction is observed. The damping of a disc oscillating in a liquid depends on the product of the density and viscosity. For HeII the appropriate density is ρ_n and so the viscosity is not zero at finite temperatures, but decreases rapidly with temperature.

In the experiment on the helium film, the exposed surfaces of the beaker are in equilibrium with the saturated vapour of the liquid of the bath and will, therefore, be covered by an adsorbed layer of helium. At temperatures below T_λ the superfluid is able to flow in the adsorbed layer or film which, therefore, acts as a sort of syphon. The driving force for the motion is the difference in gravitational potential energy of the liquid in the beaker and in the bath, which leads to a difference in the specific Helmholtz functions.

According to the two-fluid model ρ_n/ρ_s depends strongly on temperature. A rapid, local temperature fluctuation gives rise to a rapid, local variation in ρ_n/ρ_s, without appreciably altering ρ. Fluctuations in ρ_n/ρ_s correspond to second sound waves, which may be pictured as the relative movement of superfluid and normal atoms, while the total density remains constant. This is in contrast to ordinary (first) sound waves in which normal and superfluid atoms move together to give fluctuations in total density.

Chapter 5
Ideal liquids

5.1 Introduction

In Chapter 4 some of the properties of real liquids have been described. From the point of view of liquid flow, the two most important properties are that liquids are almost incompressible and that relative motion of liquid layers is opposed by viscous forces. The next stage is to try to formulate general equations to describe the motion of liquids. A description of the gross properties of liquids, in terms of large-scale parameters only, will be attempted, not a kinetic theory of liquid behaviour. Before attempting to set up these equations, it will be necessary to make a few general remarks about the properties of liquids.

5.2 Some large-scale properties of liquids

A study of the mechanics of liquids will involve consideration of the movement of small masses or elements of a liquid (liquid particles) as a result of forces acting on them.

The mass of a given element will depend on the density of the liquid in the region of the element. For any substance, if the mass of a volume V is m, the mean density $\bar{\rho}$ is defined as:

$$\bar{\rho} = m/V$$

and the substance is of uniform density if $\bar{\rho}$ has the same value for all portions of the substance. If the molecular structure of the substance is ignored and the substance is treated as a continuum, it is possible to define the density at a point, ρ, which is the limit to which the mean density for a volume surrounding the point tends as the volume tends to zero:

$$\rho = \mathop{\text{Lt}}_{V \to 0} \left(\frac{m}{V}\right).$$

[5.1]

The motion of an element of liquid may be specified in terms of the flow velocity, as described in section 4.3, remembering that this is the drift velocity of the element or liquid particle, and not a molecular velocity.

In section 2.1 a discussion was given of the internal forces that may be transmitted through a solid. The ability to transmit forces is a property of a condensed phase so that a liquid may transmit internal forces and these can be classified as for solids.

Any element of a liquid experiences forces across its surface that arise from the presence of the surrounding liquid. These forces are the contact or surface forces and arise from the molecular action between adjacent elements or particles of liquid. There may also be forces produced by the effects of long-range fields such as the gravitational field. These forces act throughout the liquid on all its elements and are called body forces.

Across any surface drawn in the interior of a liquid there will be a mutual force due to the molecular action in the liquid on either side of the surface. Because of the short-range nature of intermolecular forces this mutual force can be considered as a surface force.

In a liquid in equilibrium it is assumed that this force has a zero tangential component (a property that is often used as a definition of a liquid, indeed of fluids in general). This mutual force of the liquid on one side of the surface on that on the other side is analogous to the load in a solid, and is called the thrust. The measure of the thrust is the magnitude of the force exerted by the liquid on one side of a surface on the liquid on the other side of the surface. If the thrust on a small surface of area $\delta\alpha$ is $\delta\mathbf{F}$, the mean pressure $\overline{p}$ on the surface is defined as the thrust per unit area, that is:

$$\overline{p}\hat{\mathbf{e}} = \frac{\delta\mathbf{F}}{\delta\alpha}$$

[5.2]

where $\hat{\mathbf{e}}$ is the unit vector normal to $\delta\alpha$.

Usually the thrust in a liquid is compressive and this is taken as the positive sense. Note that the convention for loads in solids is the opposite.

The pressure at a point in the liquid, p is the limit of $\bar{p}$ as $\delta\alpha$ tends to zero, i.e.:

$$p\hat{e} = \underset{\delta\alpha \to 0}{\text{Lt}} \frac{\delta F}{\delta\alpha}. \qquad [5.3]$$

A consequence of there being no tangential forces in a liquid in equilibrium is that the pressure at any point in the (continuous) liquid is the same for all planes through the point. This may be shown as follows.

In a liquid at rest consider a cylindrical region, as shown in Fig. 5.1, that has ends of area $\delta\alpha_1$, and $\delta\alpha_2$ respectively, surrounding neighbouring points P and Q. Consider the motion in the x direction of the liquid contained in the cylinder. The

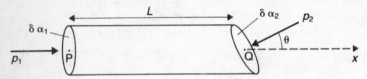

Fig. 5.1

acceleration a is finite. Let p_1 and p_2 be the values of the pressures normal to $\delta\alpha_1$ and $\delta\alpha_2$, respectively, and let F_x be the component of the body force acting in the x direction on unit mass of the liquid. The volume V of the liquid may be written:

$$V = (L + \epsilon)\,\delta\alpha_1$$

where ϵ is a positive quantity, having the dimensions of length, that allows for the variation in the length of the cylindrical generators, and that tends to zero as $\delta\alpha_1$ tends to zero. Then, if ρ is the density of the liquid, assumed constant, the equation of motion in the x direction of the liquid in the cylindrical region is:

$$p_1\delta\alpha_1 - p_2\delta\alpha_2 \cos\theta + F_x\rho(L + \epsilon)\,\delta\alpha_1 = \rho(L + \epsilon)\,\delta\alpha_1 a.$$

Now:

$$\delta\alpha_2 \cos\theta = \delta\alpha_1$$

so that:

$$p_1 - p_2 = (a - F_x) \rho (L + \epsilon) . \qquad [5.4]$$

The right hand side of equation [5.4] tends to zero as the dimensions of the cylinder tend to zero. Therefore, as P approaches Q (see Fig. 5.1), the value of p_1 tends to that of p_2. Since the choice of θ was arbitrary, the pressure of an element of surface at a given point in a liquid at rest is independent of the direction of the surface element and, therefore, it is possible to talk simply of the pressure at a point in the liquid.

Finally, in this section, a note about liquid flow. It was seen in section 4.5 that, when a liquid flows with a mean velocity less than the critical velocity, it does so in layers that, on the macroscopic scale, do not mix. Under these conditions, the behaviour of small elements of the liquid (liquid particles) can be specified in terms of streamlines. Streamlines are lines drawn in the liquid so that the tangent at any point is the direction of motion of the liquid particle at that point. Streamlines should not be confused with pathlines, which denote the actual paths of liquid particles through the bulk liquid. The components of the liquid flow velocity at any point may be functions of time as well as of position, in which case the streamlines vary with time. However, if the velocity components at any point do not.vary with time the flow is said to be steady and the streamlines and pathlines coincide.

If the streamlines through all the points on a closed curve in the liquid are drawn they enclose a stream tube. Since there is no flow across the boundary of a stream tube when conditions are steady, it behaves like a tube along which the liquid is flowing. When the stream tube is sufficiently narrow, so that the flow velocity normal to any cross-section is constant over that cross-section, and has a value u_1 over the area α_1 and u_2 over the area α_2 then continuity of the material demands that:

$$\alpha_1 u_1 \rho_1 = \alpha_2 u_2 \rho_2 \qquad [5.5]$$

where ρ_1 is the density at the cross-section of area α_1 and ρ_2 that at the cross-section of area α_2. For an incompressible liquid ρ_1 equals ρ_2 and:

$$\alpha_1 u_1 = \alpha_2 u_2 . \qquad [5.6]$$

5.3 Real and ideal liquids

In a real liquid at rest there are no tangential components of internal force but, when the shape of the liquid is changed (and this occurs essentially without change in volume and so is a shearing process), forces are set up that appear as viscous effects; the viscous effect varies with velocity gradient for a given liquid. It is often convenient to assume the existence of an ideal liquid in which no shearing forces are set up when the liquid flows. This ideal liquid then differs from a real liquid in the following ways.

1. An ideal liquid is treated as a continuous medium; the molecular structure of the real liquid is ignored.
2. There are no tangential stresses in the ideal liquid, even when flow takes place. Therefore, under all conditions, the pressure at any point in an ideal liquid is independent of direction and the coefficient of viscosity is zero.
3. If there is a rigid body in the ideal liquid the normal relative velocity is zero always, that is, the ideal liquid slips over the surface. For real liquids there is, in fact, no slip at the surface.

As a further simplification an ideal liquid is often assumed to be incompressible, but this is not an essential condition.

5.4 The acceleration of a liquid particle

The velocity of a small element of liquid, or liquid particle, has been discussed in section 4.3. This is not the velocity of the individual molecules, but the drift velocity of a small region of liquid and is approximately that of a small, light solid particle carried along with the liquid. For a complete description of the motion of the liquid the velocity $\mathbf{u}$ must be known as a function of the space variables and also the time since, at any fixed point in the liquid, the velocity is not, generally, independent of time.

Set up fixed Cartesian axes within a liquid undergoing flow and consider the behaviour of a liquid particle. If the liquid particle is at a point A, say, at a time t and at a point B at a time $t + \delta t$, the average acceleration of the liquid particle over the time interval δt is:

$$\frac{(\mathbf{u})_{t + \delta t} - (\mathbf{u})_t}{\delta t}$$

and the acceleration of the particle as it passed through A is:

$$\underset{\delta t \to 0}{\text{Lt}} \frac{(\mathbf{u})_{t+\delta t} - (\mathbf{u})_t}{\delta t}$$

where $(\mathbf{u})_t$ is the velocity of the liquid particle at time t.

This expression may be put into a more useful and instructive form by considering the behaviour of a liquid particle in the neighbourhood of the point (x, y, z).

Let the fluid particle under consideration be that contained in an element with edges δx, δy, δz, respectively, and with one corner at the point (x, y, z) in space, as in Fig. 5.2. Further, let

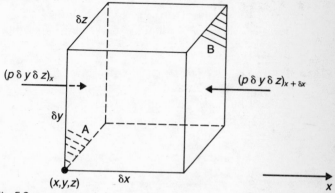

Fig. 5.2

$f(x, y, z, t)$ be some function of the state of the liquid particle at the point (x, y, z) at the time t. The change in f in a time δt, associated with this liquid particle, is:

$$\delta f = f(x + \delta x, y + \delta y, z + \delta z, t + \delta t) - f(x, y, z, t)$$

and the rate of change of f as δt tends to zero is:

$$\frac{\mathrm{d}f}{\mathrm{d}t} = \frac{\partial f}{\partial t} + \frac{\partial f}{\partial x}\frac{\mathrm{d}x}{\mathrm{d}t} + \frac{\partial f}{\partial y}\frac{\mathrm{d}y}{\mathrm{d}t} + \frac{\partial f}{\partial z}\frac{\mathrm{d}z}{\mathrm{d}t}. \qquad [5.7]$$

If the liquid velocity $\mathbf{u}$ has components u_x, u_y, u_z in the x, y, z directions, respectively:

$$u_x = \frac{\mathrm{d}x}{\mathrm{d}t}; \; u_y = \frac{\mathrm{d}y}{\mathrm{d}t}; \; u_z = \frac{\mathrm{d}z}{\mathrm{d}t}$$

and, therefore:

$$\frac{df}{dt} = \frac{\partial f}{\partial t} + u_x \frac{\partial f}{\partial x} + u_y \frac{\partial f}{\partial y} + u_z \frac{\partial f}{\partial z}. \qquad [5.8]$$

This differentiation is often called 'differentiation following the motion of the liquid' and, to bring out both the time and space dependence, it is often written Df/Dt; D/Dt is sometimes called the 'mobile operator' or the 'convective derivative'. If, for example, f denotes the density ρ of the liquid, $D\rho/Dt$ gives the rate of change of density of a particular liquid particle, but $d\rho/dt$ gives the rate of change of density at a particular point in space, i.e. part of the total change in ρ results from the lapse of time and part from the movement of the particle to a different place.

Now the velocity u of a liquid particle has components u_x, u_y, u_z:

$$\mathbf{u} = (u_x, u_y, u_z)$$

and, therefore:

$$\mathbf{u} \cdot \nabla = (u_x \mathbf{i} + u_y \mathbf{j} + u_z \mathbf{k}) \cdot \left(\mathbf{i} \frac{\partial}{\partial x} + \mathbf{j} \frac{\partial}{\partial y} + \mathbf{k} \frac{\partial}{\partial z} \right)$$

where $\mathbf{i}, \mathbf{j}, \mathbf{k}$ are unit vectors in the x, y, z directions respectively. Therefore:

$$\mathbf{u} \cdot \nabla = u_x \frac{\partial}{\partial x} + u_y \frac{\partial}{\partial y} + u_z \frac{\partial}{\partial z}$$

so that the rate of change of f (equation [5.8]) may be written:

$$\frac{Df}{Dt} = \frac{\partial f}{\partial t} + (\mathbf{u} \cdot \nabla) f \qquad [5.9]$$

and the mobile operator becomes:

$$\frac{D}{Dt} = \frac{\partial}{\partial t} + (\mathbf{u} \cdot \nabla). \qquad [5.10]$$

The acceleration of the liquid particle as it passes through the point (x, y, z) is, therefore:

$$\frac{D\mathbf{u}}{Dt} = \frac{\partial \mathbf{u}}{\partial t} + (\mathbf{u} \cdot \nabla) \mathbf{u}. \qquad [5.11]$$

The component of acceleration in the x direction is:

$$\frac{\partial u_x}{\partial t} + u_x \frac{\partial u_x}{\partial x}$$

with similar expressions for the components in the y and z directions.

When the motion is steady $\partial u_x / \partial t = 0$ and the acceleration in the x direction becomes, simply, $u_x \, \partial u_x / \partial x$.

5.5 Euler's equations of motion

Consider, as the liquid particle whose motion is to be described, the liquid contained in the element of Fig. 5.2, that is, the liquid contained in an element with edges $\delta x, \delta y, \delta z$ and with one corner located at the point (x, y, z). The liquid particle must obey Newton's laws of motion, so setting up the equations of motion involves determining the net force acting on the liquid particle and equating that to the product of its mass and acceleration.

The forces acting on the element of Fig. 5.2 are the body forces, with components, say, X, Y, Z per unit mass in the x, y, z directions, respectively, the pressure forces and the viscous forces. For the present it will be assumed that the liquid has zero viscosity (known as an inviscid liquid) and then the pressure forces are perpendicular to the boundary surface. The effect of viscosity will be considered briefly in section 5.12.

Consider first the motion in the x direction. The net force acting on the element of liquid in the x direction is:

$$(p \, \delta y \, \delta z)_x - (p \, \delta y \, \delta z)_{x + \delta x} + X \rho \, \delta x \, \delta y \, \delta z$$

where ρ is the density of the liquid in the element. This net force must equal the mass of the element multiplied by its acceleration, that is, it equals:

$$\rho \, \delta x \, \delta y \, \delta z \left(\frac{\partial u_x}{\partial t} + u_x \frac{\partial u_x}{\partial x} \right)$$

where u_x is the x component of the velocity of the liquid particle. Therefore:

$$-\delta y \, \delta z \, [(p)_{x+\delta x} - (p)_x] + X \rho \, \delta x \, \delta y \, \delta z$$

$$= \rho \, \delta x \, \delta y \, \delta z \left(\frac{\partial u_x}{\partial t} + u_x \frac{\partial u_x}{\partial x} \right) \qquad [5.12]$$

and, since:

$$(p)_{x+\delta x} = (p)_x + \frac{\partial p}{\partial x} \delta x$$

equation [5.12] may be written:

$$-\delta y \, \delta z \left[(p)_x + \frac{\partial p}{\partial x} \delta x - (p)_x \right] + X \rho \, \delta x \, \delta y \, \delta z$$

$$= \rho \, \delta x \, \delta y \, \delta z \left(\frac{\partial u_x}{\partial t} + u_x \frac{\partial u_x}{\partial x} \right).$$

To ensure that all quantities have values appropriate to the point (x, y, z), the limit is taken as δx, δy and δz each tend to zero. Then:

$$-\frac{\partial p}{\partial x} + X \rho = \rho \left(\frac{\partial u_x}{\partial t} + u_x \frac{\partial u_x}{\partial x} \right)$$

or: $X - \dfrac{1}{\rho} \dfrac{\partial p}{\partial x} = \dfrac{\partial u_x}{\partial t} + u_x \dfrac{\partial u_x}{\partial x}$. $\qquad [5.13]$

Similarly, for the y and z directions:

$$Y - \frac{1}{\rho} \frac{\partial p}{\partial y} = \frac{\partial u_y}{\partial t} + u_y \frac{\partial u_y}{\partial y} \qquad [5.14]$$

and: $Z - \dfrac{1}{\rho} \dfrac{\partial p}{\partial z} = \dfrac{\partial u_z}{\partial t} + u_z \dfrac{\partial u_z}{\partial z}$. $\qquad [5.15]$

Equations [5.13], [5.14] and [5.15] are known as Euler's equations of motion for a non-viscous liquid. They may be combined into the single vector equation:

$$\mathbf{F} - \frac{1}{\rho} \nabla p = \frac{d\mathbf{u}}{dt} = \frac{D\mathbf{u}}{Dt} \qquad [5.16]$$

where $\mathbf{F}$ is the total (vector) body force per unit mass.

Considering only liquid flow in the x direction, equation [5.13] may be written:

$$\frac{\partial u_x}{\partial t} = X - \frac{1}{\rho}\frac{\partial p}{\partial x} - \frac{\partial}{\partial x}\left(\frac{u_x^2}{2}\right).$$

Provided that ρ remains practically constant, this equation shows that, even for a liquid with a coefficient of viscosity equal to zero, a pressure gradient becomes less effective in producing acceleration in a liquid particle as the liquid velocity increases. This may be termed the Bernoulli effect.

5.6 The equation of continuity

This equation expresses the condition that, provided matter is neither created nor destroyed, a liquid as it flows does not pull apart and that different rates of flow into and out of a given region must result in changes in density of the liquid contained therein.

Consider again the liquid contained in the element of volume shown in Fig. 5.2. It will be assumed that the components of the liquid velocity $\mathbf{u}$ are u_x, u_y, u_z parallel to the x, y and z directions, respectively, and that the liquid density ρ is a function of the coordinates, i.e.:

$$\rho = \rho(x, y, z).$$

The mass of liquid flowing into the element across face **A** in the x direction in a time δt is:

$$(\rho\, u_x\, \delta y\, \delta z)_x \delta t$$

and, similarly, the mass flowing out across face **B** in the x direction in a time δt is:

$$(\rho\, u_x\, \delta y\, \delta z)_{x\,+\,\delta x}\, \delta t\,.$$

Therefore, the net mass inflow in the x direction in a time δt is:

$$-\left[(\rho\, u_x\, \delta y\, \delta z)_{x\,+\,\delta x} - (\rho\, u_x\, \delta y\, \delta z)_x\right]\delta t$$

which, on expansion gives:

$$-\delta y\, \delta z \left[(\rho\, u_x)_x + \frac{\partial}{\partial x}(\rho\, u_x)\,\delta x - (\rho\, u_x)_x\right]\delta t$$

or: $-\delta x \, \delta y \, \delta z \, \dfrac{\partial}{\partial x} (\rho \, u_x) \, \delta t$.

Taking the liquid flow in the y and z directions into account, the net mass inflow into the volume $\delta x \, \delta y \, \delta z$ in a time δt is:

$$-\delta x \, \delta y \, \delta z \left[\frac{\partial}{\partial x} (\rho \, u_x) + \frac{\partial}{\partial y} (\rho \, u_y) + \frac{\partial}{\partial z} (\rho \, u_z) \right] \delta t \ .$$

This increase in mass is also given by:

$$\frac{\partial}{\partial t} (\rho \, \delta x \, \delta y \, \delta z) \, \delta t \ = \ \delta x \, \delta y \, \delta z \, \delta t \, \frac{\partial \rho}{\partial t} \ .$$

Equating the two expressions for the change in mass of the element in a time δt gives:

$$\frac{\partial \rho}{\partial t} + \frac{\partial}{\partial x} (\rho \, u_x) + \frac{\partial}{\partial y} (\rho \, u_y) + \frac{\partial}{\partial z} (\rho \, u_z) = 0 \ . \qquad [5.17]$$

Equation [5.17] is the equation of continuity for a compressible liquid. In vector form it may be written:

$$\frac{\partial \rho}{\partial t} + \nabla \ . \ (\rho \mathbf{u}) = 0. \qquad [5.18]$$

Under conditions of steady flow $\partial \rho / \partial t = 0$ and equation [5.18] becomes:

$$\nabla \ . \ (\rho \mathbf{u}) \ = \ 0. \qquad [5.19]$$

The equation of continuity [5.17] may also be written:

$$\frac{\partial \rho}{\partial t} + \rho \frac{\partial u_x}{\partial x} + \rho \frac{\partial u_y}{\partial y} + \rho \frac{\partial u_z}{\partial z} + u_x \frac{\partial \rho}{\partial x} + u_y \frac{\partial \rho}{\partial y} + u_z \frac{\partial \rho}{\partial z} = 0$$

or: $\dfrac{D\rho}{Dt} + \rho \left[\dfrac{\partial u_x}{\partial x} + \dfrac{\partial u_y}{\partial y} + \dfrac{\partial u_z}{\partial z} \right] = 0. \qquad [5.20]$

In vector form this is:

$$\frac{D\rho}{Dt} + \rho (\nabla \ . \ \mathbf{u}) = 0 \ . \qquad [5.21]$$

If the liquid is incompressible ρ is a constant and the equation of continuity becomes:

$$\nabla \ . \ \mathbf{u} \ = \ \text{div } \mathbf{u} \ = \ 0. \qquad [5.22]$$

Equations [5.16] and [5.18] constitute Euler's equations for the flow of a compressible but inviscid liquid. They are not sufficient to describe the behaviour of an inviscid liquid, but need also a functional relationship between temperature, pressure and density of the liquid, often referred to as its equation of state. A common approximation is to treat the liquid as incompressible, when the equation of state, at constant temperature, becomes $\rho =$ constant. The solution of a simple one-dimensional problem is given in the following example.

Example 5.1

An incompressible inviscid liquid fills a length $2L$ of a horizontal tube of uniform cross-section and is acted on by an attractive force of magnitude μx per unit mass, where x is the distance measured from a fixed point O on the axis of the tube. Determine the pressure p in the liquid at a distance x from O when the nearer free surface is at a distance z from O.

Assume that the tube is sufficiently narrow that gravitational effects can be neglected.

Essentially, the solution of the problem is obtained from the equation of motion, the equation of continuity and the equation of state appropriate to the problem. This is a one-dimensional problem and so the equations are as follows. Equation of motion:

$$\frac{\partial u_x}{\partial t} + u_x \frac{\partial u_x}{\partial x} = -\mu x - \frac{1}{\rho}\frac{\partial p}{\partial x} .$$

Equation of continuity:

$$\frac{\partial u_x}{\partial x} = 0$$

making use of the equation of state:

$$\rho = \text{constant} .$$

Integration of the equation of motion, remembering that $\partial u_x/\partial x = 0$, gives:

$$x \frac{\partial u_x}{\partial t} = -\frac{1}{2}\mu x^2 - \frac{p}{\rho} + \text{Constant} .$$

The pressure in the liquid must equal the atmospheric pressure p_0 when $x = z$ and when $x = z + 2L$. Therefore:

$$z \frac{\partial u_x}{\partial t} = -\frac{1}{2} \mu z^2 - \frac{p_0}{\rho} + C \qquad [5.23]$$

$$(z + 2L) \frac{\partial u_x}{\partial t} = -\frac{1}{2} \mu (z + 2L)^2 - \frac{p_0}{\rho} + C$$

where C is a constant.

Subtraction gives:

$$2L \frac{\partial u_x}{\partial t} = -2\mu L^2 - 2\mu z L$$

or: $\quad \dfrac{\partial u_x}{\partial t} = -\mu(L + z)$.

Now:

$$\frac{\partial u_x}{\partial t} = \frac{\partial^2 z}{\partial t^2} = \frac{\partial^2 (z + L)}{\partial t^2}$$

since L is a constant. Therefore:

$$\frac{\partial^2}{\partial t^2} (z + L) = -\mu(z + L) .$$

This is the equation of simple harmonic motion and the solution is:

$$z + L = A \cos \sqrt{\mu} \, (t + \epsilon)$$

where A and ϵ are constants.

Substituting for $\partial u_x/\partial t$ in equation [5.23] gives:

$$-\mu z (L + z) = -\frac{1}{2} \mu z^2 - \frac{p_0}{\rho} + C$$

from which:

$$C = \frac{p_0}{\rho} - \frac{1}{2} \mu z^2 - \mu z L .$$

Therefore:

$$-x\mu(L + z) = -\frac{1}{2} \mu x^2 - \frac{p}{\rho} + \frac{p_0}{\rho} - \frac{1}{2} \mu z^2 - \mu z L$$

giving:

$$\frac{p - p_0}{\rho} = \mu xL + \mu xz - \frac{1}{2}\mu x^2 - \frac{1}{2}\mu z^2 - \mu zL$$

$$= -\frac{1}{2}\mu(x - z)(x - z - 2L).$$

5.7 Solutions of Euler's equations

Euler's equations of motion are not linear differential equations so that their general solution is not generally straightfoward and the principle of superposition cannot be used to obtain additional solutions. However, first integrals can readily be obtained for a number of situations and some of these will now be examined.

Hydrostatics

The simplest condition is that where the velocity $\mathbf{u}$ is zero everywhere in the liquid. Then the equations of motion become the equations of equilibrium. In vector notation:

$$\mathbf{F} = \frac{1}{\rho}\nabla p \qquad\qquad [5.24]$$

or, in components:

$$X\rho = \frac{\partial p}{\partial x} \qquad\qquad [5.25]$$

with similar equations for the y and z directions.

In the absence of any body forces, equation (5.25) becomes:

$$\frac{\partial p}{\partial x} = 0 \qquad\qquad [5.26]$$

and then p is independent of x. Similar results hold for the y and z directions, showing that p is then constant throughout the liquid.

When gravity is the only body force, and is assumed to act in the negative z direction:

$$X = Y = 0 \; ; Z = -g$$

where g is the magnitude of the acceleration of free fall. Under these conditions:

$$\frac{\partial p}{\partial x} = \frac{\partial p}{\partial y} = 0 \; ; \frac{\partial p}{\partial z} = -\rho g \qquad [5.27]$$

and p is then a function of z only, satisfying the last of equations [5.27]; in equilibrium p is a constant in $x \, y$ planes.

For a liquid of constant density, that is, an incompressible liquid:

$$p = p_0 - \rho g z \qquad [5.28]$$

if the origin of coordinates is located at the surface of the liquid, where the pressure is p_0.

Many instruments for measuring pressures in liquids measure only the increase in pressure over the pressure at the surface. Therefore, p in equation [5.28] is sometimes referred to as the absolute pressure and $p - p_0$ as the gauge pressure.

It is of interest to examine the forces exerted on a solid body that is immersed in a liquid that is at rest. Consider first the pressure on a plane area placed at any angle in a liquid of density ρ. The force on an element of this surface of area δS is $(p_0 + \rho g z) \, \delta S$, where p_0 is the pressure on the liquid surface and z is the vertical distance from the element to the surface; this force is perpendicular to the area δS. It follows that the total force over the whole surface is:

$$\Sigma(p_0 + \rho g z) \, \delta S = p_0 S + \rho g \, \Sigma z \delta S$$

where S is the total surface area and the density is assumed constant. This expression for the total force may be written:

$$p_0 S + \rho g \bar{z} S$$

or: $\quad (p_0 + \rho g \bar{z}) S$

where:

$$\bar{z} = \frac{\Sigma z \delta S}{\Sigma \delta S} .$$

The point in the immersed plane at which this force effectively acts is known as the centre of pressure of the plane. Take Cartesian axes $0x$, $0y$ in the plane of the area and let the centre of pressure have coordinates (ξ, ψ) with respect to these axes. The force on an element of sides δx and δy is $p \, \delta x \, \delta y$ and the moment of this force, about the axes $0x$ and $0y$, respectively, has the values $px \, \delta x \, \delta y$ and $py \, \delta x \, \delta y$. The corresponding moments for the whole area are:

$$\iint px \, \delta x \, \delta y \quad \text{and} \quad \iint py \, \delta x \, \delta y .$$

Since the total force acting on the plane is $\iint p \, \delta x \, \delta y$:

$$\xi \iint p \, \delta x \, \delta y = \iint px \, \delta x \, \delta y$$

and: $\psi \iint p \, \delta x \, \delta y = \iint py \, \delta x \, \delta y.$

If the plane area makes an angle α with the horizontal, and $0y$ lies along the line of intersection of the free liquid surface and the plane of the area:

$$z = x \sin \alpha$$

where z is the vertical distance to the liquid surface of an element in the plane with coordinate x. Then, using the gauge pressure $\rho g x \sin \alpha$ for p:

$$\xi = \frac{\iint x^2 \, dx dy}{\iint x \, dx dy} \; ; \; \psi = \frac{\iint xy \, dx dy}{\iint x \, dx dy} . \tag{5.29}$$

This discussion is readily extended to the case of a curved surface placed in the liquid. Consider a curved surface S that has a projection S' on any vertical plane and a projection S'' on the free surface of the liquid. Since the liquid in the cylinder with S and S' as ends is in equilibrium with the pressure on S and S' and on the surface generated by the lines which project S into S', it follows that the horizontal component of the force on S, perpendicular to S', is equal to the horizontal force on S'. This argument also holds for corresponding elements δS and $\delta S'$ and, therefore, the distribution of pressure in the given direction is the same on S and S'. Therefore, the lines of action must coincide, so that the horizontal component of the force on S acts along a line through the centre of pressure of S'.

To find the force in vertical direction, consider the equilibrium of the liquid contained between S and S''. There is no vertical force on the vertical walls of this volume. Further, S'' is in the free liquid surface so that, using gauge pressures, there is no force on S''. Therefore, the vertical force on S is equal and opposite to the gravitational force acting on the liquid in the cylinder and it acts through the centre of mass of this liquid. This force is known as the buoyancy force or upthrust. The result is known as the principle of Archimedes: the upthrust on a body immersed in a liquid is equal and opposite to the weight of liquid displaced and acts through the centre of mass of the displaced liquid.

The above principle must also apply when a body is only partially immersed in a liquid, including the case when the body is floating. Then in equilibrium, the floating body must satisfy the following conditions.

1. The weight of the body must equal the weight of liquid displaced.
2. The upthrust or buoyant force acts through the centroid of the displaced liquid (known as the centre of buoyancy).
3. The centroid of the body and the centre of buoyancy should be in the same vertical line.

An application of the principle of Archimedes to a problem in flotation will now be considered.

Example 5.2

Determine the limiting ratio of thickness to radius so that a hollow shell, made of material of density σ may float in a liquid of density ρ.

Let the external radius of the shell be a and the internal radius be b. The shell will float if, when just totally submerged in the liquid, the upthrust or buoyancy force is equal to, or greater than, the weight of the shell. The upthrust in this condition is $4/3(\pi a^3 \rho g)$ while the weight of the shell is $4/3(\pi(a^3 - b^3)\sigma g)$, where g is the acceleration of free fall. For flotation then:

$$\frac{4}{3}\pi a^3 \rho g \geqslant \frac{4}{3}\pi(a^3 - b^3)\sigma g$$

or: $\quad a^3 \geqslant (a^3 - b^3)\sigma/\rho$

or: $\quad \dfrac{b}{a} \geqslant \left(1 - \dfrac{\rho}{\sigma}\right)^{\frac{1}{3}}.$

The thickness of the shell is $a - b$ so that the limiting ratio of thickness to radius for flotation is:

$$\frac{a - b}{a} = 1 - \frac{b}{a} = 1 - \left(1 - \frac{\rho}{\sigma}\right)^{\frac{1}{3}}.$$

Steady flow

After equilibrium, the next simplest condition is that of steady flow, that is, flow in which the pattern of streamlines does not vary with time. First a general equation for steady flow will be derived and then the consequences of placing restrictions on the behaviour of the liquid particles will be examined.

1. *The Bernoulli equation*

The equation of motion for an inviscid liquid is equation [5.16] of section 5.5. When the motion is steady the liquid velocity at any point does not vary with time, $\partial \mathbf{u}/\partial t$ is equal to zero, and the equation of motion becomes:

$$\mathbf{F} - \frac{1}{\rho}\nabla p = (\mathbf{u} . \nabla)\mathbf{u} . \qquad [5.30]$$

Assume that the body force $\mathbf{F}$ is derived from a single-valued potential function. The work done by a liquid particle in a conservative field in moving from a standard position (usually infinity) to the point (x, y, z) is then a function of x, y and z only, say, $-\Omega$ per unit mass. Then $\mathbf{F}$ may be written:

$$\mathbf{F} = -\nabla\Omega .$$

In addition, assume that the pressure p is functionally related to the density ρ, i.e. at constant temperature the equation of state is:

$$p = f(\rho).$$

Define a quantity P by:

$$P = \int \frac{dp}{\rho}.$$

Then:

$$\frac{\partial P}{\partial x} = \frac{\partial P}{\partial p}\frac{\partial p}{\partial x} = \frac{1}{\rho}\frac{\partial p}{\partial x}$$

with similar equations for the y and z directions, so that:

$$\frac{1}{\rho}\nabla p = \nabla P.$$

When the results of these two assumptions are substituted in equation [5.30] the latter becomes:

$$-\nabla\Omega - \nabla P = (\mathbf{u}.\nabla)\mathbf{u}. \qquad [5.31]$$

The component of $(\mathbf{u}.\nabla)\mathbf{u}$ in the x direction may be written:

$$\left[(\mathbf{u}.\nabla)\mathbf{u}\right]_x = u_x\frac{\partial u_x}{\partial x} + u_y\frac{\partial u_x}{\partial y} + u_z\frac{\partial u_x}{\partial z}$$

which may be further expressed as:

$$u_x\frac{\partial u_x}{\partial x} + u_y\frac{\partial u_y}{\partial x} + u_z\frac{\partial u_z}{\partial x} + u_y\left(\frac{\partial u_x}{\partial y} - \frac{\partial u_y}{\partial x}\right) +$$

$$+ u_z\left(\frac{\partial u_x}{\partial z} - \frac{\partial u_z}{\partial x}\right). \qquad [5.32]$$

Now, define a vector ω by the equation:

$$\omega = \left(\frac{\partial u_z}{\partial y} - \frac{\partial u_y}{\partial z}\right)\mathbf{i} + \left(\frac{\partial u_x}{\partial z} - \frac{\partial u_z}{\partial x}\right)\mathbf{j} + \left(\frac{\partial u_y}{\partial x} - \frac{\partial u_x}{\partial y}\right)\mathbf{k}$$

$$= \text{curl } \mathbf{u}. \qquad [5.33]$$

ω is known as the vorticity vector of the liquid and vortex lines are defined as lines such that the tangent at any point gives the direction of ω.

A liquid particle in a flowing liquid may move with a velocity of translation as a whole, it may rotate and it may deform. At any instant the liquid particle may be treated as a rigid body. Then, the curl of the velocity of the liquid at the point where the particle is situated is equal to twice the angular velocity of the particle about an axis passing through it (see exercise 2).

Therefore, the vorticity vector at any point in a liquid is equal to twice the angular velocity of the liquid at that point, and the direction of a vortex line is everywhere the instantaneous axis of rotation of a liquid particle. The vorticity is solenoidal (div $\omega = 0$) so that a vortex line cannot begin and end in the liquid but must either form a closed curve or begin and end on the liquid surface. From equation [5.33] it follows that the differential equations of a vortex line are:

$$\frac{dx}{\dfrac{\partial u_z}{\partial y} - \dfrac{\partial u_y}{\partial z}} = \frac{dy}{\dfrac{\partial u_x}{\partial z} - \dfrac{\partial u_z}{\partial x}} = \frac{dz}{\dfrac{\partial u_y}{\partial x} - \dfrac{\partial u_x}{\partial y}}.$$

Using the equation [5.33], equation [5.32] may be written:

$$\left[(\mathbf{u} . \nabla)\mathbf{u} \right]_x = \frac{\partial}{\partial x}\left(\frac{1}{2}u_x{}^2 + \frac{1}{2}u_y{}^2 + \frac{1}{2}u_z{}^2 \right)$$

$$+ \omega_y u_z - \omega_z u_y$$

$$= \left[\nabla\left(\frac{1}{2}\mathbf{u}^2 \right) + \omega \times \mathbf{u} \right]_x . \qquad [5.34]$$

Substituting this result in equation [5.31] gives:

$$\nabla\left(\frac{1}{2}\mathbf{u}^2 \right) + \omega \times \mathbf{u} = -\nabla\Omega - \nabla P$$

or: $\quad \nabla\left[\frac{1}{2}\mathbf{u}^2 + \Omega + \int \frac{dp}{\rho} \right] = -\omega \times \mathbf{u} . \qquad [5.35]$

Equation [5.35] is the general equation of motion for the

steady flow of an inviscid liquid and is known as the Bernoulli equation. The effect on this equation of placing restrictions on the steady flow will now be examined.

2. *Steady irrotational flow*

If ω = curl **u** is equal to zero, the motion of the liquid is said to be irrotational. This means that a liquid particle does not rotate about an axis passing through it, i.e. it has no angular velocity; it does not mean that the liquid may not circulate around closed paths. Irrotational motion requires the liquid particles to slip past each other without setting up rotations, and this is possible only if there are no frictional (viscous) forces between the particles.

When the motion of the liquid is steady, equation [5.35] applies generally, provided that ρ is a function of pressure only and the body force is derived from a single-valued potential function. If, in addition, ω is zero, the Bernoulli equation becomes:

$$\nabla \left[\frac{1}{2} \mathbf{u}^2 + \Omega + \int \frac{\mathrm{d}p}{\rho} \right] = 0$$

or:

$$\frac{1}{2} \mathbf{u}^2 + \Omega + \int \frac{\mathrm{d}p}{\rho} = \text{Constant}. \qquad [5.36]$$

The constant in equation [5.36] has the same value at all points in the liquid at all times and is determined by the boundary conditions.

In equation [5.36], $\frac{1}{2}\mathbf{u}^2$ is the kinetic energy of unit mass of liquid while Ω is the potential energy of unit mass of liquid. The term $\int \mathrm{d}p/\rho$ may be termed pressure energy, and arises because any liquid particle may do work on its surroundings. Under steady irrotational flow conditions the sum of the three energies has the same constant value at all points in this liquid. Equation [5.36] is equivalent to the theorem of the conservation of energy in mechanics (see *Classical Mechanics* by B.P. Cowan in this series).

If the liquid density is constant, that is, for steady, irrotational, incompressible flow, equation [5.36] becomes:

$$\frac{1}{2}\mathbf{u}^2 + \Omega + \frac{p}{\rho} = \text{Constant} \, . \qquad\qquad [5.37]$$

3. *Steady rotational flow*

For steady rotational motion of an inviscid liquid equation [5.35] holds; ω is not equal to zero and each liquid particle rotates about an axis passing through that region of the liquid. However, useful results can be obtained when curl $\mathbf{u} \times \mathbf{u}$ is equal to zero. One way of satisfying this condition is to make the path of integration that is followed in the liquid coincide with a streamline. Curl $\mathbf{u} \times \mathbf{u}$ is perpendicular to $\mathbf{u}$ and, therefore, does not contribute to the integration. Then, if ds is the element of distance along a streamline:

$$\frac{\partial}{\partial s}\left[\frac{1}{2}\mathbf{u}^2 + \Omega + \int \frac{\mathrm{d}p}{\rho}\right] = 0$$

or:

$$\frac{1}{2}\mathbf{u}^2 + \Omega + \int \frac{\mathrm{d}p}{\rho} = \text{Constant.} \qquad\qquad [5.38]$$

The similarity between equations [5.36] and [5.38] is obvious, but the constant in equation [5.38] takes a different value for different streamlines. In this situation energy conservation only holds along streamlines.

If there are no external forces acting on the liquid and the liquid density is constant, equation [5.38] becomes:

$$\frac{p}{\rho} + \frac{1}{2}\mathbf{u}^2 = \text{Constant}$$

or:

$$p = p_0 - \frac{1}{2}\mathbf{u}^2 \qquad\qquad [5.39]$$

where p_0 is the pressure in the liquid at rest.

5.8 Applications of the Bernoulli equation

The Venturi meter

The Venturi meter is a device for measuring the rate of flow of a liquid. It consists of an open-ended tube, flared at both ends and shown schematically in Fig. 5.3(a). A determination of the liquid velocity can be made from the pressure difference between the centre and ends of the device. In practice the constriction is shaped as in Fig. 5.3(b). This shape reduces the pressure loss in the meter so that, after passing through the constriction, the liquid regains its original velocity. Variants of this device are the flow nozzle and the sharp-edged orifice.

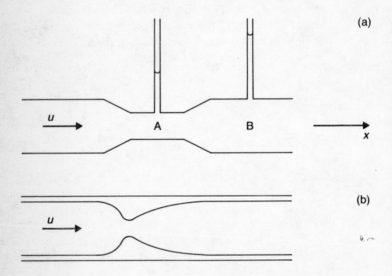

Fig. 5.3

Assume that the liquid is incompressible and that the effects of body forces may be neglected. Then, if the flow is steady and irrotational, the Bernoulli equation in the form of equation [5.37] gives:

$$p + \frac{1}{2}\rho u^2 = \text{Constant}$$

so that, if A denotes a plane in the centre of the constriction and B a plane where the liquid has regained its original velocity:

$$p_A + \frac{1}{2} \rho u_A{}^2 = p_B + \frac{1}{2} \rho u_B{}^2.$$

Now, if α is the area of cross-section of the tube, continuity demands that:

$$\rho_A u_A \alpha_A = \rho_B u_B \alpha_B$$

or, since ρ is a constant:

$$\frac{u_A}{u_B} = \frac{\alpha_B}{\alpha_A}.$$

Therefore:

$$p_A - p_B = \frac{1}{2} \rho \left(u_B{}^2 - u_A{}^2\right) = \frac{1}{2} \rho u_B{}^2 \left(1 - \left(\frac{u_A}{u_B}\right)^2\right)$$

$$= \frac{1}{2} \rho u_B{}^2 \left(1 - \left(\frac{\alpha_B}{\alpha_A}\right)^2\right)$$

so that:

$$u_B = \left[\frac{2(p_A - p_B)}{\rho(1 - (\alpha_B/\alpha_A)^2)}\right]^{\frac{1}{2}}. \tag{5.40}$$

The Pitot tube

Another instrument for determining liquid velocity is the Pitot tube. This consists of a tube with an opening facing the liquid, and connected to a manometer, as shown schematically in Fig. 5.4(a). The point S is a stagnation point in the liquid where the velocity is zero. Assume again that the liquid is incompressible, that the flow is steady and irrotational and that the effects of body forces can be neglected. Then, as for the Venturi meter, equation [5.37] gives:

$$p + \frac{1}{2} \rho u^2 = \text{Constant}$$

throughout the liquid. If p_∞ is the pressure a long way from the tube, where the liquid speed (in the x direction) is u_0:

$$p + \frac{1}{2} \rho u^2 = p_\infty + \frac{1}{2} \rho u_0{}^2 = p_0 \tag{5.41}$$

where p_0 is the pressure at the stagnation point S where the liquid is brought to rest. p_0 is measured by a manometer which, therefore, gives a measure of $p + \frac{1}{2}\rho u^2$ just outside the tube. To find p a static tube is used to measure the pressure in a region where the liquid flow is practically undisturbed (Fig. 5.4(b)). In practice the Pitot and static tubes are combined (Fig. 5.4(c)), and a differential manometer gives the value of $p_0 - p$ which is equal to $\frac{1}{2}\rho u^2$.

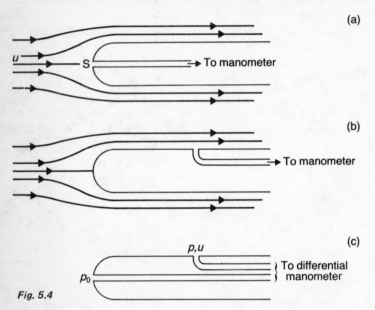

Fig. 5.4

5.9 Irrotational flow

The condition of irrotational flow is very important and needs further consideration. First, the equation for general irrotational flow will be derived and then the simplification introduced by treating the liquid as incompressible will be considered.

General irrotational flow

Making use of equation [5.34], the general equation of motion of a liquid particle (equation [5.16]) may be written in the form:

$$-\nabla\Omega - \frac{1}{\rho}\nabla p = \frac{D\mathbf{u}}{Dt} = \frac{\partial \mathbf{u}}{\partial t} + \frac{1}{2}\nabla \mathbf{u}^2 + (\nabla \mathbf{X} \mathbf{u}) \mathbf{X} \mathbf{u}\ [5.42]$$

provided that ρ is a function of the pressure only and the body force is derived from a single-valued potential function as described in section 5.7 under steady flow. The general condition for irrotational motion is that $\omega = \mathrm{curl}\ \mathbf{u} = 0$. Since curl $\mathbf{u} = 0$ if $\mathbf{u} = -\nabla\phi$, where ϕ is a scalar function, it follows that, when the flow is irrotational the vector $\mathbf{u}$ can be represented by the (negative) gradient of a scalar function ϕ, known as the velocity potential. Then, if $\mathbf{u} = -\nabla\phi$:

$$\frac{\partial \mathbf{u}}{\partial t} = -\nabla \frac{\partial \phi}{\partial t}.$$

Substitution of these two expressions in equation [5.42], together with the condition for irrotational flow, gives:

$$-\nabla\Omega - \frac{1}{\rho}\nabla p = -\nabla \frac{\partial \phi}{\partial t} + \frac{1}{2}\nabla \mathbf{u}^2$$

or: $$\nabla \left[-\frac{\partial \phi}{\partial t} + \frac{1}{2}\mathbf{u}^2 + \Omega \right] + \frac{1}{\rho}\nabla p = 0$$

or: $$\nabla \left[-\frac{\partial \phi}{\partial t} + \frac{1}{2}\mathbf{u}^2 + \Omega + P \right] = 0.$$ [5.43]

Integrating gives:

$$\frac{dp}{\rho} + \Omega + \frac{1}{2}\mathbf{u}^2 - \frac{\partial \phi}{\partial t} = \psi(t)$$ [5.44]

where $\psi(t)$ is an arbitrary function of time only, but has the same value in all regions of the liquid where the motion is irrotational. The value of $\psi(t)$ is determined by the boundary conditions and these may change with time.

Irrotational flow of an incompressible liquid

Under conditions of irrotational flow the liquid velocity $\mathbf{u}$ may be written in the form:

$$\mathbf{u} = -\nabla\phi$$

where ϕ is the velocity potential. If the liquid is incompressible, and is neither created nor destroyed in the region under consideration, the equation of continuity is:

$$\nabla \cdot \mathbf{u} = 0 .$$

Combining these two equations gives:

$$\nabla \cdot \mathbf{u} = -\nabla \cdot \nabla \phi = -\nabla^2 \phi = 0$$

or: $\quad \nabla^2 \phi = 0$ \hfill [5.45]

as the condition for the irrotational flow of an incompressible liquid. Equation [5.45] is the Laplace equation, which has applications in many branches of physics, notably in the determination of the electric fields due to static electric charges (see, for example, *Electricity and Magnetism* by E.R. Dobbs, in this series).

Using equation [5.45] the velocity field for the irrotational flow of an incompressible liquid can be determined without using the Euler equations, though these are needed to determine the pressure distribution.

Since irrotational flow is a characteristic of ideal liquids rather than of real (viscous) liquids, the solutions obtained for equation [5.45] are often not realised in practice, particularly in situations where the liquid is flowing across solid surfaces. However, there are situations where the solutions of the Laplace equation should be good approximations to what occurs in practice. Examples are the behaviour of water waves and the flow of a river on the up-stream side of a dam.

An important property of the Laplace equation, which is proved in books on vector analysis, is the uniqueness theorem which states that, if ϕ is known at each point on the boundary of a given region, and the Laplace equation is satisfied at each point within that region, there is only one function ϕ that satisfies the given conditions.

Example 5.3

As an example of one approach to the use of the Laplace equation in studying irrotational flow problems, consider the flow of an ideal, incompressible liquid past a fixed sphere.

Let the sphere, of radius R, be at rest at the origin of coordinates and let the liquid flow past in the negative z direction. At any point far from the sphere let the magnitude of the liquid velocity be u_0. The equation that must be satisfied by the velocity potential at all points where the motion is irrotational is:

$$\frac{\partial^2 \phi}{\partial x^2} + \frac{\partial^2 \phi}{\partial y^2} + \frac{\partial^2 \phi}{\partial z^2} = 0 .$$

In the absence of the sphere the flow is everywhere uniform with a velocity in the negative z direction of magnitude u_0. Inspection shows that this is represented by a velocity potential ϕ_1, where:

$$\phi_1 = u_0 z = u_0 r \cos \theta \qquad [5.46]$$

and r and θ are the polar coordinates relative to the z axis, i.e.:

$$u_z = -\partial \phi_1 / \partial z = -u_0 .$$

ϕ_1 corresponds to a uniform liquid flow parallel to the z axis and must represent the flow at large distances from the sphere when the sphere is present. To ϕ_1 must be added a potential ϕ_2 representing the disturbance introduced by the sphere. This disturbance must be symmetrical about the z axis and must vanish when r is very large. The most general form of function satisfying the Laplace equation and having the required symmetry properties is an axial harmonic so that ϕ_2 can be written as:

$$\phi_2 = \frac{A}{r} + \frac{B \cos \theta}{r^2} + \frac{C(3 \cos^2 \theta - 1)}{r^3} + \dots \qquad [5.47]$$

where A, B, C, are constants. The total velocity potential ϕ is then given by:

$$\phi = \phi_1 + \phi_2 .$$

At the surface of the sphere $r = R$ and the component of velocity normal to the surface of the solid sphere must be zero, so that $\partial \phi / \partial r$ must equal zero.

Therefore:

$$0 = \left(\frac{\partial \phi_1}{\partial r}\right)_{\substack{r = R \\ \theta = \text{constant}}} + \left.\frac{\partial \phi_2}{\partial r}\right|_{\substack{r = R \\ \theta = \text{constant}}}$$

$$= u_0 \cos \theta - \frac{A}{R^2} - \frac{2B \cos \theta}{R^3} - \frac{3C(3\cos^2 \theta - 1)}{R^4} + \dots$$

$$[5.48]$$

Equation [5.48] can be satisfied by putting:

$$B = \frac{1}{2} u_0 R^3 ; \quad A = C = \dots = 0 .$$

Therefore, the complete solution, giving the velocity potential for the flow of an incompressible, inviscid liquid past a fixed sphere under irrotational conditions is:

$$\phi = u_0 r \cos \theta + \frac{u_0 R^3 \cos \theta}{2r^2} . \qquad [5.49]$$

To change the problem to that of a sphere moving with a velocity u_0 through a liquid at rest, it is necessary to change to a coordinate system that is fixed relative to the liquid. This can be achieved by applying a velocity u_0 to the liquid and sphere, and is represented by adding a term $-\phi_1$ to ϕ. The velocity potential associated with the motion of a sphere of radius R, moving in the positive z direction with a speed u_0 through a stationary, inviscid, incompressible liquid is, therefore:

$$\phi' = \frac{u_0 R^3 \cos \theta}{2r^2} . \qquad [5.50]$$

Equation [5.50] has the same form as the electric potential around a small electric dipole and, therefore, the velocity field associated with the liquid flow around the sphere has the same form as the electric field around the dipole. The velocity is conveniently expressed in terms of the radial and transverse components u_r and u_θ, respectively. Since:

$$\mathbf{u} = -\nabla \phi'$$

$$u_r = -\frac{\partial \phi'}{\partial r} = \frac{u_0 R^3 \cos \theta}{r^3}$$

and: $u_\theta = -\dfrac{1}{r}\dfrac{\partial \phi'}{\partial \theta} = \dfrac{u_0 R^3 \sin \theta}{2r^3}$.

When:

$\theta = 0$ and $r = R$

$u_r = u_0$ and $u_\theta = 0$

when:

$\theta = \pi/2$ and $r = R$

$u_r = 0$ and $u_\theta = u_0/2$.

5.10 The stream function

The irrotational motion of an incompressible, inviscid liquid satisfies the Laplace equation. A powerful method exists for the solution of this equation in situations where the flow is two-dimensional, that is, where the Laplace equation can be written in the form:

$$\frac{\partial^2 \phi}{\partial x^2} + \frac{\partial^2 \phi}{\partial y^2} = 0 \,. \qquad [5.51]$$

Essentially, the method is based on a comparison of equation [5.51] with the one-dimensional wave equation, for which solutions are known, by putting the wave velocity to unity and replacing time by a spatial coordinate.

Put:

$$n = x + iy \,.$$

Then any function of n, w say, may be written:

$$w = f(n) = f(x + iy) = \phi(x, y) + i\psi(x, y) \qquad [5.52]$$

where ϕ and ψ are real functions. The reason for choosing ϕ will shortly become apparent.

Partial differentiation of equation [5.52] gives:

$$\frac{\partial w}{\partial x} = f'(x + iy) \,; \quad \frac{\partial^2 w}{\partial x^2} = f''(x + iy)$$

$$\frac{\partial w}{\partial y} = if'(x + iy) \; ; \; \frac{\partial^2 w}{\partial y^2} = -f''(x + iy).$$

Therefore:

$$\frac{\partial^2 w}{\partial x^2} + \frac{\partial^2 w}{\partial y^2} = 0$$

so that w satisfies the two-dimensional Laplace equation. Also:

$$\frac{\partial w}{\partial y} = if'(n) = i\frac{\partial w}{\partial x}.$$

It follows, then, from equation [5.52] that:

$$\frac{\partial w}{\partial y} = \frac{\partial \phi}{\partial y} + i\frac{\partial \psi}{\partial y} = i\left(\frac{\partial \phi}{\partial x} + i\frac{\partial \psi}{\partial x}\right).$$

Equating real and imaginary parts gives:

$$\frac{\partial \phi}{\partial y} = -\frac{\partial \psi}{\partial x} \text{ and } \frac{\partial \psi}{\partial y} = \frac{\partial \phi}{\partial x} \; .$$

These are the Cauchy–Riemann relations. If, at any point in the liquid, y is taken along a contour of constant ϕ then $\partial \psi / \partial x$ is zero, showing that in the x direction at that point ψ is a constant. This argument can be extended to all points on a curve with $\phi =$ constant. Therefore, each value of the constant in the equation $\phi(x, y) =$ constant, represents a member of a family of curves that cut orthogonally each member of the family given by $\psi(x, y)$ = constant.

It is usual to regard ϕ as the potential function so that $\psi =$ constant then represents the lines of flow, that is, the streamlines, and ψ is known as the stream function. Along a streamline $\psi =$ constant so that $\mathrm{d}\psi$ is zero. Now, since $\psi = \psi(x, y)$:

$$\mathrm{d}\psi = \left(\frac{\partial \psi}{\partial x}\right)_y \mathrm{d}x + \left(\frac{\partial \psi}{\partial y}\right)_x \mathrm{d}y \; .$$

Therefore, along a streamline:

$$\frac{\partial y}{\partial x} = -\frac{(\partial \psi / \partial x)_y}{(\partial \psi / \partial y)_x} \; . \tag{5.53}$$

The solution of equation [5.53] gives the streamlines of flow. The flow velocity **u** is given by:

$$\mathbf{u} = -\left(\frac{\partial \phi}{\partial x}\right)_y \mathbf{i} - \left(\frac{\partial \phi}{\partial y}\right)_x \mathbf{j}$$

and has a magnitude equal to:

$$\mathbf{u} = \sqrt{\left(\frac{\partial \phi}{\partial x}\right)_y^2 + \left(\frac{\partial \phi}{\partial y}\right)_x^2}.$$

Example 5.4

Any function of the form $x + iy$ gives a possible case of irrotational motion of an incompressible, inviscid liquid. For example, take:

$$\phi + i\psi = \frac{1}{2}a(x + iy)^2$$

where a is a constant. Then:

$$\phi + i\psi = \frac{1}{2}a(x^2 + 2ixy - y^2) = \frac{1}{2}a(x^2 - y^2) + iaxy.$$

Therefore, the stream function is given by $\psi = axy$, so that the streamlines are the family of rectangular hyperbolae $xy = $ constant. This stream function represents the two-dimensional flow of a liquid against a plate.

5.11 Circulation and vorticity

Construct an arbitrary closed contour C entirely within a moving inviscid liquid. The circulation Γ of the liquid is defined by:

$$\Gamma = \oint_C \mathbf{u} \cdot \mathbf{ds} \qquad [5.54]$$

where, conventionally, the contour is traced in an anticlockwise direction. Here **u** is the liquid velocity at any point and d**s** is the element of the path of the contour at the same point. If S is a surface in the liquid, bounded by C, application of the theorem of Stokes gives:

$$\Gamma = \int_S \text{curl } \mathbf{u} \cdot \mathbf{dS} \qquad [5.55]$$

where $\mathbf{dS}$ is a directed element of area, its sense being related to the direction of integration around C by the corkscrew rule.

When the liquid flow is irrotational, curl $\mathbf{u}$ is everywhere zero so that Γ is zero: the circulation vanishes over any closed path within which the liquid motion is everywhere irrotational. On the other hand, when the liquid flow is rotational, curl $\mathbf{u}$ equals ω the vorticity vector, so that:

$$\Gamma = \int_S \omega \cdot \mathbf{dS} . \qquad [5.56]$$

An important property of the circulation is contained in the result known as Kelvin's circulation theorem. This states that, when the forces acting on an inviscid liquid are conservative and derived from a single-valued potential function, and the liquid density is a function of pressure only, the time rate of change of the circulation around any closed curve moving with the liquid is zero. Here, moving with the liquid means that the contour must always be drawn through the same liquid particles.

A proof of Kelvin's theorem is as follows. Under the conditions specified, the equation of motion of an inviscid liquid is obtained by combining equations [5.16] and $\mathbf{F} = -\nabla \Omega$ to give:

$$\frac{D\mathbf{u}}{Dt} = -\nabla \Omega - \frac{1}{\rho} \nabla p \qquad [5.57]$$

where Ω is the potential from which the body force per unit mass is derived. The rate of change of the circulation is:

$$\frac{D}{Dt} \oint_C \mathbf{u} \cdot \mathbf{ds}$$

which is:

$$\oint_C \frac{D\mathbf{u}}{Dt} \cdot \mathbf{ds} + \oint_C \mathbf{u} \cdot \frac{D\mathbf{ds}}{Dt} .$$

Substituting for $\mathbf{Du}/\mathbf{D}t$ from equation [5.57] gives:

$$\oint_C \left(-\nabla\Omega - \frac{1}{\rho}\nabla p \right) . \, \mathbf{ds} + \oint_C \mathbf{u} . \frac{\partial \mathbf{u}}{\partial \mathbf{s}} \, \mathbf{ds}$$

which equals:

$$\oint_C \left(-\frac{\partial\Omega}{\partial s} - \frac{1}{\rho}\frac{\partial p}{\partial s} \right) \mathbf{ds} + \oint_C \frac{\partial}{\partial s}\left(\frac{1}{2}\mathbf{u}^2 \right) \mathbf{ds}$$

or: $$\left[-\Omega - \int\frac{\partial p}{\rho} + \frac{1}{2}\mathbf{u}^2 \right]_A^A$$

where the limits simply indicate a closed path of integration. All the terms within the square brackets are single-valued so that the value of the bracket is zero and Kelvin's theorem follows. Since D/Dt has been used it is implied that the behaviour of liquid particles is being followed.

The theorem has some interesting consequences, but it must be remembered that it holds strictly only for inviscid liquids. It follows from the theorem that if a liquid is initially stationary the circulation is zero for any closed contour, and must remain so in any subsequent motion.

In any given motion a liquid can be divided into regions where curl $\mathbf{u}$ is zero and others where curl $\mathbf{u}$ is not zero. During the subsequent motion of the liquid, those particles that are initially in regions with curl $\mathbf{u}$ equal to zero will only move into other irrotational regions; there is no exchange of liquid between irrotational and rotational regions of motion.

When the liquid motion is rotational it is associated with vortex lines which cannot end in the liquid. The strength of the vortex is measured by the vorticity vector $\omega = $ curl $\mathbf{u}$. For rotational motion, equation [5.55] may be written:

$$\Gamma = \int \omega_n \, dS$$

where ω_n is the component of ω normal to the elementary area $\mathbf{dS}$. From Kelvin's theorem, therefore, the flux of the vorticity vector through the surface S remains constant throughout the flow, provided that the contour is always associated with the same liquid particles.

The concept of the vortex line can be usefully extended to that of the vortex tube as follows. Take an element of surface dS within a region of liquid undergoing rotational motion and construct the vortex line passing through each point on the boundary. These lines form the surface of a vortex tube. From Kelvin's theorem:

$$\int_S \omega \cdot dS = \oint_C u \cdot ds$$

has a constant value for any cross-section of a vortex tube.

It is possible for the circulation to be non-zero even when the liquid motion is everywhere irrotational (see example 5.5 below). An example is when an infinite, solid, circular cylinder passes through the contour used to determine the circulation. Therefore, to decide whether a liquid flow is rotational or irrotational, the circulation must be determined with a microscopic circuit, i.e. it is necessary to examine the behaviour of individual liquid particles.

Example 5.5

The circulation of an incompressible, inviscid liquid undergoing two-dimensional irrotational flow may be examined through a suitable stream function.

Take the function:

$$\phi + i\psi = iA \ln(r\, e^{i\theta})$$

where A is a constant, r is the distance from the origin and θ is the angle measured from some reference direction. Then:

$$\phi + i\psi = -A\theta + iA \ln r$$

which gives:

$$\phi = -A\theta$$

and: $\psi = A \ln r$.

Note that ψ is not defined when $r = 0$ and ϕ is many-valued.

Streamlines are then lines satisfying $\psi = $ constant, i.e. they are concentric circles about the origin. The speed of the liquid along a streamline is given by $-\partial\phi/\partial s$, where s is measured along a streamline. Now $ds = r d\theta$ so that the speed is:

$$-\frac{1}{r}\frac{\partial\phi}{\partial\theta} = A/r.$$

Therefore, the circulation is $2\pi A$, which is independent of r. Now when r tends to zero the speed tends to infinity. Therefore, in the limit, there must be at the origin a rotating liquid element, so that the centre of the region of circulation lies outside the irrotational region. This central region is the vortex and, using equation [5.56], its vorticity vector has the magnitude $2\pi A/\pi r_0^2$, where r_0 is the radius of the vortex element.

Therefore, when an ideal, incompressible liquid that contains regions of irrotational motion also has a circulation, the irrotational region is such that a closed contour around which there is a finite circulation cannot be shrunk to a point without going out of the irrotational region at the vortex.

5.12 The Navier–Stokes equation

Equation [5.16] is not adequate to describe the motion of a viscous liquid since, in addition to the hydrostatic pressure, there are forces acting on an element of liquid arising from the viscous properties of the liquid. The necessary modification to equation [5.16] will now be considered for incompressible, viscous liquids.

Consider the element of liquid shown in Fig. 5.2 and suppose that, at a time t, the components of the body force per unit mass are X, Y, Z in the Ox, Oy, Oz directions, respectively, while the stress components are $\sigma_x, \sigma_y, \sigma_z, \tau_{yz}, \tau_{zx}, \tau_{xy}$, using the notation of section 2.3. The component in the direction Ox of the total force acting on the element is:

$$\left[\frac{\partial\sigma_x}{\partial x} + \frac{\partial\tau_{yx}}{\partial y} + \frac{\partial\tau_{zx}}{\partial z} + \rho X\right]\delta x\,\delta y\,\delta z$$

where ρ is the density of the liquid. Equating this to the product of the mass of the element and the component of the convective acceleration in the x direction gives, in the limit:

$$\rho \frac{Du_x}{Dt} = \frac{\partial \sigma_x}{\partial x} + \frac{\partial \tau_{yx}}{\partial y} + \frac{\partial \tau_{zx}}{\partial z} + \rho X .$$

Similarly:

$$\rho \frac{Du_y}{Dt} = \frac{\partial \tau_{xy}}{\partial x} + \frac{\partial \sigma_y}{\partial y} + \frac{\partial \tau_{zy}}{\partial z} + \rho Y \qquad [5.58]$$

and: $\quad \rho \dfrac{Du_z}{Dt} = \dfrac{\partial \tau_{xz}}{\partial x} + \dfrac{\partial \tau_{yz}}{\partial y} + \dfrac{\partial \sigma_z}{\partial z} + \rho Z .$

Now substitute for the stress components from the equations of motion of an incompressible viscous liquid (equations [4.9]). These give, for the x direction:

$$\rho \frac{Du_x}{Dt} = \frac{\partial}{\partial x} (2\eta \dot{e}_x - p) + \eta \frac{\partial}{\partial y} \left(\frac{\partial u_x}{\partial y} + \frac{\partial u_y}{\partial x} \right)$$

$$+ \eta \frac{\partial}{\partial z} \left(\frac{\partial u_x}{\partial z} + \frac{\partial u_z}{\partial x} \right) + \rho X \qquad [5.59]$$

where the symbols have the meanings of section 4.4. Now,

$$\frac{\partial \dot{e}_x}{\partial x} = \frac{\partial^2 u_x}{\partial x^2}$$

so that, expanding equation [5.59] gives:

$$\rho \frac{Du_x}{Dt} = \rho X - \frac{\partial p}{\partial x} + \eta \left(\frac{\partial^2 u_x}{\partial x^2} + \frac{\partial^2 u_x}{\partial y^2} + \frac{\partial^2 u_x}{\partial z^2} \right)$$

$$+ \eta \left(\frac{\partial^2 u_x}{\partial x^2} + \frac{\partial^2 u_y}{\partial y \partial x} + \frac{\partial^2 u_z}{\partial z \partial x} \right)$$

$$= \rho X - \frac{\partial p}{\partial x} + \eta \left(\frac{\partial^2 u_x}{\partial x^2} + \frac{\partial^2 u_x}{\partial y^2} + \frac{\partial^2 u_x}{\partial z^2} \right)$$

$$+ \eta \frac{\partial}{\partial x} \left(\frac{\partial u_x}{\partial x} + \frac{\partial u_y}{\partial y} + \frac{\partial u_z}{\partial z} \right) . \qquad [5.60]$$

Since the liquid is incompressible:

$$\left(\frac{\partial u_x}{\partial x} + \frac{\partial u_y}{\partial y} + \frac{\partial u_z}{\partial z} \right) = \nabla . \mathbf{u} = 0 .$$

Also:

$$\frac{\partial^2 u_x}{\partial x^2} + \frac{\partial^2 u_x}{\partial y^2} + \frac{\partial^2 u_x}{\partial z^2}$$

is $\nabla^2 u_x$. Therefore, equation [5.60] becomes:

$$\rho \frac{Du_x}{Dt} = \rho X - \frac{\partial p}{\partial x} + \eta \nabla^2 u_x. \qquad [5.61]$$

Similarly:

$$\rho \frac{Du_y}{Dt} = \rho Y - \frac{\partial p}{\partial y} + \eta \nabla^2 u_y \qquad [5.62]$$

and: $\rho \dfrac{Du_z}{Dt} = \rho Z - \dfrac{\partial p}{\partial z} + \eta \nabla^2 u_z. \qquad [5.63]$

Equations [5.61], [5.62] and [5.63] are the component equations of motion of an incompressible viscous liquid, and may be combined into the single vector equation:

$$\rho \frac{D\mathbf{u}}{Dt} = \rho \mathbf{F} - \nabla p - \eta \nabla^2 \mathbf{u} \qquad [5.64]$$

where $\mathbf{F}$ is the total body force per unit mass. Equation [5.64] is the Navier–Stokes equation for an incompressible, Newtonian viscous liquid.

Chapter 6
The slow viscous flow of liquids

6.1 Introduction

In Chapter 5 the general equation for the flow of an incompressible, Newtonian viscous liquid was obtained: the Navier–Stokes equation. For liquid flow in the x direction only the equation is:

$$\rho \frac{\mathrm{D}u_x}{\mathrm{D}t} = \rho X - \frac{\partial p}{\partial x} + \eta \nabla^2 u_x$$

using the notation of section 5.12. When the liquid flow is relatively slow $\mathrm{D}u_x/\mathrm{D}t$ may be replaced by $\partial u_x/\partial t$. In many situations the motion of the liquid is, in fact, so slow that inertial effects may be neglected completely, i.e. $\mathrm{D}u_x/\mathrm{D}t$ can be treated as zero. Solutions of the Navier–Stokes equation obtained in such situations are known as creeping solutions.

This chapter starts by considering a very simple situation where the above approximation is made and a creeping solution of the Navier–Stokes equation obtained. In situations with simple symmetry, however, it is often easier, under creeping flow conditions, to look at the problem starting with the defining equation for Newtonian viscosity (equation [4.6]) and some examples of this type are examined. A discussion of the viscosity of simple liquids in terms of the molecular behaviour follows and the chapter ends with a brief account of non-Newtonian liquids and of methods for measuring liquid viscosity.

6.2 Creeping viscous flow in a semi-infinite channel

The value of the Reynolds number is a measure of the relative importance of inertia and viscous effects in liquid flow. When Re is large the behaviour is dominated by the liquid inertia, but viscosity dominates when Re is sufficiently small. For vanishingly small Re the behaviour is creeping flow since Du_x/Dt can be neglected and the Navier-Stokes equation in one dimension can be written:

$$\frac{1}{\rho}\frac{\partial p}{\partial x} = \nu\nabla^2 u_x + X \qquad [6.1]$$

where ν is the kinematic viscosity of the liquid.

As a very simple example of the use of the Navier-Stokes equation under creeping flow conditions, consider the flow of a Newtonian liquid in a parallel-sided, semi-infinite channel in the absence of body forces. Let the boundaries be planes located at $y = \pm h$, each lying in an xz plane and let the liquid flow be in the z direction. The motion is assumed to be so slow that a creeping solution is obtained, the liquid is assumed to be incompressible and η is treated as a constant. From the symmetry of the problem the liquid flow velocity is a function of y only, so that the three components of the Navier-Stokes equation are:

$$0 = -\frac{\partial p}{\partial z} + \eta\frac{\partial^2 u_z}{\partial y^2} \qquad [6.2a]$$

$$0 = -\frac{\partial p}{\partial y} \qquad [6.2b]$$

$$0 = -\frac{\partial p}{\partial x}. \qquad [6.2c]$$

Equations [6.2b] and [6.2c] show that p is a function of z only so that the gradient of p may be written dp/dz. Further, $\partial^2 u_z/\partial y^2$ is a function of y only, and may be written $d^2 u_z/dy^2$; it follows that both dp/dz and $\eta(d^2 u_z/dy^2)$ must be constants.

Put:

$$\frac{dp}{dz} = -G$$

where G is the (constant) pressure gradient in the liquid. Then:

$$\frac{d^2 u_z}{dy^2} = -\frac{G}{\eta}$$

giving:

$$\frac{du_z}{dy} = -\frac{G}{\eta} y + \text{Constant}. \qquad [6.3]$$

By symmetry, $du_z/dy = 0$ when $y = 0$. This makes the constant in equation [6.3] equal to zero, but notice that du_z/dy is not zero at the walls.

Integrating equation [6.3] gives:

$$u_z = -\frac{Gy^2}{2\eta} + \text{Constant}. \qquad [6.4]$$

The condition of no slip at the solid boundary gives $u_z = 0$ when $y = \pm h$, so that the constant in equation [6.4] is equal to $Gh^2/2\eta$. Therefore:

$$u_z = \frac{G}{2\eta}(h^2 - y^2)$$

so that the velocity profile is parabolic. If the pressure changes from p_1 to p_2 in moving a distance L in the positive z direction $G = (p_2 - p_1)/L$ and:

$$u_z = \frac{(p_2 - p_1)(h^2 - y^2)}{2\eta L}. \qquad [6.5]$$

Creeping flow solutions may also be obtained from the defining equation for Newtonian viscosity, together with the relations arising from the symmetry of the situation. In the present example, consider the forces due to viscosity acting on the layer of liquid in an xz plane, of length L in the z direction, of unit width (in the x direction) and of thickness δy.

The net force on the layer of liquid due to viscosity is:

$$\left(\eta \frac{\partial u_z}{\partial y}\right)_{y+\delta y} L - \left(\eta \frac{\partial u_z}{\partial y}\right)_y L$$

which is:

$$\eta \frac{\partial^2 u_z}{\partial y^2} \delta y \, L .$$

The pressure force in the z direction is $(p_1 - p_2)\, \delta y$. Since the liquid element is neither gaining nor losing momentum

$$\eta \frac{\partial^2 u_z}{\partial y^2}\, \delta y\, L = (p_2 - p_1)\, \delta y$$

per unit width. Therefore:

$$\eta \frac{\partial^2 u_z}{\partial y^2} = \frac{p_2 - p_1}{L}. \qquad [6.6]$$

This pressure gradient must be independent of x by assumption, and independent of y if there is to be no motion in the y direction. Since u_z is at most a function of y it follows that:

$$\frac{p_2 - p_1}{L} = \text{Constant}, -G,$$

the constant pressure gradient in the z direction, and

$$\eta \frac{d^2 u_z}{dy^2} = -G$$

or: $\quad \dfrac{du_z}{dy} = -\dfrac{G}{\eta} y + \text{Constant}$

which is equation [6.3] and leads to:

$$u_z = \frac{G}{2\eta}(h^2 - y^2).$$

The flux of liquid per unit width is:

$$\text{Flux} = \int_{-h}^{h} u_z\, dy = \int_{-h}^{h} \frac{G}{2\eta}(h^2 - y^2)\, dy$$

$$= \frac{G}{2\eta}\left[h^2 y - \frac{y^3}{3} \right]_{-h}^{h}$$

$$= \frac{2h^3 G}{3\eta}. \qquad [6.7]$$

From this it follows that the average liquid velocity over a cross-section is:

$$\frac{2h^3 G}{3\eta} \bigg/ 2h \quad \text{or} \quad \frac{h^2 G}{3\eta}. \qquad [6.8]$$

6.3 Poiseuille flow in tubes of circular cross-section

Consider now the steady, laminar flow of an incompressible Newtonian liquid through a uniform cylindrical tube, of internal radius a and length L. Let the axis of the tube be in the z direction. If u_z is the liquid velocity component in the direction of the axis, then, assuming that there is no radial liquid flow, the equation of continuity gives $\partial u_z / \partial z = 0$ and, further, the pressure is constant over any cross-section. Since the flow is steady $\partial u_z / \partial t = 0$ and this, with $\partial u_z / \partial z = 0$, ensures that $\mathrm{D}u_z / \mathrm{D}t$ is zero and the solution obtained is a creeping solution.

Under steady flow conditions the net force acting on the liquid contained in a cylindrical element of radius r and length L, coaxial with the tube, must be zero.

Let there be a constant body force Z per unit mass, acting in the z direction. The forces acting on the liquid element in the z direction are the body force, the pressure force arising from the difference between the pressure p_1 at the inlet end of the tube and the pressure p_2 at the outlet end, and the viscous force. The magnitude of the body force acting on the liquid element is $\pi r^2 L \rho Z$, where ρ is the density of the liquid, and the pressure force is $(p_1 - p_2)\pi r^2$. Since the velocity gradient at the surface of the element is everywhere $(\mathrm{d}u_z / \mathrm{d}r)_r$, the viscous drag exerted on the curved surface of the element by the remainder of the liquid is:

$$\eta \frac{\mathrm{d}u_z}{\mathrm{d}r} 2\pi r L$$

and acts in the opposite direction to the pressure and body forces. Then, under creeping flow conditions:

$$\pi r^2 L \rho Z + (p_1 - p_2)\, \pi r^2 + \eta \frac{\mathrm{d}u_z}{\mathrm{d}r} 2\pi r L = 0$$

or: $\quad \rho Z + \dfrac{(p_1 - p_2)}{L} + \dfrac{2\eta}{r} \dfrac{\mathrm{d}u_z}{\mathrm{d}r} = 0.$ $\hfill$ [6.9]

The pressure gradient $(p_1 - p_2)/L$ must be at most a constant since it cannot vary with r. Let it be denoted by $+G$. Then:

$$\frac{2\eta}{r}\frac{du_z}{dr} = -(G + \rho Z) = -\overline{G}.$$ [6.10]

Integrating equation [6.10] gives:

$$u_z = \frac{\overline{G}r^2}{4\eta} + \text{Constant}.$$ [6.11]

Now, at the wall of the tube the liquid is at rest, i.e. $u_z = 0$ when $r = a$. Therefore:

$$u_z = \frac{\overline{G}}{4\eta}(a^2 - r^2)$$ [6.12]

showing that the velocity distribution is a paraboloid of revolution with the axis coinciding with that of the tube. The maximum value of u_z is u_{z0}, which occurs when $r = 0$ and is given by:

$$u_{z0} = \frac{\overline{G}a^2}{4\eta}.$$ [6.13]

The flux of liquid through the tube, Q, is given by:

$$Q = \int_0^a u_z 2\pi r\, dr$$

$$= \frac{2\pi\overline{G}}{4\eta}\int_0^a r(a^2 - r^2)\, dr$$

$$= \frac{\pi\overline{G}a^4}{8\eta}.$$

When the body force is zero:

$$Q = \frac{\pi G a^4}{8\eta}$$

or, as it is more usually written:

$$Q = \frac{\pi(p_1 - p_2)a^4}{8\eta L}.$$ [6.14]

Equation [6.14] is known as Poiseuille's equation.

The derivation of Poiseuille's equation assumes that, for the whole length of the tube, the liquid is travelling with constant velocity along any particular streamline, and that this velocity is not derived from the pressure difference $(p_1 - p_2)$, which merely maintains the flow. However, in many experimental arrangements, the pressure difference $(p_1 - p_2)$ is derived from a column of liquid which then flows into the tube. Close to the entrance to the tube the streamlines in the liquid converge and the liquid speeds up, so that part of the applied pressure difference is used to supply the kinetic energy of the liquid and not in opposing the viscous force. A correction, known as the kinetic energy correction, must be applied to allow for that part of the pressure difference.

The kinetic energy that the liquid receives per unit time is:

$$\int_0^a \frac{1}{2} . 2\pi r\rho u_z . u_z{}^2 \mathrm{d}r .$$

Using equation [6.12] this expression becomes, when the body force is zero:

$$\pi\rho \left(\frac{p_1 - p_2}{4\eta L}\right)^3 \int_0^a r(a^2 - r^2)^3 \mathrm{d}r .$$

This equals:

$$\pi\rho \left(\frac{p_1 - p_2}{4\eta L}\right)^3 \frac{a^8}{8}$$

which may be written:

$$\left(\frac{(p_1 - p_2)\pi a^4}{8\eta L}\right)^3 \frac{\rho}{\pi^2 a^4}$$

or: $\dfrac{Q^3 \rho}{\pi^2 a^4}$.

The total work done per unit time by the pressure difference $(p_1 - p_2)$ is $(p_1 - p_2)Q$, so that the work done against the viscous force per unit time is:

$$(p_1 - p_2)Q - (Q^3\rho/\pi^2 a^4) .$$

Therefore, the effective pressure difference is:

$$(p_1 - p_2) - (Q^2\rho/\pi^2 a^4).$$

Experiment shows, however, that this analysis is only approximate. The second term in the expression needs correction by an arbitrary factor m, whose value is close to unity, but which must be obtained by calibration in accurate work.

Even in arrangements where the liquid velocity is not derived from the measured pressure difference, it is still found that a kinetic energy correction of the form given is needed.

The converging of the streamlines at the entrance to the tube also results in the relative motion of adjacent layers of liquid, giving viscous effects that dissipate some of the work performed upon the liquid by the pressure difference before the liquid enters the tube. Consequently, the effective length of the tube is slightly greater than the geometrical length and the correction for this effect, known as the Couette correction, involves replacing L by $(L + na)$. Various values for n have been reported, most of them approximately unity. In most experiments, therefore, the Couette correction is small.

When both kinetic energy and Couette corrections are applied to Poiseuille's equation it becomes:

$$\eta = \frac{\pi a^4 (p_1 - p_2)}{8Q(L + na)} - \frac{m\rho Q}{8\pi(L + na)}. \tag{6.15}$$

In many situations Poiseuille flow occurs under a varying pressure gradient, as in the following example.

Example 6.1

A right circular vessel of area of cross-section 0.01 m² with its axis vertical, has projecting from it a horizontal tube of length 0.5 m and internal diameter 0.2×10^{-3} m. If the vessel contains a Newtonian liquid of viscosity 1.0×10^{-3} N s m⁻², calculate the time taken for the liquid level to fall from 1.0 m to 0.5 m above the axis of the horizontal tube. The density of the liquid is 1.1×10^3 kg m⁻³.

At any instant t let the height of the liquid level above the axis of the tube be y. Then, the pressure difference between the ends of the tube is $\rho g y$, where ρ is the density of the liquid and g is the acceleration of free fall. The volume rate of flow Q of liquid through the tube at the instant t is (assuming laminar flow and no kinetic energy and Couette correction) given by the Poiseuille equation:

$$Q = \frac{\rho g y \pi a^4}{8\eta L}$$

where the horizontal tube is of length L and internal radius a, and the liquid viscosity is η.

Now $Q = \mathrm{d}V/\mathrm{d}t$, where $\mathrm{d}V$ is the volume of liquid flowing through the tube in a time $\mathrm{d}t$, and $\mathrm{d}V/\mathrm{d}t = -\alpha\,\mathrm{d}y/\mathrm{d}t$, where α is the area of cross-section of the cylinder. The minus sign is introduced since it is assumed that y is measured upwards from the axis of the tube. Then:

$$-\alpha\frac{\mathrm{d}y}{\mathrm{d}t} = \frac{\rho g y \pi a^4}{8\eta L}$$

or: $-\dfrac{8\alpha\eta L}{\rho g \pi a^4}\dfrac{\mathrm{d}y}{y} = \mathrm{d}t$.

If the liquid level changes from y_1 to y_2 in a time $t_{1\,2}$:

$$-\frac{8\alpha\eta L}{\rho g \pi a^4}\ln\left(\frac{y_2}{y_1}\right) = t_{1\,2} .$$

Substituting the values given and putting $g = 9.81$ m s^{-2} makes:

$$t_{1\,2} = 8.2 \times 10^6\,\text{s} .$$

6.4 Motion of a Newtonian liquid between two coaxial cylinders

Next, consider the behaviour of a Newtonian liquid of constant density contained in the space between two coaxial cylinders, the inner one of external radius a and the outer one of internal radius b. Either or both of the cylinders can be rotated and the viscosity will cause the liquid to rotate. To derive an expression for the viscous forces it is necessary to find an expression for the rate of shear. In the arrangement being considered, this may be done as follows. When conditions are steady the streamlines in the liquid will have circular traces, concentric with the common cylindrical axis, in a plane normal to that axis. Figure 6.1 shows

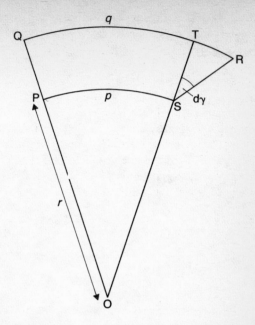

Fig. 6.1

two such streamlines p and q, a small distance δr apart; O is their common centre of curvature and OP $= r$. At a time t two very light particles are placed at P and Q on the streamlines p and q, respectively, so that OPQ is a straight line as in Fig. 6.1. If the angular velocity of the liquid particles travelling on streamline p is ω, that of liquid particles on q is:

$$\omega + \frac{d\omega}{dr}\delta r \, .$$

These are, very closely, the values for the light particles placed in the liquid. In a short time δt the particle on streamline p moves from P to S and that on streamline q moves from Q to R, where:

$$PS = r\omega\delta t$$

and:

$$QR = (r + \delta r)\left(\omega + \frac{d\omega}{dr}\delta r \, \delta t\right).$$

The shear of the liquid that occurs in the small time interval δt is measured by the angle $\delta\gamma$, i.e. by $T\hat{S}R$, which is approximately RT/ST.

Now:

$$RT/ST = (QR - QT)/ST$$

and, neglecting $\delta t(\delta r)^2$:

$$QR = r\omega\delta t + r\frac{d\omega}{dr}\delta r\,\delta t + \omega\delta r\,\delta t$$

while:

$$QT = (r + \delta r)\omega\delta t = r\omega\delta t + \omega\delta r\delta t\,.$$

Therefore:

$$\delta\gamma = r\frac{d\omega}{dr}\delta t$$

so that, in the limit as $\delta t \to 0$:

$$\frac{d\gamma}{dt} = r\frac{d\omega}{dr} \qquad\qquad [6.16]$$

which is the shear strain rate or rate of shear in this case.

Consider now a cylindrical shell of liquid lying between radii r and $r + dr$ and extending the length L of the coaxial cylinders. The condition for the steady state is that the accelerating moment or torque on the outer surface of each such elementary shell of liquid is equal and opposite to that on the inner surface. Then the moment or torque T must be constant for all values of r.

Using the defining equation for Newtonian viscosity, equation [4.6], gives for the viscous force F acting over the surface of radius r:

$$F = \eta\alpha r\frac{d\omega}{dr}$$

using equation [6.16] for the rate of shear. α is the area of the curved cylindrical surface. Now, $\alpha = 2\pi rL$ and $T = rF$. Therefore:

$$T = 2\pi\eta Lr^3\frac{d\omega}{dr}$$

or: $T\dfrac{\mathrm{d}r}{r^3} = 2\pi\eta L\,\mathrm{d}\omega$

so that:

$$-\frac{T}{r^2} = 4\pi\eta L\omega + \text{Constant} . \qquad [6.17]$$

Let the outer cylinder be rotating with an angular velocity Ω while the inner one is held stationary. Then, assuming no slippage at the walls, $\omega = 0$ when $r = a$ and:

$$-\frac{T}{r^2} = 4\pi\eta L\omega - \frac{T}{a^2} .$$

Further, $\omega = \Omega$ when $r = b$ so that, eliminating ω:

$$\frac{T}{a^2} - \frac{T}{b^2} = 4\pi\eta L\Omega . \qquad [6.18]$$

Equation [6.18] shows that the torque T on the inner cylinder varies with Ω and η. The value of T may be determined from the angle through which the inner cylinder turns when supported by a torsion wire and, therefore, the value of η may be found. It has been assumed that flow is laminar and end effects have been neglected.

When the inner cylinder is rotated with angular velocity Ω, the outer one being held stationary, the rate of shear is $-r\,\mathrm{d}\omega/\mathrm{d}r$, which gives equation [6.18] again. This is the basis of the Searle viscometer.

6.5 Bodies in liquids

When a body is placed in a liquid of lower density it sinks. At first the body accelerates, but the acceleration continuously decreases until a steady, or terminal, velocity is attained by the body. While the body is accelerating the downward force acting on it (its weight) is greater than the upward forces (the upthrust and the viscous force). While the weight and upthrust remain constant, the viscous force depends on the rate of shear of the liquid in the region of the surface of the body, and this increases with velocity. When the terminal velocity is reached the upthrust and viscous forces are, together, equal and opposite to the weight of the body. If, in a given liquid, the body has a smooth shape and surface and is light enough for it to fall very slowly through the liquid, the liquid motion is everywhere laminar and the viscous shearing of the liquid is the only dissipative process.

When the body falling through the liquid is a sphere the situation allows of a simple mathematical treatment. Let the liquid be Newtonian, let the sphere have acquired its terminal velocity and the liquid flow remain laminar. Stokes showed that under these conditions, the viscous drag exerted by the liquid on the sphere, assuming the liquid to be of infinite extent, is $6\pi\eta r v_t$, where r is the radius of the sphere and v_t is its terminal velocity.

This result is known as the law of Stokes. If the density of the liquid is ρ and that of the material of the sphere is σ, the upthrust on the sphere is $4/3(\pi r^3 \rho g)$ and its weight is $4/3(\pi r^3 \sigma g)$, where g is the acceleration of free fall. When v_t has been reached:

$$\frac{4}{3}\pi r^3 \sigma g = 6\pi\eta r v_t + \frac{4}{3}\pi r^3 \rho g$$

or:
$$\eta = \frac{2r^2 g(\sigma - \rho)}{9v_t} \qquad [6.19]$$

where the downward direction is taken as positive. Equation [6.19] holds for laminar flow in an infinite liquid. In practice, no liquid is of infinite extent and corrections must be applied. Most measurements and studies are made on spheres falling through liquids contained in long cylinders and the correction is then considered in two parts, namely, the end correction, which takes account of the finite length of the cylinder, and the wall correction, which allows for the finite radius of the cylinder. The end correction is not very important if measurements are made over the middle third of the depth of the liquid, provided, of course, that the sphere has acquired its terminal velocity before it reaches this part of the liquid.

For the wall correction Ladenburg suggested that the true viscosity is related to that obtained by direct application of equation [6.19] by

$$\eta \text{ (true)} = \frac{\eta \text{(measured)}}{(1 + 2.4 \, r/R)} \tag{6.20}$$

where R is the radius of the cylinder containing the liquid. Equation [6.20] holds approximately, but a better approach is to measure η for a range of values of R and extrapolate to R infinite.

Even when a sphere moves slowly through a viscous liquid, so that the movement of the liquid is laminar, there is a small region of 'dead' liquid immediately behind the body, and eddies are formed in this region. As the velocity increases this eddy formation becomes more pronounced until a stage is reached when the eddies break away as vortices. Other vortices grow and follow them, forming a vortex street. The vortices are detached alternately from opposite sides of the rear of the body so that the vortices in the street are staggered. If the velocity of the body increases still more the isolated vortices disappear to leave an eddying wake which extends for large distances behind the body. Similar behaviour is observed around a sphere placed rigidly in a steadily flowing liquid.

Example 6.2

A large beaker contains water to a depth of 0.1 m. Spherical particles of emery (density 4.0×10^3 kg m^{-3}) of various sizes are stirred up with the water and allowed to settle. Calculate the size of the largest particle still in suspension one hour after stirring ceases. The viscosity of water at the temperature of the experiment is 1.0×10^{-3} N s m^{-2}.

Treat water as a Newtonian liquid and assume that, in the descent of the emery particles, end and wall corrections are negligible. The largest particle still in suspension at the end of one hour will have travelled from the water surface through 0.1 m of water in that time. Assume that the terminal velocity is reached almost immediately the particle begins to descend. Then, the terminal velocity is $0.1/(60 \times 60)$ m s^{-1} and substitution of this and the other data in equation [6.19] gives:

$$10^{-3} = \frac{2 \times r^2 \times 9.81 \times 10^3 (4 - 1) \times 60 \times 60}{9 \times 0.1}$$

where r is the radius of the particle and the acceleration of free fall is taken as 9.81 m s^{-2}. Therefore:

$$r = 2.1 \times 10^{-6} \text{ m}.$$

6.6 Liquid flow and intermolecular forces

When a Newtonian liquid flows with a mean velocity less than the critical velocity it does so in layers, without mixing on the macroscopic scale. The viscosity of the liquid arises from the forces needed to maintain the relative motion of adjacent liquid layers.

On the microscopic scale, a simple liquid may be considered to be made up of local clusters or cells of molecules (see section 4.7) and liquid flow may then be described in terms of the movement of molecules from one cell to another. This process involves a migrating molecule in overcoming a potential barrier which represents the interaction between itself and those forming the remainder of the cell. Since any particular molecule can usually be considered as the occupant of one cell or as forming part of the wall of an adjacent cell, and in each case an energy barrier must be overcome for movement, the details of the model are not very crucial in a simple analysis. However, for definiteness, consider the cluster or cell of molecules shown in Fig. 6.2(a), where the positions shown represent the mean positions for the short time that the cell persists. When a particular molecule, say A, moves to positions L or R it must climb over or squeeze past its neighbours. To do so it must acquire sufficient kinetic energy in a thermal fluctuation to overcome the intermolecular forces exerted by the other members of the cell during the move. The variation of molecular potential energy E for moves to positions L and R is qualitatively as shown in Fig. 6.2(b). A molecule in a liquid may acquire the activation energy U as the result of a fluctuation of internal energy, but, in the absence of an applied shear stress there are no preferred directions for movement, so there is no net liquid flow. The effect of an applied shear stress, in the direction L-R, say, is to tilt the potential distribution, as represented in Fig. 6.2(c). Then the jump from site A to site R is more probable than that to site L, since energy barrier U_R is now less than energy barrier U_L. This general trend is true for all molecular cells and,

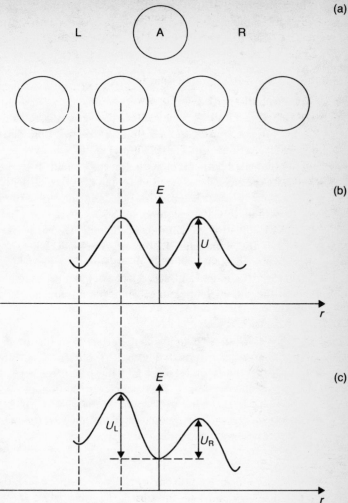

Fig. 6.2

therefore, a net liquid flow results. It can be seen from this treatment that a net flow of liquid under a shear stress is a consequence of the stress-assisted jumping of the potential energy barriers.

As the temperature of a liquid is lowered the mean kinetic

energy of the molecules decreases, and fluctuations large enough to assist a molecule over the potential barrier become less frequent. Therefore, to maintain a given flow rate the tilt of the potential barrier must be increased, and this can only be done by increasing the applied shear stress. Consequently, the viscosity increases. Experimentally, an increase of viscosity with reduction in temperature is observed in simple liquids.

The temperature-dependence of the viscosity of simple liquids can be discussed using the cell model as follows. Consider the cell of molecules shown in Fig. 6.2(a), where U is the average height of the potential barrier a molecule must surmount to escape from the cell. The molecule at A tries to climb over this barrier ν_0 times per second, where ν_0 is its vibration frequency. The probability that the molecule at A acquires sufficient energy, as a result of a thermal fluctuation, to climb over the potential barrier is proportional to the Boltzmann factor exp $(-U/kT)$, where k is the Boltzmann constant and T is the thermodynamic temperature. Therefore, the number of successful attempts per second to surmount the potential hill, known as the jump frequency ν, is:

$$\nu = \nu_0 \exp{(-U/kT)}.$$

When a shear stress is applied, the effect is to tilt the potential energy curve, as shown in Fig. 6.2(b), but for moderate shear stresses the tilt is quite small and the jump frequency is only slightly changed, though the spatial distribution of successful jumps is now biassed in the direction of the shear stress. Since the liquid viscosity will vary inversely as the jump frequency, it will show a temperature dependence of the form:

$$\eta = \frac{\text{constant}}{\exp{(-U/kT)}}$$

$$= \text{constant} \cdot \exp{(U/kT)} \qquad [6.21]$$

or: $\quad \ln \eta = A + \dfrac{B}{T} \qquad\qquad\qquad [6.22]$

where A and B are constants. This result is clearly not restricted to the particular cell model used; a similar result will be obtained for any process involving the thermally-assisted surmounting of a short-range potential barrier. Experimentally it is found that a relationship of the form of equation [6.22] represents the behaviour of simple liquids quite well over reasonable temperature ranges.

The energy barrier represents the energy needed to drag the moving molecule across its neighbours and then to squeeze into a suitable gap in the structure. When there is an applied pressure p exerted on the liquid, an additional amount of energy will be needed to allow a molecule to squeeze out of its cell and into another. This energy may be written pV_h where V_h represents the change in the size of the 'holes' in the liquid as a result of the applied pressure. Equation [6.21] is then modified in the presence of an applied pressure to read:

$$\eta = \text{constant} . \exp \left[(U + pV_h)/kT \right]$$
$$= \text{constant} . \exp (U/kT) . \exp (pV_h/kT)$$
$$= \eta_0 \exp (pV_h/kT) \qquad [6.23]$$

where η_0 is the viscosity when there is no applied pressure. Therefore, at constant temperature:

$$\ln \eta = D + Ep \qquad [6.24]$$

where D and E are constants. A relationship of the form of [6.24] is found to hold over a fairly wide pressure range for simple liquids and gives values of V_h that are a few per cent of the volume of a molecule.

6.7 Non-Newtonian liquids

The liquids that are Newtonian in their flow behaviour include water, true solutions and simple organic liquids. For all these, a graph of shear strain rate $d\gamma/dt$ (or $\dot\gamma$) against shear stress τ (known as the consistency curve or rheogram) is a straight line passing through the origin, provided that the flow is laminar, giving a coefficient of viscosity that is independent of $\dot\gamma$.

Many other liquids, however, do not show this behaviour and are known as non-Newtonian or anomalous liquids. For all these liquids the quantity $\tau/\dot\gamma$ varies with $\dot\gamma$ and sometimes with time as well, and is known as the apparent viscosity of the liquid. The flow behaviour of some non-Newtonian liquids is very complicated, but three idealised types of behaviour may be distinguished. These are:

1. time-independent or purely viscous liquids;
2. time-dependent liquids, for which $\dot{\gamma}$ depends on both τ and the duration of its application; and
3. viscoelastic liquids that possess elasticity as well as viscosity.

Many real liquids show a combination of properties from these basic types, and such liquids are termed complex rheological liquids.

Time-independent liquids

Shear-thinning or pseudo-plastic liquids have a consistency curve of the shape shown by curve 1 in Fig. 6.3. At low shear rates the curve is approximately a straight line and the slope gives the limiting low shear rate Newtonian viscosity. At higher shear rates the curve becomes concave to the $\dot{\gamma}$ axis and the apparent viscosity falls, but at still higher shear rates the curve passes through a point of inflexion and a high shear rate limiting Newtonian viscosity is

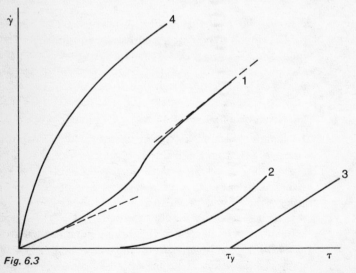

Fig. 6.3

achieved. This behaviour is commonly found with long molecular chains in solvents such as dilute polymer solutions, and in suspensions such as printing ink.

Some shear-thinning materials deform like elastic solids until a certain stress, known as the yield stress, is reached, after which they deform as normal shear-thinning liquids. These materials are described as shear thinning with yield value, and have a consistency curve like curve 2 of Fig. 6.3. Flow ceases when the stress falls below the yield stress. Materials which show this behaviour include toothpaste and muds. These substances also tend to be thixotropic.

A theoretical idealisation of pseudo-plastic with yield value behaviour is the Bingham plastic (see curve 3 of Fig. 6.3), which deforms elastically until the yield stress τ_y is reached and then flows like a Newtonian liquid with $\dot{\gamma}$ linearly related to τ. When τ is greater than τ_y:

$$\tau - \tau_y = \mu \dot{\gamma} \qquad [6.25]$$

where μ is known as the Bingham viscosity. The apparent viscosity for this material is given by:

$$\eta \text{ (apparent)} = \frac{\tau}{\dot{\gamma}} = \mu + \frac{\tau_y}{\dot{\gamma}} . \qquad [6.26]$$

A much less common type of behaviour is that of the shear-thickening or dilatant liquid, which has a consistency curve of the shape of curve 4 in Fig. 6.3. The apparent viscosity increases with shear rate and, at sufficiently high shear rates, the apparent viscosity may become so high that flow ceases, an effect known as shear blocking. Shear-thickening behaviour is associated with tightly-packed, lightly-wetted or unwetted disperse substances such as oil paint sediment and wheat starch in water.

Time-dependent liquids

Some materials show time-dependent flow effects. For example, some liquids when caused to flow at a constant rate of shear do so under a gradually decreasing shear stress. The effect is completely reversible and the apparent viscosity increases when the liquid has been allowed to rest. This behaviour is known as thixotropy. It is fairly common and is shown, for example, by tomato ketchup, margarine and shaving cream. Recovery following thixotropic behaviour may be accelerated by gentle and regular motion.

Inverse thixotropy (or negative thixotropy) is the opposite of thixotropy. Such substances show a steadily increasing apparent viscosity when sheared at a constant rate. Examples are rare, one being suspensions of vanadium oxide.

Viscoelastic liquids

In these materials both the shear rate and the apparent viscosity depend on the shear stress and the extent of the deformation of the material.

The inherent elasticity of the material can arise in several ways. In polymer melts and solutions the elasticity results from the entanglement of elastic long-chain molecules. Under stress the partially coiled molecules straighten, but tend to coil again when the stress is removed. The viscosity will depend on the orientation of the molecules relative to the direction of flow and on the strength of the interactions between the molecules. A phenomenological discussion of viscoelasticity is given in section 8.9.

6.8 Viscometers

Instruments for measuring viscosity are known as viscometers. Such instruments may be relative, requiring calibration with liquids of known viscosity, or absolute, and able to give a value for the viscosity without calibration.

Any of the flow processes described in sections 6.3, 6.4 and 6.5 can form the basis of absolute viscometers, so that there are viscometers using Poiseuille flow, rotating coaxial cylinders and the terminal velocity of falling spheres.

In routine work, relative instruments are often more convenient to use. An instrument widely used for mobile liquids is the Ostwald viscometer, in which the time taken for a given volume of liquid to pass through a capillary tube under the effect of gravity is measured. This time increases with viscosity and decreases with liquid density. The instrument, in fact, gives a value for the kinematic viscosity (see exercise 8).

A modification of the Ostwald viscometer is the Redwood viscometer, used for very viscous liquids. This viscometer consists of an open cup, through the centre of the base of which is an accurately bored hole fitted with a valve. The cup is filled to a given mark with liquid, the valve is opened, and the time taken for a given volume of liquid to discharge is noted.

In all the viscometers based on the three effects mentioned, different parts of the liquid under test undergo different rates of shear. This is of no consequence when the liquid is Newtonian, but for non-Newtonian liquids the value of the apparent viscosity depends on the rate of shear: for such liquids it is more meaningful to use a viscometer in which all parts of the test sample undergo the same rate of shear. Such an instrument is the cone and plate

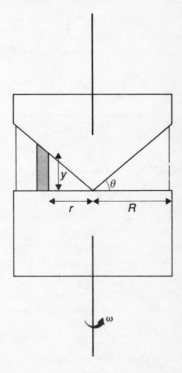

Fig. 6.4

viscometer, the essential features of which are shown in Fig. 6.4. A large-angle, fixed cone has its axis coincident with the axis of rotation of a circular plate of radius R and the sample is contained in the space between them.

Consider the liquid in the element of the space between the cone and plate surfaces and between distances r and $r + dr$ from the axis of rotation. Using the notation of Fig. 6.4, if the rate of rotation of the plate is ω rad s^{-1}, the rate of shear of the liquid in the element is $\omega r/y$. Now y/r equals tan θ, so that the rate of shear at a distance r from the axis is $\omega/\tan \theta$ which is independent of r. When θ is small, which is the usual condition, $y/r \approx \theta$ and the rate of shear is ω/θ. Let the shear stress on this element be τ. The torque exerted through the element of liquid lying between radii r and $r + dr$ is then $2\pi r dr \tau r$ and the total torque T is given by:

$$T = \int_0^R 2\pi \tau r^2 \, dr = \frac{2\pi \tau R^3}{3}$$

since τ must be constant for every element. Therefore:

$$\tau = \frac{3T}{2\pi R^3}$$

so that the apparent viscosity, which is shear stress ÷ rate of shear is:

$$\frac{3T\theta}{2\pi R^3 \omega} \, .$$

Chapter 7
Surface effects

7.1 Introduction

In solids and liquids the molecules are very close together; the bulk material shows short range order. However, at the surface of the solid or liquid the order ends rather abruptly. The surface can be considered as a two-dimensional defect in the molecular arrangement in the sense that the environment of a molecule in the surface region is markedly different from that of a molecule in the bulk.

It is implicit in the above paragraph that the condensed phase is in contact with a vapour phase. However, this need not be so. One condensed phase may be in contact with another, and, generally, the boundary region separating two bulk phases is known as an interface, although, where one of the phases is a vapour, the term surface is normally used.

Different types of interface show rather different physical properties, so that it is convenient to discuss them separately. This chapter is largely concerned with the properties of the liquid–vapour interface, and, to a lesser extent, the solid–vapour interface, of pure (one-component) simple materials.

The limitation means that the question of adsorption at interfaces will not be considered. However, some situations, such as the spreading of liquids on solids, are considered, where liquid–vapour, solid–vapour and solid–liquid interfaces are all present.

7.2 Excess surface free energy and surface tension of liquids

An important feature of the behaviour of a drop of a one-component liquid in equilibrium with its vapour is that, in the absence of external forces (as in free fall), it spontaneously assumes a spherical shape, which is the form that has the minimum surface area for a given volume. This indicates that the surface of the liquid is a seat of potential energy; work must be done on a drop of liquid to increase its surface area.

When the formation of new liquid surface is done reversibly and isothermally, the work needed to increase the liquid surface area by unity is called the specific excess surface free energy or, frequently, the specific surface free energy, having units $J\ m^{-2}$ and symbol γ (specific here means per unit area). This is not the total energy of the molecules in unit area of the surface region (see section 7.3), but the excess which the molecules have over those in the bulk by virtue of being in the surface region.

The explicit thermodynamic definition of the specific surface free energy for a one-component (pure) liquid in contact with its vapour is:

$$\gamma = \left(\frac{\partial A}{\partial \alpha} \right)_{T,V} \qquad [7.1]$$

where A is the Helmholtz function of the system and α the area of its surface, with temperature T and volume V held constant. A similar definition can be used for the specific interfacial free energy when two immiscible liquids are in contact.

Dupré's experiment, in which a liquid film is formed on a frame, one side of which can slide, practically without friction, on the adjacent sides (see Fig. 7.1(a)), shows that the molecular interactions that give rise to the surface free energy result in the liquid being in tension, since a force F_a, parallel to the liquid surface, must be applied to the movable part of the frame to maintain equilibrium. The force F_a does not change when the liquid evaporates, making the film of liquid thinner (except when the film is so thin that molecules in the two surface regions interact), showing that the liquid tension is, in fact, confined to the surface regions of the liquid, and may be called a surface tension. Further, F_a is proportional to the length of the part of the movable frame in contact with the liquid, showing that the value of γ does not depend on the area α of the liquid surface.

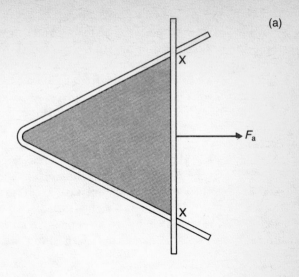

Fig. 7.1

To obtain a quantitative measure, the surface tension of a liquid may be defined in the following way. Make a cut in a plane liquid surface, extending only a short way into the liquid. If the liquid surface is to remain in equilibrium, equal and opposite forces, which are in the plane of the surface, must be applied to the faces of the cut. The force, per unit length of the cut, applied to one face of the cut, is the surface tensile 'stress' that existed across the line of the cut and is known as the surface tension of the liquid, units $N\,m^{-1}$. It follows from this definition that surface tension in liquids may be studied by determining the force exerted on some solid object either placed in, or terminating, a liquid surface.

There is a formal similarity between the definition of the surface tension of a liquid surface and stress in an elastic solid.

However, the stress in an elastically deformed solid increases as the surface area is increased and no additional molecules are brought to the surface in the stretching process. In contrast the surface tension of a liquid does not depend on the surface area since the increase in area results from additional molecules being brought from the bulk to the liquid surface.

Let the arm XX of the frame in Fig. 7.1(a) move without friction and let the liquid film (shown shaded) be in equilibrium under the external force F_a. When the arm XX is moved through a distance dx in the direction of F_a the surface area is increased by $2(XX)dx$, the factor 2 arising because the liquid film has two surfaces (see Fig. 7.1(b)). If the increase in surface area is carried out reversibly and isothermally, the surface free energy of the liquid film is increased by an amount $2(XX)dx\gamma$. The applied force F_a does work on the liquid film equal to $F_a dx$. Therefore:

$$F_a dx = 2(XX)dx\gamma$$

or: $\quad F_a = 2\gamma(XX).$ [7.2]

Equation [7.2] shows that a liquid surface exerts a mechanical force on any solid surface with which it is in contact. The length of the terminated liquid surface is $2(XX)$ so that the force per unit length, i.e. the surface tension, is numerically equal to γ. Therefore, for a pure liquid in equilibrium with its vapour, the specific surface free energy, in J m^{-2}, is numerically equal to the

Table 7.1 *Values of the specific surface free energy γ at room temperature for some common simple liquids in equilibrium with their vapour*

Liquid	$\gamma(m\ J\ m^{-2})$
Benzene	28
Bromine	43
Carbon tetrachloride	26
Chloroform	26
Glycerol	61
Glycol	48
Mercury	490
Methanol	22
Turpentine	27
Water	73

surface tension, in N m^{-1}. For liquids, both will be represented by the symbol γ. Values of γ at room temperature for some common simple liquids are given in Table 7.1.

7.3 The total surface energy of liquids

The total change in energy of a liquid surface when its area changes is not, in general, equal to the change in surface free energy. Essentially this is because the specific surface free energy decreases as the temperature rises so that, when a liquid surface is enlarged isothermally, heat flows to the liquid from the surroundings. This can be seen from a simple thermodynamic analysis.

Let a liquid surface of area α be increased by dα under reversible conditions. Assume that there is no mass transfer from the liquid to the vapour in this process, so that the liquid (bulk plus surfaces) may be treated as a closed system. The work done on the liquid during the increase in area is γdα so that, if volume changes are negligible, the first law of thermodynamics may be written:

$$\mathrm{d}U = T\mathrm{d}S + \gamma\mathrm{d}\alpha \qquad [7.3]$$

where U is the internal energy and S the entropy of the liquid. Now the entropy may be treated as a function of the temperature T and the surface area α, i.e.:

$$S = S(T, \alpha)$$

so that:

$$T\mathrm{d}S = T\left(\frac{\partial S}{\partial T}\right)_{\alpha} \mathrm{d}T + T\left(\frac{\partial S}{\partial \alpha}\right)_{T} \mathrm{d}\alpha \,.$$

It may readily be shown (see *Thermal Physics* by C.B.P. Finn in this series) that one of the Maxwell relations for a liquid surface is:

$$\left(\frac{\partial S}{\partial \alpha}\right)_{T} = -\left(\frac{\partial \gamma}{\partial T}\right)_{\alpha}$$

Now, $T(\partial S/\partial T)_{\alpha}$ is the heat capacity C_{α} of the liquid when the surface area is held constant, so that:

$$TdS = C_\alpha dT - T\left(\frac{\partial \gamma}{\partial T}\right)_\alpha d\alpha \, .$$

The Dupré experiment shows that γ does not depend on α so that γ is a function of T only. Therefore:

$$TdS = C_\alpha dT - T\frac{d\gamma}{dT}\,d\alpha \qquad [7.4]$$

is the general equation relating heat flow under reversible conditions (TdS) to changes in T and α of a liquid whose surface area may change, but whose volume is kept constant.

In a reversible, isothermal change of surface area at constant volume $dT = 0$ and:

$$TdS = -T\frac{d\gamma}{dT}\,d\alpha \, . \qquad [7.5]$$

Substituting for TdS in equation [7.3] gives:

$$dU = \left(\gamma - T\frac{d\gamma}{dT}\right)d\alpha \, .$$

For a finite change in area from α_i to α_f at constant temperature and volume (in which U changes from U_i to U_f):

$$\frac{U_f - U_i}{\alpha_f - \alpha_i} = \gamma - T\frac{d\gamma}{dT} \, . \qquad [7.6]$$

Now the internal energy of the bulk liquid does not change; the quantity $(U_f - U_i)/(\alpha_f - \alpha_i)$ is the energy per unit area associated with the surface only and is known as the specific total surface energy, symbol σ. Unless $d\gamma/dT = 0$, the change in energy of the surface when the area is changed isothermally is not simply the work done on the liquid, there is also a heat flow to maintain T constant.

For pure liquids both γ and σ decrease with increasing temperature, and both become zero at the critical temperature.

7.4 Surface tension and intermolecular forces

In both the solid and liquid phases the free surface is the termination of the closely packed molecular arrangement. It was shown in section 1.4 that, for solids, where the molecules are effectively fixed in a three-dimensional array, a consequence of this termination is that the variation of potential energy E of a molecule with distance r along a row of molecules perpendicular to the free surface is as shown schematically in Fig. 7.2. In particular, the energy of the surface layers is less negative than those in the bulk.

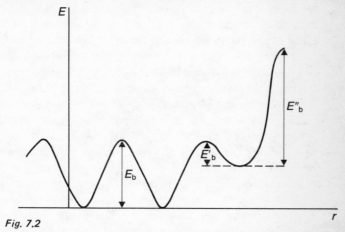

Fig. 7.2

Figure 7.2 can still be used to represent the variation of potential energy of a molecule as it moves from the bulk of the liquid to the surface, provided that the surface layer is assumed to have the same intermolecular separation as in the bulk. The liquid phase, however, has fluidity and the molecules are able to diffuse through the liquid.

It can be seen that, for a molecule to move in the bulk of the liquid it must obtain, as a result of a thermal fluctuation, an energy E_b. This is the activation energy of diffusion, and represents the energy needed by the molecule under consideration to push apart and climb over the two molecules in its way and escape from the attractions of the other molecules forming the cell that contains it. In the bulk of the liquid, on average, such movement is equally probable for all directions, so that the average molecular separation is unchanged by the molecular movement.

A molecule in the surface region has, in contrast, a smaller energy barrier E'_b, to surmount to move from the surface to the bulk of the liquid, since it has fewer molecules pulling back on it, but a much higher barrier E_b'' for movement into the vapour. Therefore, if energy fluctuations are distributed according to the Maxwell–Boltzmann law, jumps towards the bulk of the liquid are more likely than jumps into the surface region, leaving the liquid with vacancies or holes in the surface region. It is this increase in the molecular separation that causes the liquid surface to be put in tension. However, this depletion of the surface layer has the effect of increasing the energy barrier to the movement of molecules from the surface to the bulk. When a surface is freshly formed, each surface molecule has, say, six nearest neighbours, each approximately at the mean equilibrium separation r_0. In the depleted surface, however, though each molecule has a smaller number, say five, nearest neighbours, the mean separation r_s between them is larger than r_0, so that there is a strong attractive force, with a component normal to the surface, that has to be overcome.

This means that the magnitude of E_b', increases and, neglecting molecular movement into the vapour, it continues to do so until $E_b = E_b'$. When this condition is achieved, the probability for molecular motion into the bulk is the same as that for motion into the surface layer and a state of dynamic equilibrium is reached with the surface layer in tension.

It is of interest to consider the problem in terms of the separation of a column of material. This approach can be applied to solids, pure liquids and to interfaces between solids and between pure immiscible liquids.

Consider the work w that must be done to break a column of material of cross-section α and separate the two parts to infinity under reversible, isothermal conditions; the work done is then the increase in the Helmholtz function of the material resulting from the separation. Initially, all the molecules in the neighbourhood of the plane along which the separation is going to take place are 'bulk' molecules. Separation, however, changes the environment of these molecules and they become 'surface' molecules with quite different energies. This increase in energy, measured by the isothermal, reversible work of separation, arises from the difference in the intermolecular forces experienced by molecules in the new surfaces, compared with those acting on them when they were part of the bulk material. The extra (or excess) energy is equal to $2\alpha\gamma$, since the new surface created has twice the area of the column. Provided that the effects of kinetic energy can be neglected, this approach can readily lead to an estimate of the specific surface free energy in terms of the parameters in the intermolecular potential.

Before attempting this a few remarks must be made about the surface energy of solids.

7.5 Solid surfaces

When a fresh solid surface is formed, say by cleavage, the molecules in the freshly generated surface may take a long time to reach their equilibrium positions, so that the new surface is a non-equilibrium structure. This is in contrast to the situation with liquids, where the mobility of the molecules enables the surface to reach an equilibrium configuration almost as soon as it is formed. For a solid surface a free energy can be defined in terms of the reversible, isothermal work needed to produce the new surface, while it is convenient to define surface tension in terms of the forces needed to bring the freshly exposed surface to an equilibrium state.

The existence of surface tension in solids composed of neutral molecules can be attributed to the effects of attractive interactions between other than nearest neighbours. These next-nearest-neighbour and more distant attractions ensure that a plane of molecules is more closely packed than a row of molecules, but less closely packed than a large three-dimensional array. If a layer of molecules is produced separately it has to contract to fit onto the bulk phase and must therefore be put into compression. The balancing tension in the bulk phase falls rapidly to zero over a few molecular diameters.

The surface area of a condensed phase may be increased either by creating a fresh surface, having the properties of the original, or by stretching the surface already present. Almost invariably the extension of the surface of a pure liquid is an example of the first process, as is the extension of a cleavage crack in a brittle solid, while the increase of a solid surface by stretching is an example of the second.

Stretching a solid changes both the surface area α and the specific excess surface free energy γ_S. For a one-component, isotropic solid, let dw be the reversible isothermal work needed to extend the surface area by $d\alpha$. Then, if the surface is stretched in the same proportion in all directions:

$$dw = d(\gamma_S \alpha) = \gamma_S d\alpha + \alpha d\gamma_S.$$

If the surface tension of the solid surface is T_S, i.e. the force per unit length in the surface:

$$dw = T_S d\alpha.$$

Therefore:

$$\gamma_S d\alpha + \alpha d\gamma_S = T_S d\alpha$$

or: $\quad T_S = \gamma_S + \alpha \dfrac{d\gamma_S}{d\alpha}.$ \hfill [7.7]

Clearly, the surface tension T_S is only equal to γ_S when $d\gamma_S/d\alpha$ is zero. This condition holds for a one-component liquid, but not for a freshly-formed solid surface, where the magnitudes of γ_S and $\alpha(d\gamma_S/d\alpha)$ may be comparable. In solids an increase in an existing area forces the molecules further apart so that $d\gamma_S/d\alpha$ is negative.

7.6 Specific surface free energy and the intermolecular potential

While bearing in mind the conclusions that liquid surfaces contain a fraction of vacancies and that solid surfaces are seldom equilibrium structures, an estimate of the specific surface free energy of a condensed phase can be made using the method of separating a column of material into two parts.

Let the mean equilibrium spacing of the molecules in the condensed phase be r_0. Then, in a column of cross-sectional area α, the number of molecules in any layer perpendicular to the axis of the column is α/r_0^2. When the column is separated under reversible, isothermal conditions, the area of new surface produced is 2α, which corresponds to an increase in surface free energy of $2\alpha\gamma$. If q is the number of nearest neighbours in the bulk material, the number of nearest neighbours in the surface layer is approximately $q/2$. Then, if the energy of interaction between any pair of molecules is ϵ (the chemical bond energy), the total energy needed to break completely all the bonds in the surface of separation is:

$$\frac{\alpha}{r_0^2} \frac{q}{2} \epsilon$$

which equals $2\alpha\gamma$. Therefore:

$$\gamma = \frac{q\epsilon}{4r_0^2}. \tag{7.8}$$

For solids and liquids q is approximately 10 and, at sufficiently low temperatures, ϵ is approximately the potential energy of a pair of molecules at the equilibrium separation, U_0. For the Mie potential (see section 1.3):

$$U_0 = -\frac{A}{r_0^m} \left(1 + \frac{m}{n}\right)$$

giving:

$$\gamma = \frac{10A}{4r_0^{m+2}} \left(1 + \frac{m}{n}\right). \tag{7.9}$$

Sublimation, for solids, and vaporisation, for liquids, correspond to the breaking of all the bonds between a molecule and its neighbours. Therefore, the molar enthalpy for sublimation or vaporisation (as is appropriate) L_m, is equal to $q\epsilon N_A/2$, where N_A is the Avogadro constant. Hence:

$$q\epsilon = 2L_m/N_A$$

and, from equation [7.8]:

$$\gamma = \frac{2L_m}{4r_0^2 N_A} = \frac{L_m}{2r_0^2 N_A}. \tag{7.10}$$

Now the density ρ is $M_r/N_A r_0^3$, where M_r is the relative molecular mass, so that:

$$r_0 = \left(\frac{M_r}{\rho N_A} \right)^{\frac{1}{3}}$$

and: $\gamma = \frac{L_m}{2N_A} \left(\frac{\rho N_A}{M_r} \right)^{\frac{2}{3}}$. [7.11]

7.7 Liquid surfaces and the Laplace–Young equation

In the absence of electrical of other long-range external fields, a small vapour bubble in a one-component liquid assumes a spherical shape when equilibrium is reached. The bubble does not collapse, even though this would give a reduction in surface free energy, because the effects of the surface tension forces are balanced by those of an internal excess pressure that is set up in the vapour of the bubble. This result is, in fact, more general: across any curved interface between two bulk fluid phases there is a change in pressure that is a consequence of the interfacial free energy, independent of any gravitational or other effects. For example, beneath a liquid surface, in contact with its vapour, that is concave towards the bulk liquid, the pressure is greater than that in the vapour. This pressure difference, arising from the intermolecular forces, builds up in the thin interfacial region and is then constant throughout the bulk fluids on either side. A general expression for the pressure difference across a curved fluid interface may be derived as follows.

Any region of a surface has its geometry specified by the algebraic values of the two principal radii of curvature in that region. Consider a very small element of the free surface of a one-component liquid in equilibrium with its vapour, having principal radii of curvature r_1 and r_2 as shown in Fig. 7.3(a). A sign convention is needed here. For a liquid–vapour interface take the origin of coordinates in the liquid phase and let the positive direction of the normal at the interface be from the liquid phase to the vapour phase.

A radius of curvature is then considered positive when its centre of curvature is in the liquid phase. In Fig. 7.3(a), both r_1 and r_2 are positive if the surface is concave towards the liquid. This situation will now be analysed. Let the pressure on the

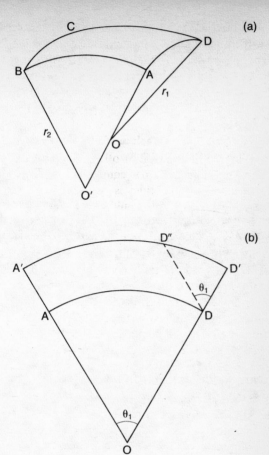

(a)

(b)

Fig. 7.3

concave side of the surface be p_1 and that on the convex side be p_2. It has been shown above that $p_1 > p_2$. If the curvature of the surface is not too great and the surface element is sufficiently small, the element is essentially a small rectangle to which curvatures have been applied. Take the local x axis parallel to AD and the y axis parallel to AB, in Fig. 7.3(a). Since the chosen element is very small, AD and AB are effectively straight and the region ABCD is effectively planar, and of area $\alpha = AB.AD = xy$. Now let the surface area be expanded reversibly and isothermally by a very small amount by allowing each radius of curvature to increase by δr, the centres of curvature remaining stationary.

Ignoring gravitational and other effects, the work that must be done on the liquid to produce the increase in area is given by $(p_1 - p_2)xy\delta r$; the corresponding increase in the surface free energy is $\gamma\delta\alpha$. These two quantities are equal so that:

$$(p_1 - p_2)xy\delta r = \gamma\delta\alpha . \qquad [7.12]$$

The change in area is $\delta\alpha$, given by:

$$\delta\alpha = \delta(xy) = x\delta y + y\delta x . \qquad [7.13]$$

Figure 7.3(b) shows A'D', the new position of AD after the expansion of the surface, and has DD'' drawn parallel to AA', making A'D'' equal to AD ($= x$) and D''D' equal to δx. Then, using the notation in the figure:

$$\theta_1 = \frac{x}{r_1} = \frac{\delta x}{\delta r}$$

so that:

$$\delta x = \frac{x}{r_1} \delta r .$$

Similarly, for the section O'DC:

$$\delta y = \frac{y}{r_2} \delta r .$$

Therefore:

$$\delta\alpha = \frac{xy}{r_1} \delta r + \frac{xy}{r_2} \delta r . \qquad [7.14]$$

Substituting for $\delta\alpha$ from equation [7.14] gives:

$$\Delta p = p_1 - p_2 = \gamma\left(\frac{1}{r_1} + \frac{1}{r_2}\right) . \qquad [7.15]$$

Equation [7.15] gives the pressure drop that occurs on crossing the liquid–vapour interface in the positive direction, and is known as the Laplace–Young equation. When r_1 and r_2 are both positive Δp is positive, i.e. $p_1 > p_2$, and there is a decrease in pressure on passing through the liquid–vapour interface from liquid to vapour. However, if both r_1 and r_2 are negative, i.e. the surface is concave towards the vapour, Δp is negative ($p_1 < p_2$) and the pressure increases on crossing the interface from liquid to vapour. Therefore when both curvatures are of the same sign the pressure is always greater on the concave side of the surface, irrespective of whether or not this is the liquid phase. Equation [7.15] also holds for any liquid–liquid interface, provided that the appropriate specific interfacial free energy is used.

For a spherical liquid drop, where $r_1 = r_2 = r$, say:

$$\Delta p = \frac{2\gamma}{r}. \hspace{4cm} [7.16]$$

When a thin liquid film is considered, two pressure differences occur. These have the same sign and magnitude so that the pressure difference in crossing both surfaces is:

$$\Delta p = 2\gamma\left(\frac{1}{r_1} + \frac{1}{r_2}\right).$$

For a spherical bubble $r_1 = r_2 = r$, say, and:

$$\Delta p = \frac{4\gamma}{r}. \hspace{4cm} [7.17]$$

Some indication of the relatively large forces that can be brought into play as a result of the Laplace–Young pressure drop is given in example 7.1.

Example 7.1

Two circular glass plates, each of 0.05 m radius, are separated by a water film 0.01×10^{-3} m thick. Find the minimum direct pull needed to separate the plates. The specific surface free energy of water, at the temperature of the experiment, is 72 m J m^{-2} and the angle of contact of water with glass is zero (see section 7.8).

If the plates are of radius R and the separation of the plates is $2r$, the pressure drop in going through the liquid–vapour interface in the positive direction is:

$$\Delta p = \gamma \left(\frac{1}{R} + \frac{1}{r} \right).$$

If $R \gg r$, this is closely equal to:

$$\Delta p = \frac{\gamma}{r}.$$

With the sign convention adopted, r is negative, so that the pressure inside the liquid is less than that of the surroundings by the amount Δp. Therefore, if the plates are of area α the force F_a that must be applied to both plates to separate them is:

$$F_a = \alpha \Delta p = \frac{\alpha \gamma}{r} = \frac{\pi R^2 \gamma}{r}.$$

Substituting the given values:

$$F_a = \frac{72 \times 10^{-3} \times \pi \times (0.05)^2}{0.005 \times 10^{-3}}$$

$$= 113 \text{ N (approximately } 11.5 \text{ kg wt).}$$

7.8   Liquid spreading

The molecular environment in the surface layer of a solid is not the same as that in the bulk material, giving rise to the concept of the surface free energy of the solid. When the surface of a solid is covered by a liquid, the free energy of the resulting solid–liquid interface is less than that of the solid–vapour interface, because the 'one-sidedness' of the environment of the surface molecules is reduced. Therefore when a liquid is placed on part of a solid surface, it may spread over the surface and so reduce the surface free energy of the solid. As the liquid spreads, however, it increases the solid–liquid interfacial free energy and also its own surface free energy. Neglecting gravitational effects, spreading will continue as long as the sum of the interfacial free energies is reduced as a result, and will cease if this sum reaches a minimum value.

Consider a drop of a pure liquid resting on a plane solid surface of area α_0, such that the liquid covers an area α, the remainder of the space being filled by the vapour of the liquid. Let the specific surface free energy of the solid–vapour interface be γ_{SV}, that of the liquid–vapour interface be γ_{LV} and that of the solid–liquid interface be γ_{SL}. The sum of the interfacial surface free energies is closely equal to:

$$\alpha(\gamma_{SL} + \gamma_{LV}) + (\alpha_0 - \alpha)\gamma_{SV}$$

and this quantity will decrease as α increases if:

$$\gamma_{SL} + \gamma_{LV} < \gamma_{SV} \qquad [7.18]$$

assuming that the liquid layer is of sufficient thickness for the values of γ_{SL} and γ_{LV} to be independent of liquid layer thickness. Therefore, neglecting changes in gravitational potential energy, relation [7.18] is the condition for the liquid to spread completely over the whole of the solid surface. Should:

$$\gamma_{LV} < \gamma_{SL} - \gamma_{SV} \qquad [7.19]$$

a condition that is mutually exclusive to relation [7.18], for a given pair of fluids, the liquid will endeavour to minimise its contact with the solid surface.

Since the liquid–vapour interface must have γ_{LV} positive, there is a third possibility:

$$\gamma_{LV} > | \gamma_{SL} - \gamma_{SV} | \qquad [7.20]$$

and here it is possible to have an equilibrium in which the three surfaces of separation coexist, intersecting in a line on the solid surface. Figure 7.4 shows a possible situation where the solid surface is, in fact, plane. It is usual to refer to the angle between the solid and the tangent to the liquid surface at the line of contact with the solid, measured in the liquid, as the contact angle θ,

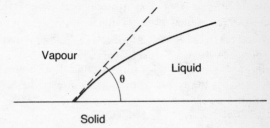

Fig. 7.4

for the particular combination of solid and liquid. Strictly the only vapour present should be that of the liquid substance, but θ is insensitive to the nature of the vapour and measurements are usually made in air. For a given solid–liquid combination the value of θ depends to some extent on whether the liquid is advancing or receding over the solid surface, advancing angles of contact usually being slightly larger than receding ones; θ is also very sensitive to surface contamination.

When, for a given solid–liquid pair, θ is greater than $\pi/2$ the liquid is said to be non-wetting with respect to the solid; when $\pi/2 > \theta > 0$ the liquid is said to be partially wetting and when $\theta = 0$ the liquid is said to wet the solid. In practice, θ is zero only when the liquid has already wetted the surface, so that a very thin layer of liquid is adsorbed to the surface.

The angle of contact is the only directly measureable quantity which gives information about interfacial free energies. One method of determining θ is to take a flat plate of the appropriate solid and partially immerse it in the required liquid. The plate is then rotated about an axis, lying in the plate and parallel to the liquid surface, until the liquid meets the solid on one surface without curvature of the liquid surface. θ is then the angle of the plate from the horizontal on that side. Another method uses the sessile drop, discussed in section 7.11.

Consider now a small amount of a liquid A placed on a large amount of a liquid B, with which it does not mix. There are three possible processes that may occur:
1. the liquid A may remain as a non-spreading drop on liquid B and will then take up an equilibrium configuration in which it is lens-shaped;
2. liquid A may spread as a monolayer over liquid B, with or without a residual lens of liquid;
3. liquid A may spread as a relatively thick film, known as a duplex film.

For a duplex film γ_A and γ_{AB} retain their bulk values and the condition for the spreading of liquid A on liquid B is (see equation [7.18]):

$$\gamma_A + \gamma_{AB} < \gamma_B \qquad [7.21]$$

or: $S > 0$.

Here γ_A is the specific surface free energy of liquid A, γ_B that of liquid B and γ_{AB} the specific interfacial free energy of the contact surface. The quantity S, defined as $\gamma_B - \gamma_A - \gamma_{AB}$, is known as the spreading tension or spreading coefficient. In practice, liquid A will, in time, become saturated with liquid B, even though they do not mix, and a distinction should be made between the initial spreading tension and the equilibrium value when the liquids are mutually saturated.

When a column of liquid A, having unit area of cross-section, is separated reversibly and isothermally into two parts in equilibrium at infinity, the work done, neglecting gravity, is:

$$W_C{}^A = 2\gamma_A$$

and is known as the work of cohesion for liquid A. A similar quantity exists for liquid B. If a column of liquid A rests on a column of an immiscible liquid B, both of unit area cross-section, the work to separate these reversibly and isothermally at the interface is, neglecting gravity:

$$W_a{}^{AB} = \gamma_A + \gamma_B - \gamma_{AB} \; .$$

$W_a{}^{AB}$ is called the work of adhesion of the two liquids. The spreading tension S may then be written:

$$S = W_a{}^{AB} - W_C{}^A \qquad [7.22]$$

where the values of γ are measured in the pure or saturated condition as is appropriate.

7.9 Young's relation

A work of adhesion $W_a{}^{SL}$ can be defined for a solid–liquid interface in a similar way to that for a liquid–liquid interface, namely:

$$W_a{}^{SL} = \gamma_{SV} + \gamma_{LV} - \gamma_{SL} \qquad [7.23]$$

using the notation of the previous section. The quantity γ_{SL} is experimentally inaccessible, but this difficulty can be overcome by introducing the angle of contact through an equation known as Young's relation. This may be derived in the following way:

A fixed mass of liquid is contained in a conical vessel as shown in Fig. 7.5, the semi-angle of the cone being $\pi/2 - \theta$ where θ is the angle of contact for the particular solid–liquid pair. Consequently, the surface of the liquid is plane, right up to the solid, and there is no pressure change due to intermolecular forces on passing through the surface. The cone communicates via a narrow vertical tube to a drop of the liquid that is suspended at its lower end.

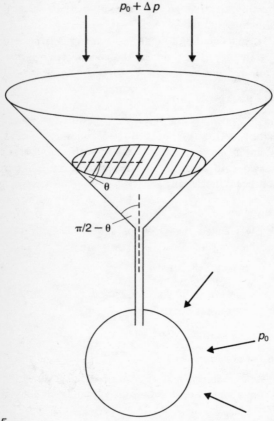

Fig. 7.5

If gravitational effects are ignored, equilibrium will be achieved for a drop of radius r, when the pressure around the drop is p_0 and that acting on the surface of the liquid in the cone is $p_0 + 2\gamma_{LV}/r$.

This situation arises because there is a pressure drop $2\gamma_{LV}/r$ in crossing the surface of the drop, but no pressure drop in crossing the surface of the liquid in the cone. Assume that the liquid is incompressible, so that the Helmholtz function is independent of pressure. Now let the radius of the drop be increased by a very small amount δr by transferring liquid from the cone to the drop reversibly and isothermally, and assume that there is no additional evaporation as a result of this. The volume of liquid transferred is $4\pi r^2 \delta r$ and the work done is:

$$\left(p_0 + \frac{2\gamma_{LV}}{r}\right) 4\pi r^2 \delta r - 4\pi r^2 p_0 \delta r$$

where the left hand term represents the work done by the surroundings at a pressure $p_0 + 2\gamma_{LV}/r$ on the plane surface of the liquid in the cone, and the right hand term is the work done on the surroundings at a pressure p_0 by the expanding drop. The net work done is $8\pi r\gamma_{LV}\delta r$. However this is just the change in surface free energy of the drop and, therefore, the net change in surface free energy of the liquid in the cone must be zero. When the liquid level in the cone falls so that the radius of the surface decreases by δr, the change in surface free energy is:

$$(\gamma_{SV} - \gamma_{SL}) \frac{2\pi r \delta r}{\cos \theta} - 2\pi r \delta r \, \gamma_{LV}$$

and this must equal zero. Therefore:

$$(\gamma_{SV} - \gamma_{SL}) = \gamma_{LV} \cos \theta$$

or: $$\cos \theta = \frac{\gamma_{SV} - \gamma_{SL}}{\gamma_{LV}}. \qquad [7.24]$$

Using this relationship the work of adhesion $W_a{}^{SL}$ may be written:

$$W_a{}^{SL} = \gamma_{SV} + \gamma_{LV} + \gamma_{LV} \cos \theta - \gamma_{SV}$$

$$= \gamma_{LV}(1 + \cos \theta) \qquad [7.25]$$

so that $W_a{}^{SL}$ may be determined from γ_{LV} and θ. Equation [7.24] is known as Young's relation. It applies to the liquid in equilibrium, so that the liquid should be saturated with solid which, in general, leads to a reduction in γ_{LV} in comparison with the pure liquid. The vapour and solid must be at adsorption equilibrium.

7.10 Capillary effects

One of the most striking effects associated with surface tension is the rise (sometimes a fall) of a liquid in a vertical tube partly immersed in it, to a height above (or below) that predicted by simple hydrostatic conditions.

A uniform cylindrical tube is shown in Fig. 7.6(a) dipping into a one-component liquid of specific surface free energy γ. When the tube dips into the liquid a meniscus is formed. This meniscus is curved since the liquid surface must meet the tube walls at the angle of contact and yet be horizontal on the axis of the tube. If the angle of contact θ between the liquid and the solid of which the tube is made is less than $\pi/2$, as shown, the meniscus will be convex towards the liquid. Therefore the pressure just below the surface of the liquid will be less than the pressure of the vapour and the liquid will then rise in the tube until the drop in pressure found on passing through the liquid surface from vapour to liquid is just compensated by the additional hydrostatic pressure of the elevated column of liquid. (While, strictly, the atmosphere should consist of the vapour only, to eliminate adsorption considerations, in practice it makes a negligible difference if the experiment is carried out in air.) The situation can be analysed in the following way.

The meniscus in the tube will be a surface that is symmetrical about the axis of the tube and, on the axis of the tube, the two principal radii of curvature will be equal and have a value R, say. Take the origin of coordinates at C, a point that is on the axis of the tube and at the same level as the plane liquid surface, and let the positive y direction be upwards along the axis of the tube. At the point G, which is just above the plane surface of the liquid the pressure is p_0, the pressure of the atmosphere and, for equilibrium, it must also have this value at the point C, since C and G are on the same level. The change in pressure dp on moving a distance along the axis of the tube in the positive direction is given by:

$$dp = -\rho g dy$$

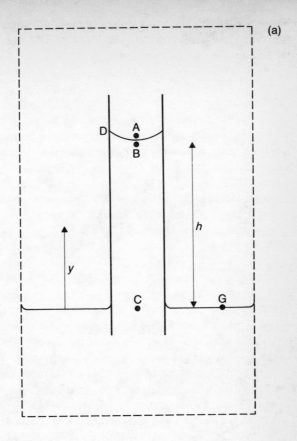

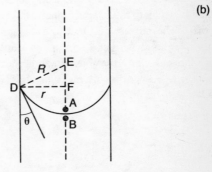

Fig. 7.6

where ρ is the density of the liquid and g is the acceleration of free fall. Then, assuming ρ constant, the pressure at B, just below the lowest point of the meniscus is:

$$p_{\mathrm{B}} = p_0 - \int_0^h \rho g \mathrm{d}y = p_0 - \rho g h$$

where h is the height of the liquid column above the plane liquid surface. On passing through the meniscus in the positive direction there is a drop in pressure of $2\gamma/R$, so that the pressure at A, just above the lowest part of the meniscus is p_{A} and is equal to $p_0 - \rho g h - 2\gamma/R$.

If it is assumed that variations in atmospheric pressure over the height h can be neglected, p_{A} must also be equal to p_0. Therefore:

$$h = -\frac{2\gamma}{\rho g R}. \qquad [7.26]$$

Note that, in the example of Fig. 7.6(a), R is negative so that h is positive. Equation [7.26] gives h in terms of R, the radius of curvature of the lowest part of the meniscus. The equation is valid whatever the internal radius of the tube or the angle of contact, but, unfortunately, R cannot be measured directly. One approach to this difficulty is as follows.

If the tube is narrow the height BD is small and, therefore, the change in hydrostatic pressure in the liquid in going from B to D is small. Then, Δp in equation [7.15] remains practically constant and so does $(1/r_1 + 1/r_2)$. If, in addition, it is assumed that r_1 and r_2 individually remain constant, then the meniscus may be considered as part of a spherical surface. An enlarged view of the meniscus when these approximations are valid is shown in Fig. 7.6(b). The tangent to the liquid surface along the line of contact with the solid defines the angle of contact θ and the normal to this tangent along the line of solid–liquid contact meets the axis of the tube at the point E. Then DE is equal to R, and DF is the radius r of the tube. Now:

$$\frac{\mathrm{DF}}{\mathrm{DE}} = \cos\theta$$

so that:

$$R = r/\cos\theta$$

and:
$$h = \frac{2\gamma\cos\theta}{\rho g r} .$$
[7.27]

Equation [7.27] is a very good approximation when r is small. When θ is greater than $\pi/2$ the value of $\cos\theta$ is negative and h is negative; the liquid is depressed in the tube. If the liquid wets the material of the tube θ is zero and $\cos\theta$ is unity so that:

$$h = \frac{2\gamma}{\rho g r} .$$
[7.28]

Since h is measured to the bottom of the meniscus in the tube the hydrostatic pressure of the liquid above that level is not taken into account. It can be shown that, for narrow capillaries, a good correction is simply to add $r/3$ to h.

7.11 The sessile drop

When a small volume of a liquid is placed on a plane horizontal surface of a material that it does not wet, it collects into a shape that is almost spherical. The effect of the intermolecular forces in trying to minimise the surface area is much more important than that of the gravitational force in trying to lower the centre of mass. As more liquid is added to the drop it grows larger but becomes flattened as the effect of gravity becomes more important. The depth of the drop increases as more liquid is added to it until a certain value is reached. Then, adding more liquid causes the depth to decrease slightly before reaching a steady value with the surface of the drop flat. Large drops in this condition are known as sessile drops, and their dimensions give information about the free energy of the liquid–vapour interface and of the angle of contact of the liquid with the solid.

Consider a very large sessile drop, part of a principal vertical section of which is shown in Fig. 7.7. Any small part of the circumference in a plane parallel to the solid surface may be taken as straight, so that only curvatures in a vertical plane need be considered.

Let s be the distance along the profile of the drop in a given

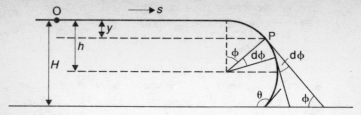

Fig. 7.7

vertical plane, measured from some arbitrary point O on the horizontal surface of the drop. At a point P on the profile the local radius of curvature is r and the line joining P to the local centre of curvature makes an angle ϕ with the vertical. The value of r is given by $\partial s/\partial \phi$. Just outside the liquid surface at P the pressure is atmospheric, while just inside the surface, because of the curvature, it is atmospheric plus γ/r. However this latter pressure is also equal to atmospheric pressure plus the hydrostatic pressure at the level of P, i.e., atmospheric pressure plus $\rho g y$, where y is the vertical distance from the horizontal top surface of the drop to P, and ρ is the density of the liquid. Therefore:

$$\rho g y = \frac{\gamma}{r} = \gamma \frac{\partial \phi}{\partial s}$$

that is:

$$\rho g y = \gamma \frac{\partial \phi}{\partial y} \frac{\partial y}{\partial s} .$$

Now:

$$\frac{\partial y}{\partial s} = \sin \phi$$

so that:

$$\rho g y = \gamma \frac{\partial \phi}{\partial y} \sin \phi$$

or separating the variables:

$$\sin \phi \, d\phi = \frac{\rho g y}{\gamma} \, dy .$$

Integrate now from the top of the liquid drop, where ϕ and y are both zero, to the point of maximum bulge, where y equals h and ϕ is $\pi/2$. Then:

$$\left[-\cos\phi \right]_0^{\pi/2} = \frac{\rho g}{2\gamma} \left[y^2 \right]_0^h$$

so that:

$$1 = \frac{\rho g h^2}{2\gamma}$$

or: $\quad \gamma = \frac{\rho g h^2}{2} \qquad\qquad\qquad [7.29]$

a result that is independent of the angle of contact.

If the integration is performed over the range $y = 0$ to $y = H$, the total height of the drop, ϕ, varies from zero, when y is zero, to θ, the angle of contact, when y equals H. Then:

$$1 - \cos\theta = \frac{\rho g H^2}{2\gamma} \qquad\qquad\qquad [7.30]$$

a result that can be used to give a value for θ if γ is known.

7.12 Vapour pressure and liquid-surface curvature

Since surface tension is a manifestation of intermolecular forces, it is to be expected that the curvature of a liquid–vapour interface will affect the ease of evaporation and, therefore, the vapour pressure. A relationship between the vapour pressure over a curved surface and the curvature of the surface may be obtained as follows.

Consider a closed volume containing only a one-component liquid and its vapour, as in Fig. 7.6(a). When a narrow bore tube is placed so as to dip in the liquid, the liquid rises or falls in the tube depending on the value of the angle of contact.

For definiteness, consider the situation illustrated in Fig. 7.6(a), in which the liquid rises in the tube. Assume that the liquid wets the material of the tube and that the radius r of the tube is very small. Then the liquid surface in the tube is part of a sphere, also of radius r.

Let y be the distance measured vertically upwards from the plane liquid surface outside the tube. In equilibrium, the pressure at G, just above this plane surface, and at C, on the same level but on the axis of the tube, must be equal. Let this value be p_0. The change in pressure dp, experienced on moving a vertical distance dy through the vapour is:

$$dp = -\sigma g dy$$

where σ is the density of the vapour. Therefore, if p is the pressure at the point A, just above the curved liquid surface:

$$p = p_0 - \int_0^h \sigma g dy . \qquad [7.31]$$

Similarly, in moving a vertical distance dy through the liquid:

$$dp = -\rho g dy$$

where ρ is the density of the liquid. Therefore, the pressure at B, immediately below the meniscus and on the axis of the tube, is equal to:

$$p_0 - \int_0^h \rho g dy .$$

On passing through the meniscus there is a pressure drop of $2\gamma/r$ (r is actually negative in Fig. 7.6(a), so that the pressure drop is negative, i.e. it is a pressure increase). p is also given by:

$$p = p_0 - \int_0^h \rho g dy - 2\gamma/r . \qquad [7.32]$$

Eliminating p and p_0 from equations [7.31] and [7.32] gives:

$$\int_0^h (\rho - \sigma) g dy = -\frac{2\gamma}{r} . \qquad [7.33]$$

Now $dp = -\sigma g dy$ so that equation [7.33] becomes:

$$\int_{p_0}^p \left(\frac{\rho - \sigma}{\sigma} \right) dp = \frac{2\gamma}{r} . \qquad [7.34]$$

Assume now that the vapour behaves as an ideal gas. Then:

$$pV_m = RT$$

applies to the vapour, where V_m is the molar volume of the vapour phase. If M is the mass of one mole of molecules of the substance, σ is equal to M/V_m and substituting for V_m gives:

$$\sigma = \frac{pM}{RT}.$$

Substituting this value in equation [7.34] gives:

$$\frac{2\gamma}{r} = \int_{p_0}^{p} \left(\frac{\rho RT}{pM} - 1 \right) dp$$

which integrates to give:

$$\frac{2\gamma}{r} = \frac{\rho RT}{M} \ln\left(\frac{p}{p_0} \right) - (p - p_0).$$

When $p - p_0$ is small:

$$\frac{2\gamma}{r} \approx \frac{\rho RT}{M} \ln \frac{p}{p_0}.$$

Now ρ is equal to M/V_{ML}, where V_{ML} is the molar volume of the liquid phase. The final expression is then:

$$\ln\left(\frac{p}{p_0} \right) = \frac{2\gamma V_{ML}}{rRT}. \qquad [7.35]$$

Equation [7.35] is one form of an equation known as Kelvin's equation. In the example of Fig. 7.6(a), r is negative so that $p < p_0$, i.e. evaporation from a surface convex to the liquid is more difficult than from a plane surface.

7.13 The measurement of surface free energies

Any effect for which the specific surface free energy γ appears in the equations describing it can be used for the measurement of γ, but only a few such methods give reliable results. Some of these will now be considered.

Solid surfaces

For brittle solids an estimate of the specific surface free energy can be made by the method of controlled cleavage. A cleavage crack is produced along the middle of a long specimen of thickness $2t$, as shown in Fig. 7.8. In equilibrium, a crack of length L is just on the point of moving when forces F_a are applied at right angles to the cleavage plane, the separation of the cleaved ends being $2y$.

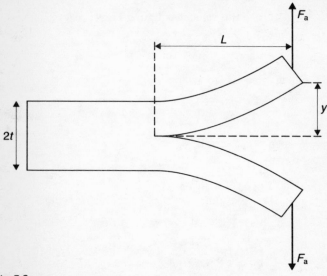

Fig. 7.8

The material on each side of the cleavage plane may be treated as a bent beam, a cantilever in fact, and, if only elastic deformation is considered to occur, it can be shown that:

$$F_a = \frac{yEt^3z}{4L^3}$$

where E is Young's modulus of the material and z is the width of the crack. The elastic energy stored in each beam is $F_a y$, which is equal to:

$$4L^3F_a{}^2/Et^3z \ .$$

When the crack increases its length from L to $L + \delta L$ the new surface produced is $2z\delta L$ and, if this is done reversibly and isothermally, the energy needed is:

$$w_S = 2z\gamma_S\delta L .$$

The spreading of the crack results in the storage of additional elastic energy of amount:

$$w_E = [(L + \delta L)^3 - L^3] \, 4F_a{}^2/Et^3z$$

which is approximately:

$$12 \, F_a{}^2 L^2 \delta L/Et^3z .$$

All the energy needed for the change, w_F, is provided by the forces F_a, which do work $2F_a\delta y$ which is:

$$24 \, F_a{}^2 L^2 \delta L/Et^3z .$$

In equilibrium there is no net change in the total energy for a small displacement and, therefore, $w_F = w_S + w_E$, giving:

$$\gamma_S = \frac{6F_a{}^2 L^2}{Et^3 z} . \qquad [7.36]$$

This theory assumes no shear deformation (i.e. $t \ll L$) and no plastic deformation and is, therefore, best for long, thin specimens at low temperatures.

For ductile solids γ_S can be obtained at high temperatures by finding the load that gives zero creep rate. A metal specimen in the form of a very thin foil (to give increased sensitivity) is loaded by suspending a weight from it and is entirely surrounded by similar material to retain chemical equilibrium. The stress arising from the surface energy will tend to contract the foil and the applied load will counteract this. An X-ray technique is used to monitor the change in dimensions of the specimen and the condition adjusted so that the dimensions of the loaded specimen do not change with time. Then, if σ is the stress that just balances the surface tension in a specimen of thickness t:

$$\gamma_S = \sigma t . \qquad [7.37]$$

Liquid surfaces

Methods for determining the specific surface free energies of liquid surfaces fall into two categories: dynamic methods, in which the surface is continuously renewed, and static methods, in which there is no such renewal.

The use of capillary rise to measure γ is a static method. To use equation [7.27] the tube must have a very narrow bore and θ must be known. If the method is to give accurate results θ must be zero, so that equation [7.28] may be used; non-zero contact angles are both difficult to measure and reproduce.

However, narrow bore tubes are difficult to clean and there are difficulties in ensuring that the cross-section is circular, but the method gives reliable values for the surface tension of pure liquids and, by using a U-tube, is readily adapted for measuring the variation of γ with temperature.

Another static method uses measurements of a sessile drop. Equation [7.29] can be used, though h is quite difficult to measure, and the risk of the surface becoming contaminated is high. Unless empirical corrections are applied to equation [7.29], drops of very large diameter must be used. Once γ is known, θ can be obtained from equation [7.30].

A method that is neither truly static nor dynamic is the drop weight method, which utilises the result that, when drops of a liquid are allowed to form slowly at the end of vertical capillary tube of small diameter and then break away, they are of constant size. The break-away, in fact, usually produces several drops: the main drop is followed by one or more much smaller satellite drops.

As a very crude approximation to the behaviour of the drop it might be expected that the weight W of the drop when it is about to break away is just supported by the surface tension forces around the tip of the tube of radius r. This gives the so-called law of Tate:

$$W = mg = 2\pi r \gamma \qquad [7.38]$$

where m is the mass of the drop. This argument ignores the fact that, just before break-away, the surface tension forces are acting at an angle to the vertical around the tip, and also neglects the pressure difference across the curved liquid surface.

A complete analysis would involve a discussion of the dynamics of flow during break-away, but Harkins and Brown developed an empirical correction to the Tate law in the following way. They considered that W does not depend only on r and γ, but also on the shape of the drop which, itself, depends on the ratio of some linear dimension of the tip and a linear dimension of the drop, or a related quantity. Harkins and Brown then wrote two 'corrected' forms of equation [7.38], one of which is:

$$mg = 2\pi r \gamma f(r/a)$$

where a is the capillary constant, given by:

$$a^2 = 2\gamma/g\Delta\rho$$

and $\Delta\rho$ is the difference in density between the drop and its surroundings. f is a function that must be determined experimentally. They analysed their drop weight measurements by plotting $f(r/a)$ against r/a for four liquids. The points all lie on a smooth curve that goes through a maximum at $r/a \approx 1.86$, though, for $r/a \gtrsim 1.6$ the correction curve is subject to uncertainty.

In a commonly used experimental arrangement the liquid is forced slowly through a capillary tube attached to a micro-syringe as the result of a piston being moved by a micrometer screw. The movement of the screw between the break-away of consecutive drops enables the drop volume to be determined. Since the drop forms slowly it is important to prevent evaporation, and this is achieved by performing the measurement in an enclosed volume.

A simple dynamic method due to Jaeger involves the formation of a bubble at the end of a tube dipping into the liquid concerned. The tube has a radius R and dips a distance d below the surface of the liquid, which has a density ρ. As the gas pressure in the tube is increased a bubble is produced on the end of the tube dipping into the liquid. The pressure in the bubble is a maximum when its radius of curvature is a minimum, i.e. when it is equal to the radius of the tube. When this size is reached, any increase in bubble size corresponds to a lower pressure inside the bubble for equilibrium so the bubble rapidly becomes unstable and breaks away. If Δp_m is the maximum pressure registered on the manometer during the bubble formation and break-away:

$$\Delta p_{\mathrm{m}} = \frac{2\gamma}{R} + \rho g d .$$ [7.39]

Equation [7.39] is, in fact, approximate since the bubble is flattened by the variations in hydrostatic pressure across its surface and it has a tendency to spread across the thickness of the tube wall. For these reasons, the method is most widely used for the comparison of surface free energies. It is very convenient for the study of the temperature variation of γ and has been used for measurements on molten metals. The bubble surface is always freshly formed.

Chapter 8
High polymers and liquid crystals

8.1 Introduction

Practically all of the book so far has dealt with the properties of aggregations of simple molecules, that is, of molecules that consist of, at most, a few atoms or ions. From the point of view of their interactions, these simple molecules can be treated more or less as Newtonian particles. There are, however, many molecules that consist of a large number of component atoms or ions and consequently show some rather different properties from the simple solids and liquids. Some properties of two types of molecule, high polymers and liquid crystals, will be examined briefly in this chapter.

8.2 High polymers

High polymers are long-chain molecules with relative molecular masses of from thousands to many millions. The polymer molecule may consist of a single chain (known as a linear polymer), it may have secondary chains branching from the main molecular chain (a branched polymer) or the polymer chains may be bonded together at various points by covalent bonds (a cross-linked polymer).

A polymer molecule is composed of a large number of repeating units (each of which is known as a mer) supplied by a molecule known as a monomer in a process called polymerisation. The bonds between adjacent mers are strong covalent bonds but, in the absence of cross-linking, the chains themselves only interact through weak van der Waals forces.

8.3 The mechanisms of polymerisation

Two mechanisms are known to operate in the process of polymerisation; addition polymerisation and condensation polymerisation. Each results in the formation of a certain type of polymeric structure.

In addition polymerisation the monomers are simply added together. This process involves the breaking down of a double covalent bond between two carbon atoms and the subsequent redistribution of these bonds as single bonds between a whole series of carbon atoms. In the formation of polyethylene (polythene) from ethylene this occurs as shown below.

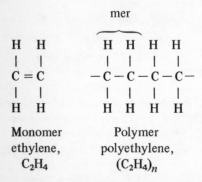

In contrast, polymerisation by condensation involves a reaction between active groups, of which there must be at least two in each molecule. During the polymerisation process simple, non-polymerisable, molecules are condensed out as byproducts. In the case of the formation of nylon 66 from diamine and dicarboxylic acid, for example, water is the small molecule that is eliminated or condensed, as shown below:

$$HO_2C(CH_2)_4CO_2H + H_2N(CH_2)_6NH_2$$
$$\downarrow$$
$$\text{+}CO.(CH_2)_4.CO.NH.(CH_2)_6NH\text{+}_n + H_2O$$

Addition polymers can be produced by opening a double bond by the application of sufficiently high temperatures and pressures to the material, but most processes involve the addition of a small amount of a very reactive substance, called an initiator, to the material. The initiator effectively 'opens' the double bonds of a few monomer molecules. When these molecules polymerise the initiator is released and can then open further double bonds. Once a particular polymer chain is started it proceeds rapidly to a higher relative molecular mass, even though the complete conversion of all the monomer present to polymer may take a considerable time. This may be contrasted with condensation polymerisation, where all the polymer molecules grow simultaneously at about the same rate.

8.4 The size and shape of polymer molecules

Polymers are long-chain molecules, the repeating units of which are more-or-less flexibly joined together. This latter property is a consequence of the relative freedom of rotation of chemical bonds, such as the single C—C bond, with respect to neighbouring bonds in the chain. In solution, in the melt and even in the solid if the temperature is high enough, the internal energy of the molecules ensures that a range of configurations is taken up, and any particular molecule undergoes fluctuations of form.

A linear polymer consists of N monomers, each of length L, joined end to end to give a total length NL. Information regarding the size and shape of the polymer molecule is usually obtained from measurements made on dilute solutions of the polymer in a suitable solvent. The nature of polymers and the methods of production normally give a distribution of chain lengths and, therefore, of relative molecular mass. Different types of measurement give different quantities that are related to the size (strictly, to the relative molecular mass) of the polymer. For example, measurements of properties such as the lowering of the osmotic pressure and of the freezing point give a value for the number average relative molecular mass $\overline{M}_n$, given by:

$$\overline{M}_n = \frac{\Sigma X_i M_{ri}}{\Sigma X_i} \qquad [8.1]$$

where, in unit mass of solution, there are X_i molecules with relative molecular mass M_{ri}.

The intensity of light scattering is proportional to the square of the mass of a particle and provides a value for the mass average of the relative molecular mass $\overline{M}_m$ defined by:

$$\overline{M}_m = \frac{\Sigma X_i M_{ri}^2}{\Sigma X_i M_{ri}} . \qquad [8.2]$$

If η_s is the viscosity of a polymer solution of concentration c and η_0 is that of the pure solvent, the specific viscosity η_{sp} is defined as:

$$\eta_{sp} = \frac{\eta_s - \eta_0}{\eta_0} .$$

It is found that η_{sp} varies linearly with c, and its value, extrapolated to zero concentration, is known as the intrinsic viscosity η_{int}. For long-chain molecules in neutral solvents:

$$\eta_{int} = K(\overline{M}_v)^a$$

where $\overline{M}_v$ is the viscosity average relative molecular mass and K and a are constants for a given polymer. $\overline{M}_v$ is given by:

$$\overline{M}_v = \left(\frac{\Sigma X_i M_{ri}^{1+a}}{\Sigma X_i M_{ri}} \right)^{\frac{1}{a}} . \qquad [8.3]$$

The flexibility of a long-chain polymer leads to problems in specifying the shape in a useful way. One approach is to treat the polymer as infinitely thin and assume that the orientation of each flexible segment has a random orientation unaffected by the orientations of its neighbours. The problem is then that of the Einstein random walk so that, if one end of a molecule has a position vector $\mathbf{R}_0$ and the other end has a position vector $\mathbf{R}_N$, a measure of the space occupied by the molecule is $| \mathbf{R}_0 - \mathbf{R}_N |$. For the problem specified:

$$<(\mathbf{R}_0 - \mathbf{R}_N)^2> = NL^2 \qquad [8.4]$$

i.e. the most probable mean length is $N^{\frac{1}{2}}$ of the total, or fully extended, length. Real molecules, of course, have a finite thickness and the monomers cannot get closer than touching. The interactions between touching chain segments (van der Waals and dipole interactions, which are both usually attractive) must be taken into account. Then:

$$\langle (\mathbf{R_0} - \mathbf{R}_N)^2 \rangle = f(N, L, T) \qquad [8.5]$$

where f is some function of the total length NL and the temperature T.

8.5 The structure of solid polymers

A linear polymer is one in which the individual long-chain molecules are quite distinct from one another and only interact, in general, through relatively weak secondary bonds. In the molten or solution condition these polymer molecules are randomly oriented and free to move, though the molten material is very viscous. When a polymer melt is rapidly cooled this random orientation is retained, giving a solid material with an amorphous structure. Slower cooling of the melt gives a solid that has some regions where the structure is amorphous and others where the polymer chains are aligned to some extent, so that there are regions that exhibit long-range order or crystallinity. Many polymers show a tendency to exist in a crystalline condition but few ever show complete crystallinity, and then only when produced under rather specially controlled conditions. The earliest model for the partial crystallinity usually observed in bulk solid polymers was the fringed micelle model, illustrated in Fig. 8.1(a), where the continuous lines represent long-chain molecules. In this model different polymer chains are arranged so that small regions show a regular packing of part of the chains. However, the observation that plate-like single crystals can be obtained by careful crystallisation from dilute solutions lead to the folded-chain model (Fig. 8.1(b)), in which the crystallinity is produced by one polymer chain folding backwards and forwards on itself to produce a regular pattern. Except in crystalline regions, linear polymers commonly have a tangled structure which plays an important role in their mechanical behaviour.

It is possible, under well-defined conditions, to cause normally simple linear polymer molecules to grow into branched chains. When this branching is extensive, the solid polymer shows a considerable interlocking of the branched chains and this gives a material that is both denser and stronger than the unbranched form.

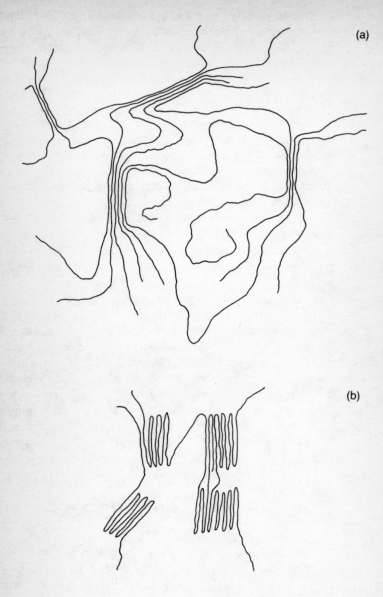

(a)

(b)

Fig. 8.1

A linear polymer may also become cross-linked, which is the binding together of polymer chains at various places by means of strong covalent bonds, usually through the presence of foreign atoms. The result is a three-dimensional network of polymer chains in which the movement of the individual molecules is quite restricted. Network and cross-lined polymers are rarely crystalline, even to a limited extent, and may be treated as amorphous.

Crystallinity is greatly affected by polymer chain perfection. Copolymerisation (the formation of a polymer with more than one chemical unit) and chain branching greatly reduced crystallinity, as does a random arrangement of side groups that can take up more than one configuration (giving an atactic polymer) whereas highly stereoregular polymers tend to show considerable crystallinity.

8.6 The glass transition temperature

In many polymers the atoms and atomic groups in the long chains are held together by strong covalent bonds, while neighbouring chains only interact through weak van der Waals forces. Polymers of this nature, in which strong cross-links are effectively absent, are rigid at low temperatures but become soft and rubbery, showing viscoelastic behaviour, at high temperatures, the transition being reversible. This transition from rigid (or glass-like) behaviour is found in both amorphous and partially crystalline types of un-branched polymers, and takes place over a fairly narrow temperature range, usually called the glass transition range. One manifestation of the glass transition is a fairly abrupt change in the volume expansivity, as shown in Fig. 8.2, and this can be used to define a temperature T_g, known as the glass transition temperature.

At temperatures in excess of T_m in Fig. 8.2, the not very well-defined melting temperature, these polymers are completely amorphous and show many of the features characteristic of liquids, the condition being termed viscofluid. Rapid cooling of the polymer from state A (Fig. 8.2) causes it to follow the path ABC, whether it it cross-linked or not. The polymer is amorphous at all stages along ABC, shows little or no change in specific volume at T_m and when the temperature is below T_g it is essentially glassy.

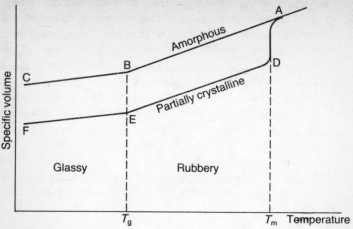

Fig. 8.2

During slow cooling however, the material follows the path ADEF. There is a marked change in specific volume at T_m and the material shows partial crystallinity. At temperatures between T_m and T_g the polymer chains have considerable freedom of relative movement and are able to slide over one another, while below T_g their relative positions are fixed. The actual value of T_g is largely determined by the stiffness of the polymer chains. Flexible molecules, such as polybutadiene, have a low value of T_g, while stiff molecules, such as polystyrene, have a high value of T_g. The cohesive energy of the molecule is also important in determining T_g, while the symmetry of the molecule plays a minor role.

Polymers that show a glass transition are called thermoplastics. At temperatures above T_g they extend readily under tension, the main effect being a straightening of the polymer chains. They retain this different shape when the load is removed, though the original shape can be recovered simply by raising the temperature sufficiently.

Linear and branched polymers that have a few strong cross-links do not show a glass transition. They can undergo large extensions under tension, but regain their original dimensions completely when the load is removed. Such materials are known as elastomers; rubber is probably the best-known example. They must contain molecules with freely-rotating links and weak inter-chain forces so that the molecules have considerable freedom of motion. There must, however, be certain strong links between the chains to reconcile the need for local changes in chain configuration with the maintenance of a coherent structure.

When a polymer is heavily cross-linked it forms a rigid three-dimensional arrangement that deforms very little under load. As these materials polymerise, a process accelerated by raising the temperature, the monomers group themselves into a rigid framework that is not softened when the temperature is raised again. Materials of this sort, for example, urea formaldehyde, are known as thermosetting plastics.

8.7 Young's modulus of solid polymers

One of the simplest mechanical tests that can be carried out on a solid polymer is to deform it in axial tension. For all polymers, the stress–strain curve for the initial stages of such a test is linear, so that a value for Young's modulus of the material may be obtained. Typical results for a high polymer, e.g. polystyrene, that is available in amorphous, partially crystalline and cross-linked forms is shown in Fig. 8.3, where Young's modulus E is shown as a function of temperature T. For all the conditions of the material E is high in the glassy region and practically independent of temperature.

In the partially crystalline condition there is a small change in E as the temperature is raised through T_g. With further increase in temperature there is a gradual decrease in E until T_m, the melting temperature of the crystallites, is reached. There is then a rapid fall in E as the material becomes essentially a very viscous liquid, the condition being referred to as viscofluid.

For the amorphous material (typically quenched from the melt) E falls by several orders of magnitude as the temperature is raised through T_g, and above that temperature the material is rubbery or, strictly, viscoelastic. When the temperature exceeds T_f (see Fig. 8.3), known as the viscofluid transition temperature, E

falls sharply. Note that T_f is not equal to T_m since the viscofluid is produced from different structures in the two cases.

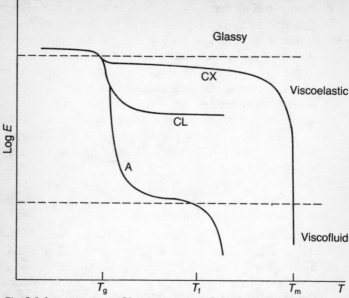

Fig. 8.3 A = amorphous, CL = cross-linked, CX = partially crystalline.

The cross-linked material shows a marked drop in E as the temperature is raised through T_g and then E is relatively constant for a wide range of temperature, only decreasing rapidly when the viscofluid region is reached.

8.8 Stress–strain curves of polymers

Typical stress–strain curves at different temperatures relative to T_g are shown for an amorphous polymeric material in Fig. 8.4(a) and for the partially crystalline condition in Fig. 8.4(b).

For both types of material, the graph of axial stress σ against linear strain ϵ is a straight line for temperatures well below T_g and the material is brittle.

At temperatures up to T_g amorphous polymers deform elastically in tension until the so-called yield stress σ_y is reached, when the stress falls to a lower value σ_d, known as the draw stress,

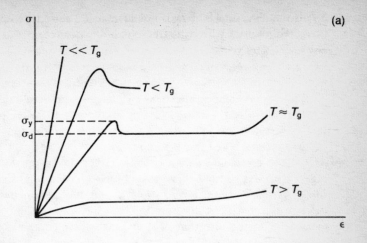

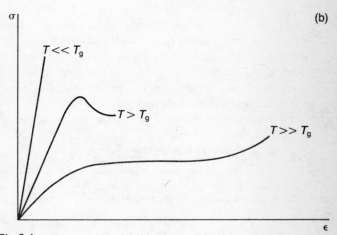

Fig. 8.4

and a neck appears in the specimen. With further deformation this neck propagates along the specimen. At temperatures below T_g the specimen usually fractures during this process but, when the temperature is about T_g, the neck propagates along the whole of the gauge length and, when this is complete, the stress rises again. In this process the polymer chains are oriented in the direction of the applied stress and the material becomes stronger in that direction. When the deforming forces are removed the polymer chains remain in their new positions but this strain can be completely recovered by gently raising the temperature of the material above T_g, when the polymer chains revert to their random distribution. At temperatures above T_g large strains develop from the start of the test and no yield drop is observed. If the temperature is raised above the viscofluid transition temperature the material is suitable for drawing into fibres.

Partially crystalline polymers show rather similar curves (see Fig. 8.4(b)) but brittle behaviour is observed for temperatures up to T_g. At temperatures above T_g a neck is produced during tensile deformation, but it results from the recrystallisation of the polymer chains in the direction of stress, since the melting point of the aligned chains is higher than that of the unaligned chains. Consequently, no recovery of the strain takes place when the temperature of the material is raised. At temperatures around T_g the propagation of the neck is usually terminated by flaws in the material, but well above T_g the neck propagates along the entire length of the specimen at constant stress. The stress rises again when the aligned polymer chains become strained. When the temperature reaches T_m the material behaves in a viscofluid manner similar to that of an amorphous polymer.

Data for some common polymeric materials are given in Table 8.1.

Table 8.1 *Properties of some common high polymers*

Material	Condition at room temperature	E(MPa)	T_g(K)
Polyethylene	Partially crystalline	70–280	153
Polyvinyl-chloride (PVC)	Amorphous/slightly crystalline	2500–3500	353
Polymethyl-methacrylate (PMMÅ)	Amorphous	2500–4000	380
Nylon 6	Partially crystalline	2000–3000	323
Phenol formaldehyde resin	Thermosetting glass	7000	—

8.9 Viscous flow in polymers

Molten polymers and polymer solutions are, in general, non-Newtonian in their flow behaviour, with an apparent viscosity that decreases as the rate of shear is increased at constant temperature.

In section 6.6 a simple discussion of liquid flow, in terms of the cell model was given, and it is of interest to apply similar considerations to the flow of polymer melts and solutions. Since a polymer molecule is not even approximately spherical, but very long, it might be expected that the activation energy needed to allow a polymer molecule to break away from its surroundings would be proportional to the length of the polymer chain and would, therefore, be much greater for a polymer molecule than for a small molecule containing the same sort of atoms. However, experiment shows that the temperature dependence of the apparent viscosity of polymers obeys the exponential law of simple liquids and that the activation energy is not very much larger. Therefore, the basic unit in the flow process, the 'particle' which jumps the energy barrier in the simple model, has dimensions of the same order of magnitude as in simple liquids. This is, perhaps, not really too surprising, since a polymer can be thought of as a flexible chain of randomly jointed links, in which the orientation of any one link bears no definite relationship to that of its neighbours. The chain, therefore, cannot move as a rigid entity, but individual short segments can move more or less, independently of each other. These segments are the 'particles' for which the activation energy must be provided.

Though the temperature coefficient of polymer viscosity, and the activation energy derived from it, are independent of chain length (to a good approximation), this is not true of the viscosity coefficient itself. Viscosity is determined by the movement of the polymer chain as a whole and this depends not only on the rate of jumping of individual segments, but also on the way these jumps are related to each other in direction. Because of the complicated form of the molecules in space, and the mutual entanglements between molecules, not all jumps are equally effective in producing a resultant displacement of the molecule.

Polymer viscosity η increases with relative molecular mass M_r

for a given polymer. The graph of log η against log M_r shows a sharp 'knee', below which the molecules move more or less individually, as in a simple liquid, but above which the molecules become so entangled that any one molecule can move only by dragging others along with it.

When a polymer solution or melt is made to flow at a high rate of shear, the tangled chain arrangement behaves as a temporary molecular network since the imposed flow rate cannot be accommodated simply by the thermally assisted jumping of molecular segments. To accommodate the flow process the polymer chain arrangement becomes elastically deformed, in addition to undergoing rearrangements, and this elastic deformation generates stresses additional to the shearing stresses producing flow. These additional stresses are equivalent to an internal tension in the polymer, acting parallel to the planes of macroscopic sliding.

If the polymer solution or melt is placed in the space between two coaxial cylinders, one of which is kept fixed while the other is rotated, the liquid is not only subjected to a rate of shear, which generates a shear stress on the inner and outer cylinders, but, in addition, there is a tensile stress set up in the direction of the streamlines. In this case the stress is a hoop stress. This hoop stress produces an internal pressure in the liquid. It is as if the liquid were surrounded by a stretched elastic membrane. Consequently, the liquid is forced up the wall of the inner cylinder to give what is known as the Weissenberg effect.

The Weissenberg effect is one of a general class of effects that may be termed viscoelastic, a term that is used to describe the condition of a material when it shows a combination of solid-like and liquid-like behaviour. More precisely, it is the condition in which the material can show both energy storage and dissipation during deformation. Since this behaviour can be shown by both solids and liquids, the term viscoelastic is usually restricted to deformations that are repeatable, so that plastic deformation, for example, is excluded. A viscoelastic material, then, is one in which the time dependence of stress and strain is important. In high polymer melts, though not solutions, the elastic properties arise from the entanglements between the long-chain molecules forming a loose network. For example, the bouncing properties of 'potty putty' arise from the presence of a network of entangled long-chain molecules. At room temperature and above, these entanglements have relatively short lifetimes. Under low stresses, that give low shear rates, e.g. the gravitational field, the material flows like a very viscous liquid. However, for deformations of short duration but high shear rate, as in bouncing, the entangled networks persist during the deformation and the material shows essentially elastic behaviour.

Materials, and, in particular, polymers, that show viscoelastic behaviour, can be modelled by a combination of perfectly elastic Hookean springs and Newtonian viscous dashpots. For many polymers the behaviour at temperatures above T_g when strains are small ($\leqslant 1$ per cent) is approximately represented by the so-called standard linear substance. This consists of a dashpot and spring in series (called a Maxwell element) and this combination in parallel with a second spring of different elastic modulus. In deformation, the strain of the Maxwell element and of the spring will be the same, say ϵ. At a time t let σ_1 be the stress in the Maxwell element and σ_2 that in the spring. Then, if E_1 is the Young's modulus of the Maxwell element and E_2 that of the spring:

$$\sigma_2 = E_2\epsilon \qquad\qquad [8.6]$$

and:
$$\frac{d\epsilon}{dt} = \frac{1}{E_1}\frac{d\sigma_1}{dt} + \frac{\sigma_1}{\eta} \qquad\qquad [8.7]$$

where η is the viscosity of the liquid in the dashpot. Since the total stress σ in the model is the sum of σ_1 and σ_2:

$$\sigma = E_2\epsilon + \eta\left[\frac{d\epsilon}{dt} - \frac{1}{E_1}\frac{d\sigma_1}{dt}\right]$$

or since:
$$\frac{d\sigma}{dt} = \frac{d\sigma_1}{dt} + \frac{d\sigma_2}{dt}$$

$$\sigma + \frac{\eta}{E_1}\frac{d\sigma}{dt} = E_2\left[\epsilon + \eta\frac{(E_1 + E_2)}{E_1 E_2}\frac{d\epsilon}{dt}\right]. \qquad\qquad [8.8]$$

If a constant stress σ_0 is abruptly applied to the material at time equal to zero, when the substance is unstrained, there is an instantaneous strain ϵ_0 equal to $\sigma_0/(E_1 + E_2)$, and solving equation [8.8] with this initial value of ϵ gives:

$$\epsilon = \frac{\sigma_0}{E_2} \left[1 - \frac{E_1}{E_1 + E_2} \exp(-t/t_0) \right] \qquad [8.9]$$

where $t_0 = \eta(E_1 + E_2)/E_1E_2$. It can be seen from equation [8.9] that the strain approaches σ_0/E_2 exponentially. The relaxation time is defined as the time for the value of a quantity that decreases exponentially with time to fall to $1/e$ of its initial value. The general linear substance has two principal relaxation times: for relaxation of the stress at constant strain the value is η/E_1; for relaxation of the strain at constant stress it is $\eta(E_1 + E_2)/E_1E_2$.

8.10 Liquid crystals

Liquid crystals belong to a range of materials, termed meso-morphic phases, that are intermediate between crystalline solids and simple, isotropic liquids. They are formed from compounds whose molecules have a strongly non-spherical shape, by heating or by dissolution in a suitable solvent. Many liquid crystals are formed from molecules that are, in fact, rod-shaped.

The phases formed by liquid crystals may be classified according to the structure existing in the liquid. In nematic liquid crystals the molecules have their long axes aligned statistically parallel to one another within macroscopic volumes of the phase, but they have no positional order, as shown schematically in Fig. 8.5(a). This statistically averaged direction defines a unique direction in the liquid crystal and the unit vector in this direction is known as the director. At a sufficiently high temperature the nematic structure breaks down to give a true liquid.

In smectic liquid crystals, not only is there a statistical ordering parallel to the long axis of the molecules but, in addition, the molecules are ordered into layers, within which there is some freedom of motion. A schematic representation of the structure is given in Fig. 8.5(b). The type of motion possible, coupled with an orthogonal or tilted arrangement of the molecules in the layers allows a subdivision into several smectic subtypes. As the

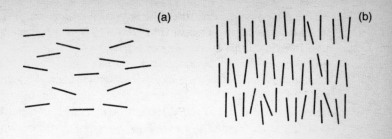

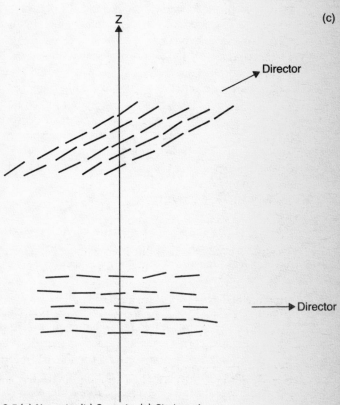

Fig. 8.5 (a) Nematic. (b) Smectic. (c) Cholesteric.

temperature is raised the weak bonds break first and the smectic structure goes over to a nematic structure.

Cholesteric liquid crystals are formed only from materials which are optically active. The structure is similar to that of a nematic but, instead of the molecules remaining parallel, a twist is imposed upon the structure, resulting in a helical disposition of the molecular axis, i.e. the direction of the director varies in a helical fashion around the z axis. Two layers of a cholesteric liquid crystal are shown in Fig. 8.5(c), but it must be remembered that the distribution of molecules is a continuous function of z, with the direction of the director rotating continuously as z varies.

In materials that form more than one liquid crystalline phase, a nematic phase and a cholesteric phase never occur together, while a cholesteric phase and a nematic phase may produce the same smectic phase on cooling.

The coupling of the axis of rod-shaped molecules is the basic characteristic that leads to a liquid which displays many of the properties of a crystalline solid, such as birefringence and electric and diamagnetic anisotropy. The response of liquid crystals to applied forces may be weakly elastic but, in nematics at least, true flow is retained. This combination of anisotropy and liquid flow leads to some interesting properties of liquid crystals, since it becomes possible to reorient the director by imposing an external electric field.

An interesting property of liquid crystals is that, when a non-spherical molecule is dissolved in a liquid crystal, it takes on the ordering of the solvent. In a nematic liquid crystal, for example, solute molecules of anisotropic shape are aligned parallel to the director and their orientation may be changed by the application of an external electric field.

One application of liquid crystals that has received much attention is their use as temperature-measuring elements. The basis of this effect is a cholesteric phase with a very short pitch. When this pitch corresponds with the wavelength of light, Bragg-like reflection of a single wavelength (or colour) is seen. Carefully blended mixtures of liquid crystals have a pitch which varies rapidly with temperature in a well-defined range, and it is possible to design mixtures which successively reflect each spectral colour over a total temperature range that can be 1 °C or less.

An interesting use of nematic liquid crystals is in display devices based on the so-called twisted nematic cell. The rod-like molecules may be aligned either perpendicular to the solid–liquid interface (homeotropic ordering) or parallel to it (homogeneous ordering), by suitable treatment of the solid surfaces. In the twisted nematic cell the two opposite faces through which light is passed are treated to give homogeneous ordering and are arranged so that the alignment directions of the faces are at right angles. When there is no applied electric field E (or, strictly when E is less than some critical value E_c) the homogeneous ordering is not disturbed and the director rotates through $90°$ in going from one cell wall to the opposite one. If the incoming light is plane polarised using a sheet of polaroid, its plane of vibration is rotated through $90°$ on passing through the cell. The light passes through a second piece of polaroid with its vibration direction at right angles to the first, and is then reflected by a plane mirror. On the return path the behaviour is the reverse of that on the first traverse and, therefore, the device reflects radiation and appears light.

When a sufficiently large field is produced across the cell ($E \gg E_c$) the molecules, except those very close to the solid surfaces, are mostly ordered with their axis parallel to the applied field, i.e. perpendicular to the two opposite faces of the cell. Then, the plane of vibration is not rotated by $90°$ and the radiation is unable to pass through the second sheet of polaroid. No light is reflected by the mirror and the device appears dark.

This elementary introduction to the properties of solids and liquids is now concluded. It is hoped that the reader who has worked through the book will have a sound understanding of the macroscopic behaviour of solids and liquids and will also, perhaps, have some inkling of the answer to the final question in Newton's *Opticks*: 'Have not the small particles of Bodies certain Powers, Virtues or Forces by which they act at a distance . . . upon one another for producing a great Part of the Phaenomena of Nature?'

Appendix 1
Exercises

Chapter 1

1   In 1827 the botanist Robert Brown observed that pollen particles suspended in water perform a continuous random motion now known as Brownian motion. Give a detailed qualitative interpretation of this observation as evidence for the existence of molecules.

2   An alternative to the Mie potential for representing the interaction energy between two molecules is the Morse potential:

$$U(r) = U_0 \left[\exp[-2a(r - r_0)] - 2 \exp[-a(r - r_0)] \right]$$

where r is the separation of the molecules and a, r_0 and U_0 are constants. Determine the equilibrium separation of atoms in a long-chain molecule composed of equally spaced atoms at a temperature close to absolute zero for which the Morse potential is applicable. Also, find the significance of U_0.

3   The Lennard-Jones potential:

$$V(r) = 4U_0 \left[\left(\frac{a}{r} \right)^{12} - \left(\frac{a}{r} \right)^6 \right]$$

where U_0 and a are constants, is useful for many simple molecules, including van der Waals solids and metals. Determine the significance of U_0 and a.

4   Show that the proportion of the total volume actually occupied by hard spheres in contact is $\sqrt{2}\,\pi/6$ for face centred cubic packing (see Fig. 1.3(a)).

5   Copper crystallises in the f.c.c. structure and has a bulk density of about 8885 kg m^{-3} at room temperature. The copper atom has a

relative atomic mass of 63.54. If the Avogadro constant is 6.025 $\times 10^{23}$ mol^{-1}, calculate: (a) the number of copper atoms in one cubic metre of crystalline copper; (b) the mass of a copper atom; (c) the atomic radius of copper.

6   Show that the gravitational attraction between two molecules is much too small to provide the binding energy of a condensed phase. In condensed phases the intermolecular distance is typically of the order of 10^{-9} m, molecular masses are of the order of 10^{-26} kg and the gravitational constant is 6.67×10^{-11} N m^2 kg^{-2}.

Chapter 2

1   The axial modulus of elasticity χ for a solid is defined as:

$$\chi = \frac{\text{Axial load per unit area of cross-section}}{\text{Increase in length per unit length}}$$

subject to the condition that there is no change in the area of cross-section during deformation, i.e. lateral forces must be applied to maintain the area constant. Show that, for an isotropic solid:

$$\chi = \frac{3K + 4G}{3}$$

where K is the bulk modulus of the material and G is its rigidity modulus.

2   A uniform wire suspended vertically from a rigid support extends 0.5 mm when a mass of 1 kg is suspended from the lower end. Calculate the elastic energy stored in the wire and the change in potential energy of the mass. Comment on these values.

3   A uniform wire of circular cross-section has an unstretched length of 2.0 m and a radius of 1.0 mm. The material is isotropic, with Young's modulus of 81×10^9 Pa. The wire is suspended vertically from a rigid support and a mass of 1.5 kg is suspended from the lower end. Calculate the change in elastic energy stored in the wire when the mass is increased in small increments by a further 1 kg.

4   A wire is stretched elastically by balanced applied forces and simultaneous measurements are made of its resistance R and length L. If the resistivity of the material of the wire is assumed unchanged

by elastic deformation, show how to obtain the value of Poisson's ratio v of the material from these measurements.

5   An aluminium bar, initially at room temperature, has its temperature increased by 1 °C. Calculate the stress which must be set up in the bar to restore it to its original length. This is the stress set up in the bar if its temperature is raised while its length is kept constant. Linear expansivity of aluminium at room temperature $= 2.4 \times 10^{-5}\,°C^{-1}$; Young's modulus of aluminium at room temperature $= 6.9 \times 10^{10}$ Pa.

6   A metal tube 2.0 m long and of internal and external radii 0.040 m and 0.043 m, respectively, is clamped at one end. Calculate the magnitude of the couple that must be applied to the other end to twist it through 30°. The metal is isotropic with a rigidity modulus of 25×10^9 Pa.

7   One half of a right circular rod of length $2L$ has a radius r and the other half has a radius $2r$. Derive an expression for the torsional rigidity of the complete rod if the modulus of rigidity of the material, which is assumed to be isotropic, is G. State the assumptions made in obtaining the expression.

8   A thin wire of isotropic material is of length $2L$ and area of cross-section α. It is stretched between two rigid supports so that it is horizontal and has a tension F_0. When a mass M is suspended from the midpoint of the wire the equilibrium position of that point is a distance y below its original position. If the effects of the mass of the wire can be neglected, show that, approximately:

$$\frac{MgL}{2y} = \frac{E\alpha y^2}{2L^2} + F_0\left(1 - \frac{y^2}{2L^2}\right)$$

where E is Young's modulus of the material of the wire and g is the acceleration of free fall. This expression is the basis of Gravesande's method for determining E.

9   A thin ring of mean radius R is made of a material that has a density ρ and a Young's modulus E. Determine the increase in the mean radius of the ring when it is rotated about an axis through its centre, perpendicular to its plane, with an angular velocity ω.

10   A certain simple cubic crystal consists of identical molecules that interact with their nearest neighbours only. If the potential energy of the interaction is given by:

$$U = -\frac{A}{r^6} + \frac{B}{r^{12}}$$

where A and B are constants and r is the nearest neighbour distance, determine the values of A and B if Young's modulus measured in a cube direction is 2.5×10^{10} Pa and the equilibrium spacing of the molecules is 0.5 nm.

Chapter 3

1 When a solid deforms plastically by slip it does so without change of volume. Show that under this condition the Poisson ratio is equal to $\frac{1}{2}$.

2 An ideal elastic-plastic solid is one that deforms elastically until the yield stress is reached and thereafter deforms plastically under that stress without hardening. One such material is isotropic, with Young's modulus 80×10^9 Pa and yield stress 12×10^6 Pa. A right circular cylinder of this material, initially 0.2 m long and of radius 1.0×10^{-3} m is extended axially to give a total extension of 6.0×10^{-3} m, and is then unloaded. Calculate: (a) the permanent extension; and (b) the elastic energy recovered on unloading.

3 In a given crystal there is a uniform density ρ of edge dislocations, with Burgers vector $\mathbf{b}$. If the dislocations all slip with a velocity $\mathbf{u}$ in the direction of $\mathbf{b}$, show that the shear strain rate is $\rho u b$.

4 A thin sheet of a crystalline solid is bent to form part of the wall of a right circular cylinder of mean radius of curvature r, by introducing into it a uniform density of edge dislocations. If each dislocation has a Burgers vector $\mathbf{b}$ parallel to the neutral plane of bending of the sheet and perpendicular to its axis of bending, show that, in the absence of long-range stresses, the density of dislocations needed is $1/rb$.

5 For solid argon, which may be treated as a cubic solid in which only nearest neighbour interactions are important, the equilibrium interatomic spacing is 5.31×10^{-10} m and the binding energy is -7.76×10^3 J mol^{-1}. If the energy of interaction U between two atoms is given by:

$$U(r) = -\frac{A}{r^6} + \frac{B}{r^{12}}$$

where r is the separation of the atoms, estimate the theoretical brittle strength. A and B are constants.

Chapter 4

1   When the tensile strength of a liquid of density ρ is determined by means of a rotating Z-shaped capillary tube (see section 4.2) show that, if the liquid ruptures at an angular velocity ω_0 when the radial distance to either free meniscus is r_0, the maximum tension per unit area in the liquid is $\omega_0^2 \rho r_0^2$.

2   Use dimensional analysis to show that the critical velocity of a liquid with kinematic viscosity ν, flowing in a channel of lateral dimension d, is proportional to ν/d.

3   According to the Hertzfeld–Mayer model of melting, a solid will melt when the amplitude of vibration of the molecules is so large that the intermolecular separation r exceeds the value r_m, which is the separation at which the potential energy $U(r)$ has a point of inflexion and the attractive force starts to decrease. For a solid in which only nearest neighbour attractions are important and for which:

$$U(r) = -\frac{A}{r^6} + \frac{B}{r^9}$$

where A and B are constants: (a) calculate the value of r_m in terms of r_0, the equilibrium intermolecular distance; (b) derive an expression for the melting temperature T_m by equating the energy of a molecule oscillating with amplitude $(r_m - r_0)$ to $3kT_m$, the average energy per molecule at temperature T_m. k is the Boltzmann constant.

4   Give a qualitative explanation of the thermomechanical and mechanocaloric effects in liquid HeII, using the two-fluid model.

Chapter 5

1   A prism of material of density σ, whose cross-section is a right-angled isosceles triangle OAB, with OA $=$ OB and $A\hat{O}B = \pi/2$, floats in a liquid of density ρ. If it floats with O immersed in the liquid, find the position of equilibrium.

2 Show that, when a rigid body is in motion, the curl of its velocity at any point gives twice its angular velocity in magnitude and direction.

3 An incompressible, inviscid liquid escapes from a vessel through a small hole in the side of the vessel so that the flatness of the free surface of the liquid is not disturbed. Show that the speed of emergence corresponds to that attained by a body falling freely in space through a vertical distance equal to the depth of the hole below the free surface. This is the theorem of Torricelli.

4 An ideal, incompressible liquid flows in a streamline manner through a horizontal tapering tube of circular cross-section, the section of the exit end having half the inlet area. If the length of the tube is L, the inlet area of cross-section is α, the input velocity is u, the pressure at the entrance to the tube is p and the liquid has a density ρ, determine: (a) the liquid velocity v at a distance x from the inlet; (b) the pressure p_x at the same cross-section; and (c) the pressure p_e at the exit end of the tube.

5 A submarine submerged in seawater travels at 10 km hr^{-1}. Estimate the pressure at the front stagnation point when it is 1.5 m below the sea surface. The density of seawater may be taken as constant and equal to 1026 kg m^{-3}.

6 A pipe carrying water tapers from a cross-sectional area of 0.3 m^2 at A to 0.15 m^2 at B. At A the velocity, assumed uniform, is 2.0 m s^{-1} and the gauge pressure is 120 kPa. If water is treated as an ideal, incompressible liquid of density 1000 kg m^{-3} determine the pressure at B, which is 6 m above A.

7 A U-tube consists of two open limbs joined by a straight horizontal section. Let the horizontal section be parallel to the x axis and let the tube contain liquid of density ρ. Show that, if the tube suffers uniform acceleration a in the positive x direction, then there is a pressure gradient along the horizontal section, given by:

$$\partial p / \partial x = -\rho a.$$

Further, show that:

$$a = hg/L$$

where L is the length of the horizontal section, h is the difference in the free surface levels of the liquid in the vertical limbs and g is the acceleration of free fall.

8   Show that the complex potential

$$\phi + i\psi = -\ u_0\left(z + \frac{a^2}{z}\right)$$

represents the symmetrical flow of an incompressible, inviscid liquid around an infinite cylinder of radius a in a stream of undisturbed velocity u_0.

Chapter 6

Unless otherwise stated, assume that the liquids involved are Newtonian and that the flow is laminar.

1   Calculate the shear stress needed to slide a flat plate at a rate of 0.07 m s^{-1} over a large flat surface separated from it by a film of oil of uniform thickness 0.3×10^{-3} m and having a viscosity of 0.45 N s m^{-2}.

2   Use dimensional analysis to establish the form of the Stokes law (section 6.5).

3   Two cylindrical vessels of equal area of cross-section α and with their axes vertical are joined near their bases by a uniform, horizontal, capillary tube of length L and internal radius r. The vessels contain liquid of density ρ and, initially, the liquid surfaces are at heights $3h$ and h, respectively, above the axis of the horizontal tube. Show that the time taken for the difference in levels to become h is:

$$\frac{4\eta L\alpha}{\pi r^2 \rho g}\ \ln(2)$$

where g is the acceleration of free fall, and η is the liquid viscosity.

4   A sphere of radius 0.5×10^{-3} m, made of material of density 7.9×10^3 kg m^{-3}, falls along the axis of a vertical right circular cylinder of internal radius 0.01 m containing a liquid of density 1.26×10^3 kg m^{-3}. When the sphere has reached its terminal velocity it takes 68.3 s to travel a 0.15 m length of the middle section of the cylinder. Calculate the viscosity of the liquid both with and without the Ladenburg correction.

5   Two equal circular discs A and B, of radius r, are placed separately in a liquid of viscosity η. The discs are in parallel planes at a small separation d, and are so positioned that a line passing normally through the centre of A passes through the centre of B. Disc A is rotated about this line as axis with constant angular velocity ω. Determine the torque needed to keep disc B at rest, neglecting any edge effects.

6   A thin rod of radius b is placed coaxially in a narrow tube of length L and internal radius a. Show that, if the tube is horizontal, the volume rate of flow Q of a liquid of viscosity η through the tube when conditions are steady is:

$$Q = \frac{\pi \Delta p}{8 \eta L} \left[\frac{a^4 - b^4 - (a^2 - b^2)^2}{\ln a - \ln b} \right]$$

where Δp is the pressure difference between the ends of the tube.

7   A long circular cylinder of length L and radius a is immersed in a large vessel containing a liquid of viscosity η. Show that, when the cylinder is rotating about its axis with a constant angular velocity ω, the torque that must be applied continuously is $4\pi \eta a^2 \omega L$, neglecting end effects.

8   A uniform vertical tube of length L and internal radius a is joined to a cylinder of large radius in which a liquid of viscosity η and density ρ stands to a depth h. Show that the instantaneous volume rate of flow of liquid through the tube is:

$$\pi a^4 \rho g (L + h) / 8 \eta L.$$

9   A Bingham plastic is placed in a cylindrical tube and the pressure difference between the ends is gradually increased from zero. Show that flow first occurs at the wall of the tube, causing the material to flow as a 'plug' along the tube.

10 A liquid flows down a channel of rectangular cross-section that is inclined to the horizontal at an angle θ. If the flow velocity has a value u at a depth z below the surface of the liquid, show that the velocity gradient with respect to depth is given by:

$$\frac{du}{dz} = - \left(\frac{zg \sin \theta}{\nu} \right)$$

where ν is the coefficient of kinematic viscosity of the liquid.

Chapter 7

1   A tube has a circular cross-section which varies in diameter from d_1 at one end to d_2 at the other $(d_1 > d_2)$. Plane soap films are formed across the ends of the tube and the pressure in the tube is then slowly increased by admitting air through a side tube. What happens to the two soap films?

2   Two equal soap bubbles are formed on the two ends of a short cylindrical tube. Both bubbles are larger than one hemisphere. Describe what happens when a small disturbance makes the radius of one bubble change slightly. What would happen if both bubbles were initially smaller than one hemisphere?

3   A vertical capillary tube of internal radius a stands vertically with its lower end dipping into a liquid of density ρ and specific surface free energy γ_1. The upper end of the tube is closed by a soap bubble of radius b, the specific surface free energy of the soap solution being γ_2. Derive an expression for the height of the liquid column, assuming that the liquid wets the material of the tube.

Note that in problems 1, 2 and 3 above it is assumed that the specific surface free energy does not depend on the area of the solution surface, i.e. the surface is maintained at constant composition.

4   A capillary tube of internal diameter 0.4×10^{-3} m stands vertically in water of density 1.0×10^3 kg m^{-3} and specific surface free energy 72 m J m^{-2}. The angle of contact for water and the material of the tube is zero. The tube is slowly lowered into the liquid until only 0.02 m is above the outside water level. Describe what happens.

5   A small quantity of water is placed in a glass tube that has a narrow conical bore. The angle of contact between glass and water is zero. When the tube is held vertically it is found that the water is retained in the mid-position of the tube. Which end of the tube is uppermost when the water is retained in this way?

6   Calculate the minimum radius a drop of water can have if it is free to evaporate, but is thermally isolated. The specific enthalpy of vaporisation of water is 2270×10^3 J kg^{-1}, its density is 1.0×10^3 kg m^{-3} and its specific surface free energy is 72 m J m^{-2}.

7   A loop of fine thread is placed upon a plane liquid film and the

film inside the loop is then broken. Show that the loop will form a circle and derive an expression for the tension in the thread.

8   A single bubble of radius R is formed from the coalescence of two bubbles of radii r_1 and r_2 respectively. If the external pressure is p_0, show that the specific surface free energy of the liquid is:

$$\frac{p_0(R^3 - r_1^3 - r_2^3)}{4(r_1^2 + r_2^2 - R^2)}.$$

Discuss the assumptions that must be made to give this result.

9   Two small bodies A and B float in the surface of a liquid. Discuss whether A and B attract or repel each other in the following conditions: (a) both bodies are wetted by the liquid; (b) the liquid wets neither body; (c) the liquid wets A but not B.

10 The temperature dependence of the surface tension of a pure liquid in equilibrium with its vapour is often represented by an equation of the form:

$$\gamma_t = \gamma_0 \left(1 - \frac{t}{t'}\right)^n$$

where γ_t is the surface tension at a temperature of $t\,^\circ C$, γ_0 is that at $0\,^\circ C$, t' is a temperature a little below the critical temperature and n is a constant.

Test this relationship using the data for water given below. Take t' as $374\,^\circ C$.

$t(^\circ C)$	0	10	20	25	30	40	50	60
$\gamma(mJ\ m^{-2})$	75.7	74.2	73.5	72.0	71.2	69.6	67.9	66.2

$t(^\circ C)$	70	80	100
$\gamma(mJ\ m^{-2})$	64.4	62.6	58.8

Chapter 8

1   Which of the following polymer structures could, in principle, be made by the polymerisation of the monomer shown as A?

A

(a)

$$-NH-\langle\bigcirc\rangle-NH-CO-\langle\bigcirc\rangle-CO-NH-\langle\bigcirc\rangle-NH-$$

$$-CO-\langle\bigcirc\rangle-+H_2O$$

(b)

$$-NH-\langle\bigcirc\rangle-CO-NH-\langle\bigcirc\rangle-CO-NH-\langle\bigcirc\rangle-CO-+H_2O$$

2   The substance formed by the polymerisation of the compound vinyl chloride ($CH_2 = CH.Cl$) does not show chemical reactions typical of the group:

$$-\underset{\underset{Cl}{|}}{CH}-\underset{\underset{Cl}{|}}{CH}-$$

What conclusion about the polymer structure can be deduced from this result?

3   What structures are expected from the following reactions? (a) The self-addition of propylene:

$$\underset{\underset{H}{|}}{\overset{\overset{H}{|}}{C}}=\underset{\underset{H}{|}}{\overset{\overset{CH_3}{|}}{C}}$$

(b) The condensation of the di-acid:

$$\underset{\underset{HO}{|}}{\overset{\overset{O}{\|}}{C}}-\langle\bigcirc\rangle-\underset{\underset{OH}{|}}{\overset{\overset{O}{\|}}{C}}$$

with the dihydroxy compound:

$$\underset{\underset{H}{|}}{O}-CH_2-CH_2-\underset{\underset{H}{|}}{O}$$

4   Which two of the monomers (a)–(d) would condense together to give a linear polymer?

(a)

$$HO-\overset{\displaystyle O}{\underset{\displaystyle }{C}}\!\!-\!\!\!\!\!\!\!\!\!\!-\!\!\!\!\!\!\!\!\!\!-\overset{\displaystyle O}{\underset{\displaystyle }{C}}-OH$$

(b)

$$OH-\overset{\displaystyle }{\underset{\displaystyle O}{C}}\!\!-\!\!\!\overset{\displaystyle }{\underset{\displaystyle HO}{C}}\!\!=\!\!O$$

(c) $CH_2 - CH - CH_2$
         $\ \ \ |$ $\ \ \ |$ $\ \ \ |$
         $OH\ \ \ OH\ \ \ OH$

(d) $CH_2 - CH_2$
         $\ \ \ |$ $\ \ \ |$
         $OH\ \ \ OH$

5   The perfectly linear elastic or Hookean substance can be represented by a spring in which:

$$\sigma = E\epsilon$$

where σ is the stress, ϵ is the strain and E is the Young's modulus of the material.

The perfectly viscous or Newtonian substance can be presented by a dashpot in which the stress σ is related to the strain rate $d\epsilon/dt$ by:

$$\sigma = \eta d\epsilon/dt$$

where η is the viscosity.

A reasonable model for the behaviour of some high polymers is the Voigt or Kelvin substance, which may be represented by a spring in parallel with a dashpot. Show that, for such a substance:
(a) if at time zero when the strain is zero, a constant stress is applied

abruptly, the strain that would have been obtained instantaneously in the absence of the dashpot is approached exponentially; (b) if the system is extended to a given strain and then released the strain decreases exponentially to zero; (c) the relaxation time of the process described in (b) is η/E.

Appendix 2

Answers to exercises

Chapter 1

2   Equilibrium separation $= r_0$. The potential energy when $r = r_0$ is $-U_0$.

3   Equilibrium separation $= a(2)^{\frac{1}{6}}$. The potential energy when $r = r_0$ is $-U_0$.

5   (a) 8.42×10^{28} atoms. (b) 1.06×10^{-25} kg. (c) 1.28×10^{-10} m.

Chapter 2

2   Energy stored in the wire $= 0.25 \times 10^{-3}$ J. Change in potential energy of the mass $= -0.5 \times 10^{-3}$ J.

3   Change in elastic energy $= 1.5 \times 10^{-3}$ J.

4    $\dfrac{\mathrm{d}R}{R} = (1 + 2\nu)\dfrac{\mathrm{d}L}{L}$.

5   Stress set up in the wire is -1.7 MPa.

6   The magnitude of the torque is 8.8×10^3 N m.

7   Torsional rigidity $= \dfrac{8\pi Gr^4}{17L}$.

9    $\Delta R = \rho R^3 \omega^2 / E$.

10   $A = 1.35 \times 10^{-77}$ J m^6.

     $B = 1.05 \times 10^{-133}$ J m^{12}.

Chapter 3

2 (a) The permanent extension is 5.97 mm. (b) The energy stored elastically is 5.7×10^{-4} J.

5 Theoretical brittle strength $= 3.3 \times 10^7$ Pa.

Chapter 4

3 $r_m = r_0 \left(\dfrac{10}{7} \right)^{\frac{1}{3}}$.

$T_m = 0.08 E r_0^3 / k$. $E =$ Young's modulus

Chapter 5

1 Let α be the distance from O to the liquid level along OA and β the corresponding distance along OB. In the symmetrical floating position:

$$\alpha = \beta = a(\sigma/\rho)^{\frac{1}{2}} .$$

Provided that $\sigma/\rho < \frac{1}{4}$, there are two non-symmetrical positions of equilibrium given by:

$$\alpha, \beta = \frac{a \pm (a^2 - 4a^2 \sigma/\rho)^{\frac{1}{2}}}{2}$$

4 (a) $v = 2Lu/(2L - x)$

(b) $p_x = p - \dfrac{\rho u^2 x (4L - x)}{2(2L - x)^2}$

(c) $p_e = p - 3\rho u^2/2$

5 Pressure at the stagnation point $= 154.9$ kPa (gauge).

6 Pressure at B $= 55.14$ kPa (gauge).

Chapter 6

1 Shear stress $= 105$ Pa.

4 Uncorrected viscosity $= 1.65$ N s m^{-2} Corrected value $= 1.47$ N s m^{-2}.

5 Torque $= \pi \eta \omega r^4 / 2d$.

Chapter 7

1   The radii of curvature must remain equal for the two soap films as long as their surfaces remain parts of spheres. When the bubble at the end of the larger bore becomes hemispherical its excess pressure is at a maximum, so that a further increase in its size needs a drop in pressure for equilibrium. If air continues to be supplied, instability of the larger bubble is likely.

2   The smaller bubble decreases in size and the larger one increases until their radii of curvature are again equal. In situation two, the bubbles would return to their original sizes and radii.

3   $\text{Height} = \left(\dfrac{2\gamma_1}{a} - \dfrac{4\gamma_2}{b} \right) \Big/ \rho g$

where g is the acceleration of free fall.

4   The meniscus reaches the top of the tube and, in equilibrium, has a radius of curvature of 0.73×10^{-3} m.

5   The narrow end is uppermost.

6   The minimum radius is 64×10^{-12} m assuming that γ has a meaning for such small drops.

7   Tension in thread = $2\gamma r$, where γ is the specific surface free energy of the liquid and r is the radius of the loop.

9   (a) Attract. (b) Attract. (c) Repel.

Chapter 8

1   (b)

2   Molecules are only linked 'head-to-tail' and not 'head-to-head' or 'tail-to-tail'.

3   (a) Polypropylene:

$$-CH_2 - CH - CH_2 - CH -$$
$$| \qquad\qquad |$$
$$CH_3 \qquad\quad CH_3$$

(b) Terylene:

$$-O - \overset{\displaystyle O}{\overset{\|}{C}} - \bigcirc - \overset{\displaystyle O}{\overset{\|}{C}} - O - CH_2 - CH_2 -$$

4   A and D condense together to give terylene.

Index

RELATIVITY PHYSICS

Relativity Physics covers all the material required for a first
course in relativity. Beginning with an examination of the paradoxes
that arose in applying the principle of relativity to the two great
pillars of nineteenth-century physics — classical mechanics and
electromagnetism — Dr Turner shows how Einstein resolved these
problems in a spectacular and brilliantly intuitive way. The implications
of Einstein's postulates are then discussed and the book concludes
with a discussion of the charged particle in the electromagnetic field.

The text incorporates details of the most recent experiments and
includes applications to high-energy physics, astronomy, and solid state
physics. Exercises with answers are included for the student.

R. E. Turner

Dr Roy Turner is Reader in Theoretical Physics at the University of
Sussex.

ISBN 0-7102-0001-3

ELECTRICITY AND MAGNETISM

Electromagnetism is basic to our understanding of the properties of matter and yet is often regarded a difficult part of a first degree course. In this book Professor Dobbs provides a concise and elegant account of the subject, covering all the material required by a student taking such a course. Although concentrating on the essentials of the subject, interesting applications are discussed in the text. Vector operators are introduced at the appropriate points and exercises, with answers, are included for the student.

E. R. Dobbs

Professor Roland Dobbs is Hildred Carlile Professor of Physics at the University of London.

ISBN 0-7102-0157-5

CLASSICAL MECHANICS

A course in classical mechanics is an essential requirement of any first degree course in physics. In this volume Dr Brian Cowan provides a clear, concise and self-contained introduction to the subject and covers all the material needed by a student taking such a course. The author treats the material from a modern viewpoint, culminating in a final chapter showing how the Lagrangian and Hamiltonian formulations lend themselves particularly well to the more 'modern' areas of physics such as quantum mechanics. Worked examples are included in the text and there are exercises, with answers, for the student.

B. P. Cowan

Dr Brian Cowan is in the Department of Physics, Bedford College, University of London

ISBN 0-7102-0280-6